Python Bootcamp

A Rapid Crash Course Featuring Q&A Sessions, Exercises, and Projects

Vaskaran Sarcar

Apress®

Python Bootcamp: A Rapid Crash Course Featuring Q&A Sessions, Exercises, and Projects

Vaskaran Sarcar
Kolkata, West Bengal, India

ISBN-13 (pbk): 979-8-8688-1515-7   ISBN-13 (electronic): 979-8-8688-1516-4
https://doi.org/10.1007/979-8-8688-1516-4

Copyright © 2025 by Vaskaran Sarcar

This work is subject to copyright. All rights are reserved by the Publisher, whether the whole or part of the material is concerned, specifically the rights of translation, reprinting, reuse of illustrations, recitation, broadcasting, reproduction on microfilms or in any other physical way, and transmission or information storage and retrieval, electronic adaptation, computer software, or by similar or dissimilar methodology now known or hereafter developed.

Trademarked names, logos, and images may appear in this book. Rather than use a trademark symbol with every occurrence of a trademarked name, logo, or image we use the names, logos, and images only in an editorial fashion and to the benefit of the trademark owner, with no intention of infringement of the trademark.

The use in this publication of trade names, trademarks, service marks, and similar terms, even if they are not identified as such, is not to be taken as an expression of opinion as to whether or not they are subject to proprietary rights.

While the advice and information in this book are believed to be true and accurate at the date of publication, neither the authors nor the editors nor the publisher can accept any legal responsibility for any errors or omissions that may be made. The publisher makes no warranty, express or implied, with respect to the material contained herein.

Managing Director, Apress Media LLC: Welmoed Spahr
Acquisitions Editor: Celestin Suresh John
Development Editor: James Markham
Editorial Assistant: Gryffin Winkler

Cover designed by eStudioCalamar

Cover image designed by Freepik (www.freepik.com)

Distributed to the book trade worldwide by Springer Science+Business Media New York, 1 New York Plaza, New York, NY 10004. Phone 1-800-SPRINGER, fax (201) 348-4505, e-mail orders-ny@springer-sbm.com, or visit www.springeronline.com. Apress Media, LLC is a Delaware LLC and the sole member (owner) is Springer Science + Business Media Finance Inc (SSBM Finance Inc). SSBM Finance Inc is a **Delaware** corporation.

For information on translations, please e-mail booktranslations@springernature.com; for reprint, paperback, or audio rights, please e-mail bookpermissions@springernature.com.

Apress titles may be purchased in bulk for academic, corporate, or promotional use. eBook versions and licenses are also available for most titles. For more information, reference our Print and eBook Bulk Sales web page at http://www.apress.com/bulk-sales.

Any source code or other supplementary material referenced by the author in this book is available to readers on GitHub. For more detailed information, please visit https://github.com/Apress/Python-Bootcamp.

If disposing of this product, please recycle the paper

I dedicate this book to all the unsung heroes and volunteers who fought on the front lines of the COVID-19 battle to save humanity and this beautiful world.

Table of Contents

About the Author xv

About the Technical Reviewer xvii

Acknowledgments xix

Introduction xxi

Part I: Foundations 1

Chapter 1: Getting Ready 3

What Is Python? 3

Setting Up the Programming Environment 4

    Installing Python 4

    Checking the Installation Status 6

    Troubleshooting 7

    Checking Multiple Python Versions 8

Running the Code 8

    Using the Command Prompt 9

    Using IDLE 10

    Using Popular IDEs 12

Using Comments 23

    Useful Notes 25

Summary 27

Exercise 1 28

    Keys to Exercise 1 28

v

TABLE OF CONTENTS

Chapter 2: Variables and Operators..31

Understanding Variables 31

Assigning Variables 31

Types of Variables...38

Reassigning Variables 40

Naming Conventions..43

Operators 50

Types 51

Precedence of Operators..51

Operators Associativity 55

Summary...57

Exercise 2 57

Keys to Exercise 2 58

Chapter 3: Simple Data Types 63

Strings...64

Playing with Strings...64

Using Built-In Functions 67

Numbers 75

Playing with Numbers 75

Using Built-In Functions 79

Importing the math Module 81

Booleans 84

Playing with Booleans 84

Making Interactive Programs...86

Accepting User Inputs 86

Summary...89

vi

TABLE OF CONTENTS

Exercise 3 89

Keys to Exercise 3 90

Case Studies 91

CS3.1 Problem Statement 92

CS3.2 Problem Statement 93

Sample Implementations 94

CS3.1 Implementation 94

CS3.2 Implementation 95

Part II: Building Smart Programs 97

Chapter 4: Decision-Making 99

Understanding Conditional Structures 99

Using an if Statement 99

Using the if-else Statements 100

Using the if-elif-else Statements 102

Alternative Designs 107

Pattern Matching Using the match Statement 109

Tautology and Contradictions..111

Summary...112

Exercise 4 112

Keys to Exercise 4 114

Case Study 116

CS4.1 Problem Statement 116

CS4.2 Problem Statement 117

Sample Implementations 117

CS4.1 Implementation 118

CS4.2 Implementation 119

vii

TABLE OF CONTENTS

Chapter 5: Loops 123

The Purpose of Iteration 123

The while Loop 125

    Notable Characteristics 125

The for Loop 129

    Is range a Function or a Type? 130

    Introducing Lists 134

    Use of the break Statement 136

    Use of the continue Statement 138

    Using Built-In Functionalities 139

    The iter and next Functions 139

    The enumerate Function 141

    Nested Loop 141

Summary 143

Exercise 5 144

    Keys to Exercise 5 144

Case Study 146

    CS5.1 Problem Statement 146

    CS5.2 Problem Statement 147

Sample Implementations 148

    CS5.1 Implementation 148

    CS5.2 Implementation 149

Chapter 6: Advanced Data Types 151

Lists 151

    Playing with Lists 151

Tuples 165

    Playing with Tuples 167

viii

TABLE OF CONTENTS

Dictionaries 172

    Playing with Dictionaries 172

Summary 174

Exercise 6 175

    Keys to Exercise 6 176

Case Study 178

    CS6.1 Problem Statement 178

    CS6.2 Problem Statement 179

Sample Implementations 180

    CS6.1 Implementation 180

    CS6.2 Implementation 181

Chapter 7: Functions and Modules 183

Function Overview 183

    Characteristics 183

Discussion on Function Arguments 188

    Positional Argument 188

    Keyword Arguments 189

    Use of Default Values 190

    Variable Arguments 193

Lambda Functions 197

    How to Use? 197

Modules 199

    Creating a Module 200

    Importing Partial Contents 201

    Importing Entire Contents 202

    Alias 205

ix

TABLE OF CONTENTS

Additional Notes..206

General Form of Import 206

Executing a Program as the Main Program..207

Summary..209

Exercise 7 210

Keys to Exercise 7 212

Case Study 216

CS7.1 Problem Statement 216

CS7.2 Problem Statement 218

Sample Implementations 218

CS7.1 Implementation 218

CS7.2 Implementation 221

Chapter 8: Exception Management..223

General Philosophy 224

Common Terms 225

Exception Handling in Python 226

Hierarchical Structure 226

Key Points...231

Using try-catch-finally...233

Using the else Block..236

Using the pass Statement 238

Arranging Multiple except Blocks..240

Summary..245

Exercise 8 246

Keys to Exercise 8 247

x

TABLE OF CONTENTS

Case Study 249

    CS8.1 Problem Statement 249

Sample Implementation 251

    CS8.1 Implementation 251

Chapter 9: Programming with Files 253

Processing Text Files 253

    Reading from a File 254

    Writing to a File 261

Processing Binary Files 267

    Copying an Image 267

    Pickling and Unpickling 268

Handling Exceptions 272

    FileNotFoundError 272

Exercise 9 274

    Keys to Exercise 9 275

Case Study 281

    CS9.1 Problem Statement 281

    CS9.2 Problem Statement 282

Sample Implementations 284

    CS9.1 Implementation 284

    CS9.2 Implementation 285

Part III: Introduction to OOP 291

Chapter 10: Classes and Objects 293

Basic Concepts and Common Terms 293

Modeling a Class 294

Creating Objects 295

    Alternative Code 296

xi

TABLE OF CONTENTS

Initializer 298

   Using Initializers 299

   Changing an Attribute Value 302

Default Attributes 304

   Applying the Concept..304

   Class Variables versus Instance Variables..306

Importing Classes 307

   Importing a Single Class...307

   Importing Multiple Classes 309

   Importing the Whole Module 310

   Alternative Code 311

Summary..313

Exercise 10 314

   Keys to Exercise 10 315

Case Study 316

   CS10.1 Problem Statement 317

   CS10.2 Problem Statement 317

Sample Implementations 317

   CS10.1 Implementation 317

   CS10.2 Implementation 318

Chapter 11: Inheritance 321

Basic Concepts and Terminologies 321

Types of Inheritance..322

   Single Inheritance..323

   Multiple Inheritance...327

   Investigating the Super Call 331

   Hierarchical Inheritance 334

xii

TABLE OF CONTENTS

Multilevel Inheritance 334

Hybrid Inheritance 335

Private Variables and Methods.. 336

Does Python Have Private Variables? 336

Accessing Private Data.. 338

Final Thoughts.. 341

Summary.. 342

Exercise 11 342

Keys to Exercises 11 347

Case Study 351

CS11.1 Problem Statement 351

CS11.2 Problem Statement 352

Sample Implementations 353

CS11.1 Implementation 353

CS11.2 Implementation 354

Appendix A: Supplementary Material...**357**

Appendix B: What's Next?..**385**

Appendix C: Other Books by the Author **387**

Index..**389**

xiii

About the Author

Vaskaran Sarcar obtained his master's in engineering from Jadavpur University, Kolkata (India), and his master's in computer application from Vidyasagar University, Midnapore (India). He was a National Gate Scholar (2007-2009) and has over 12 years of experience in education and the IT industry. He devoted his early years (2005–2007) to the teaching profession at various engineering colleges, and later, he joined HP India PPS R&D Hub in Bangalore. He worked there for more than 10 years and became a senior software engineer and team lead. After that, he pursued his passion and has already authored 17 Apress books that can be found at the link amazon.com/author/vaskaran_sarcar or the link `https://link.springer.com/search?newsearch=true&query=vaskaran+sarcar&content-type=book&dateFrom=&dateTo=&sortBy=newestFirst`. You can also find him on LinkedIn at `https://www.linkedin.com/in/vaskaransarcar`.

About the Technical Reviewer

Shibsankar Das is currently working as a senior data scientist at Microsoft. He has more than 10 years of experience working in IT where he has led several data science initiatives, and in 2019, he was recognized as one of the top 40 data scientists in India. His core strength is in GenAI, Deep Learning, NLP, and Graph Neural Networks. Currently, he is focusing on his research on AI Agents and Knowledge Graph. He has experience working in the domain of foundational research, FinTech, and ecommerce.

Before Microsoft, he has worked at Optum, Walmart, Envestnet, Microsoft Research, and Capgemini. He has pursued a master's from the Indian Institute of Technology, Bangalore.

Acknowledgments

At first, I thank the Almighty. I extend my deepest gratitude and thanks to the following people:

Celestin and the Apress team: I sincerely thank each of you for giving me another opportunity to work with you and Apress.

Shibsankar: I appreciate your time and effort in reviewing the book.

Gryffin Winkler, Deepa Tryphosa, Jagathesan, Vinoth, and the copy editor Leah Bitong: Thanks to each of you for your exceptional support in this book's development and for beautifying my work. Your efforts are extraordinary.

Finally, I thank the Python community for sharing their knowledge in various forms. In fact, I thank everyone who directly or indirectly contributed to this work.

Introduction

Python Bootcamp: A Rapid Crash Course Featuring Q&A Sessions, Exercises, and Projects is an introductory guide to Python programming. To give you an overview of the book, let me highlight a few points:

- The primary aim of this book is to make you familiar with Python programming as quickly as possible. I believe that you can enjoy learning when you analyze case studies, ask questions (about the doubts), and do some exercises. So, throughout this book, you will see interesting program segments, "Q&A sessions", and exercises. By analyzing these Q&As and doing the exercises, you can verify your progress. As said before, these are presented to make your future learning easier and enjoyable, but most importantly, they make you confident as a developer.

- Toward the end of each chapter, you'll see the exercises. Chapter 3 onward, you'll start solving case studies (a.k.a. projects). Once you finish reading the chapter, you'll get the complete implementation of the projects. The exercises and case studies are neither too easy nor too tough. These are within your optimal zone of difficulty. These will help you test your understanding and raise your confidence level.

INTRODUCTION

- Each question in these Q&A sessions is marked with **Q<Chapter_no>.<Question_no>.** For example, Q2.1 means question number 1 from Chapter 2. Similarly, each question in these exercises is marked with **E<Chapter_no>.<Question_no>.** For example, E5.3 means exercise number 3 from Chapter 5. **The case studies also have a similar format, but for them, you will see the prefix CS**. For example, CS5.1 means case study 1 from Chapter 5.

- Many of us are afraid of fat books because they do not promise that we can learn the subject in 1 day or 7 days. But you know that learning is a continuous process. It is hard to achieve any real mastery in 24 hours or 7 days. So the motto of the book is *to learn the core topics of Python; whatever effort I need to put in, I am okay with that*. Still, simple arithmetic says that if you can complete one chapter in 1 day, you can complete the book within 11 days (your learning speed depends only on your concentration level, focus, and dedication). But this arithmetic calculation is secondary! I have designed the book in such a way that upon completion of the book, you will know the core concepts in Python. Most importantly, you'll know how to learn further.

- Python is a very popular computer language and is widely used. Like other popular programming languages, it grows continuously to give us support with additional features and functionalities. In this book, you'll see me using **Python 3.13**. At the time of this writing, it is the latest version. So everything in this book should run in Python 3.13 and upcoming versions.

xxii

INTRODUCTION

How Is the Book Organized?

The book has eleven chapters and three appendixes. Let me give you a quick overview of them:

Chapter 1 is a warm-up session for you. Here, you'll set up your programming environment and learn about code comments that will help you understand the programs better.

Chapter 2 makes you familiar with variables and operators.

Chapter 3 discusses the common data types such as strings, numbers, and Booleans. This chapter also helps you make interactive programs.

Chapter 4 talks about decision-making in your program.

Chapter 5 discusses iterations. Here, you'll learn about loops and the usage of break and continue statements.

Chapter 6 shows the usage of some advanced data types such as lists, tuples, and dictionaries.

Chapter 7 teaches you how to use functions to make your code more Pythonic. It also discusses modules along with their usage.

Chapter 8 talks about exceptions and how to manage them.

Chapter 9 teaches you file-handling mechanisms.

Chapters 10 and 11 briefly cover the object-oriented programming basics and show you the usage of classes, objects, and inheritance.

Appendix A provides some extra material that was not discussed in the previous chapters.

Appendix B suggests a list of recommended books, courses, and online resources that can help you learn more on this topic.

Appendix C lists my other books.

You can download the source code of the book from the link: `https://github.com/Apress/Python-Bootcamp`.

INTRODUCTION

Prerequisite Knowledge

The target readers for this book are those who are new to Python programming. The book will be super easy for the readers with the least coding experience in any other high-level computer language. I assume that you can download a software installer following the instructions (or you have already installed Python on your computer). So I do not spend too much time on this topic. It is because you can find them easily both online and offline.

Who Is This Book For?

In short, you can pick the book if the answer is yes to the following questions:

- Are you learning Python for the first time?

- Do you want to explore the Python basics step by step but as quickly as possible?

- Would you like to cover a brief overview of object-oriented programming and want to know how Python supports the concept?

- Do you like to review your knowledge before you use Python in advanced fields such as data science and machine learning?

You probably should not read this book if the answer is yes to any of the following questions:

- Are you confident about the Python fundamentals?

- Are you looking for the advanced concepts, excluding the topics mentioned previously?

xxiv

INTRODUCTION

- Do you dislike a book that has an emphasis on Q&A sessions, exercises, and case studies?

- "I dislike Windows OS and PyCharm. I want to learn and use Python without them only." Is this statement true for you?

Guidelines for Using This Book

Here are some suggestions so you can use the book more effectively:

I suggest you read these chapters sequentially. The reason is that some fundamental techniques/concepts may be discussed in a previous chapter, and I do not repeat the same in a subsequent chapter.

I also suggest that you complete the exercises in a chapter before you enter a new chapter. This process can give you confidence, which can give you a better payoff soon.

Indentation is an important part of Python programming. We consider anything indented as a block of code in Python. Based on your device's screen size, you may not see the correct indentation in some programs. I suggest that you refer to the actual code in those cases.

I used PyCharm 2024.2.4 (Community Edition) in the Windows 10 environment for this book. PyCharm has many interesting features. When you work with large projects, those features are useful. The Community Edition of PyCharm is also free of cost. If you do not use the Windows operating system (OS), you can also use Visual Studio Code, which is also a source-code editor developed by Microsoft to support Windows, Linux, or Mac operating systems. This multiplatform integrated development environment (IDE) is also free. However, I recommend that you check the license and privacy statement as well. This is because this statement may change in the future.

As said before, I used Python 3.13 for this book. This is the latest version (at this time of writing). You can surely predict that version updates will come continuously, but I strongly believe that these version details

INTRODUCTION

should not matter much to you because I have used the fundamental constructs of Python. So these codes should execute smoothly in the upcoming versions of Python/PyCharm as well. I also believe that the results should not vary in other environments, but you know the nature of software that is naughty. So, if you like to see the same output, it is better to mimic the same environment.

Remember that you have just started on this journey. As you learn about these concepts, try to write your code. It helps you write better programs.

Author's note: Python 3.x (commonly known as Python 3) is the current and actively developed version, but Python 2.x (also known as Python 2) is the legacy. You may see some old Python projects with Python 2, but I recommend that you learn and use Python 3.

Conventions in This Book

Here, I mention only two points: In some places, I have used only the pronoun "he" to refer to a person when the context is generic, for example, a customer, an executive, etc. Please treat it as "he" or "she" – whichever applies to you.

Second, all the outputs and codes of the book follow the same font and structure. To draw your attention, in some places, I have made them bold. Here is a sample code fragment that is taken from Chapter 8:

```
// The previous portion is not shown here
except ValueError as e:
    print("Invalid input! Provide a correct input next time!")
    print(f"Error details: {e}")
else:
    print(f"The result of the division is: {result}")
finally:
    print("The program completes successfully.")
```

xxvi

INTRODUCTION

Final Words

You are an intelligent person. You have chosen a topic that can assist you throughout your career. As you learn and review these concepts, I suggest you write your code; only then will you master this area. There is no shortcut for this. Do you know the ancient story of Euclid and Ptolemy, the ruler of Egypt? Euclid's approach to mathematics was based on logical reasoning and rigorous proofs, and Ptolemy asked Euclid if there was an easier way to learn mathematics. Euclid's reply to the ruler? **"There is no royal road to geometry."** Though you are not studying geometry, the essence of this reply applies here. You must study these concepts and code. Do not give up when you face challenges. Don't forget that they'll make you a better developer.

Errata: I have tried my level best to ensure the accuracy of the content. However, mistakes can happen. So I have a plan to maintain the "Errata," and if required, I can also make some updates/announcements there. So I suggest that you visit those pages to receive any important corrections or updates.

An appeal: You can easily understand that any good-quality work takes many days and many months (even years!). Many authors like me invest most of their time in writing and heavily depend on it. You can encourage and help these authors by preventing piracy. If you come across any illegal copies of our works in any form on the Internet, I would be grateful if you would provide me/the Apress team with the location address or website name. In this context, you can use the link `https://www.apress.com/gp/services/rights-permission/piracy` as well.

Share your feedback: I believe that once you finish reading this book, you will be confident about Python programming. I hope that you will value the effort. Please provide your valuable feedback on the Amazon review page or any other platform you like.

xxvii

PART I

Foundations

Part I consists of three chapters. In this part, you'll set up your programming environment and execute simple programs. This part will make you familiar with variables, operators, and common primitive data types such as strings, numbers, and Booleans. A careful study of this part will help you understand the remaining part of the book easily.

CHAPTER 1

Getting Ready

This chapter briefly talks about the Python language and its importance. Shortly, you'll learn how to set up your programming environment before you execute the programs.

What Is Python?

Python is a computer programming language that was created by Guido van Rossum in the late 1980s. It is a popular programming language and is rapidly growing. The primary reasons for its popularity are simplicity and readability. The official site (see What is Python? Executive Summary | Python.org) states the following:

> *Python is an interpreted, object-oriented, high-level programming language with dynamic semantics.*

At this moment, you do not need to dig further. You can simply note that since it is a high-level language, you can avoid direct interaction with registers, memory addresses, call stacks, etc. Instead, you write your program in plain English. Most importantly, you can use Python for various purposes. For example, you may notice its usage in game programming, business applications, tools development, etc. As an interpreted language, Python offers rapid prototyping and development. So it saves developers time and energy. In recent years, we have noticed

© Vaskaran Sarcar 2025
V. Sarcar, *Python Bootcamp*, https://doi.org/10.1007/979-8-8688-1516-4_1

CHAPTER 1   GETTING READY

its usage in emerging fields like data science and machine learning too. Finally, I'd also like to mention that the Python community is very strong and supportive, and they help you grow faster.

Setting Up the Programming Environment

At this stage, you need to get the Python interpreter and install it before you write your programs. You need to pick the correct interpreter based on your operating system.

POINT TO NOTE

Nowadays, lots of alternative options are available. For example, you can directly jump into coding using an online editor. To illustrate, I can head over to `https://www.online-python.com/` and easily execute some code. Still, I recommend that you install Python on your system. You should not worry about the early setup issues (if any). Sorting out these issues can provide long-term benefits in the future.

Installing Python

Get the Python installer from `https://www.python.org/`. Once you click the **Downloads** tab, you should see the latest Python version. For example, once I followed these steps, I could see the following (see Figure 1-1).

4

CHAPTER 1 GETTING READY

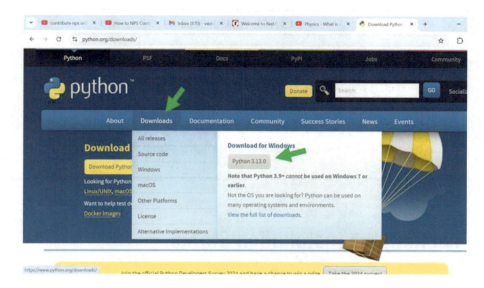

Figure 1-1. *Official Downloads page for Python*

Download the appropriate installer and run it. Since I used Python for Windows, I downloaded the installer for Windows. While running the installer, I suggest you select the Add python.exe to PATH option for convenient access to Python across environments like command-line interface (CLI), editor, etc.

Author's note: I assume that you're probably familiar with installing software on a machine. There are lots of YouTube videos and online materials that show how to install Python on your computer. Showing all these steps with screenshots will make the chapter lengthy. If needed, you can check those materials.

5

CHAPTER 1 GETTING READY

> **GENTLE REMINDER**
>
> As the book's "Introduction" stated, the programs of this book were developed and tested on a Windows (64-bit) machine. To make the chapter short, I'll keep the instructions only for Windows. There is no wondering that the specifics can vary for a machine that uses a different OS. So, while downloading software, you must read the OS-specific instructions from the corresponding Downloads page.

Checking the Installation Status

Once you download and install Python, the first step is to verify whether it is installed properly. Open the command prompt and type python --version. Using this command, I could see that Python version 3.13.0 was installed on my computer (see Figure 1-2).

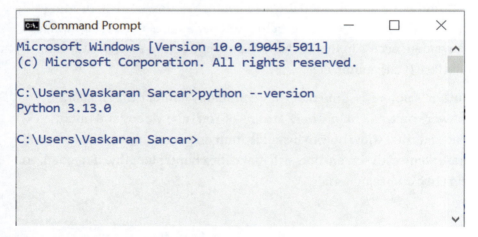

Figure 1-2. Checking the Python version on a Windows machine

CHAPTER 1   GETTING READY

POINT TO NOTE

You can see that Python 3.13.0 is installed on my computer. When this chapter was written, Python 3.13.0 was the latest version. Later, I got updates. Before the release of this book, I was able to test my programs in version 3.13.2 as well. From the online link `https://www.python.org/downloads/`, you can learn about the different Python versions along with their release dates.

Troubleshooting

If the previous command does not work and you notice something like `python is not recognized as an internal or external command`, you probably forgot to select the **Add python.exe to PATH** option when you ran the installer. When I installed Python 3.12 on my computer, I chose the default installation path, and the following two variables were added to the Path environment variable:

```
C:\Users\Vaskaran Sarcar\AppData\Local\Programs\Python\
Python312\
C:\Users\Vaskaran Sarcar\AppData\Local\Programs\Python\
Python312\Scripts\
```

However, when I installed Python 3.13 on my computer, I chose a different installation path, and the following two variables were added to the Path environment variable:

```
C:\Python313\
C:\Python313\Scripts\
```

So, if you find any problem after the installation, I suggest that you first find out the Python interpreter installation path and edit the environment variable accordingly.

CHAPTER 1   GETTING READY

Checking Multiple Python Versions

If you have installed multiple Python versions on your computer, you can check those installations as well. For example, when I wrote my first Python book, I used Python 3.8. In between, I installed Python 3.12.4 and now I installed Python 3.13.0 for this book. I can check all these Python versions by executing the command **py -0** as follows:

```
C:\Users\Vaskaran Sarcar>py -0
 -V:3.13 *        Python 3.13 (64-bit)
 -V:3.12          Python 3.12 (64-bit)
 -V:3.8-32        Python 3.8 (32-bit)
```

PYTHON 2 IS A LEGACY

The online link `https://www.python.org/doc/sunset-python-2/#:~:text=We%20have%20decided%20that%20January,as%20soon%20as%20you%20can.` states the following:

We have decided that January 1, 2020, was the day that we sunset Python 2. That means that we will not improve it anymore after that day, even if someone finds a security problem in it. You should upgrade to Python 3 as soon as you can.

This is why this book also focuses on Python 3.x (known as Python 3), but not on Python 2. Even if you see some old Python projects with Python 2, I recommend you to learn and use Python3.

Running the Code

You can write and execute a Python program in various ways. Probably, one of the simplest ways is to use a text editor (such as Notepad) to write a Python program. For now, let me show you a few ways to run the Python code.

8

CHAPTER 1   GETTING READY

Using the Command Prompt

Open the command prompt, type py, and then press the **Enter** key to open
the Python shell. Notice the arrow tip in the following figure (Figure 1-3).

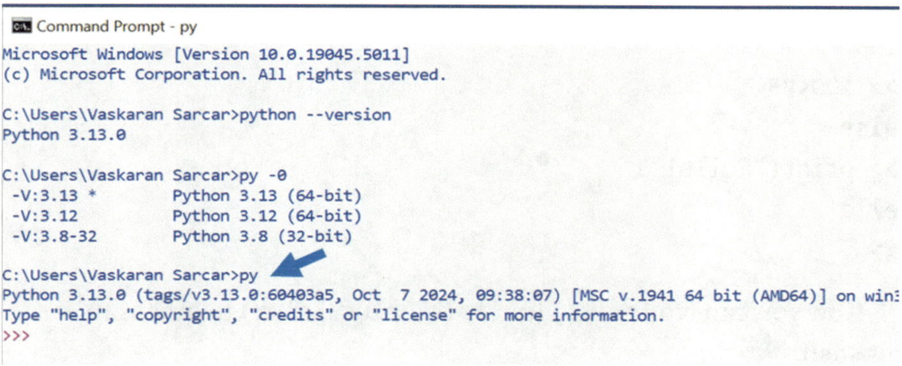

Figure 1-3. *Checking the Python version in the command prompt,
then listing the available versions, and finally entering into the
Python shell*

Q&A Session

Q1.1 What is a shell?

In simple terms, it is an environment that is used to run other programs.
We can use shells for both the command-line interface and the graphical
user interface (GUI). Normally, we use it to refer to the command-line
interface of the operating system (OS). Developers often call the terms
"shells" and "terminals" in the same context interchangeably.

Let us try running some code snippets. You start typing the code after
the >>> prompt. Then you press the Enter (or Return) key and execute
the code. Here are some examples:

```
C:\Users\Vaskaran Sarcar>py
Python 3.13.0 (tags/v3.13.0:60403a5, Oct  7 2024, 09:38:07)
[MSC v.1941 64 bit (AMD64)] on win32
```

9

CHAPTER 1   GETTING READY

```
Type "help", "copyright", "credits" or "license" for more
information.
>>> 12+3
15
>>> 7>5
True
>>> 100<95
False
>>> print("Hello!")
Hello!
>>>
```

Now you can type exit() (or Ctrl+Z plus Enter) to quit from this shell.

Using IDLE

You can also launch IDLE to get a Python shell where you can execute Python commands. To get IDLE in Windows 10, you can type IDLE in the search box as shown in Figure 1-4.

CHAPTER 1 GETTING READY

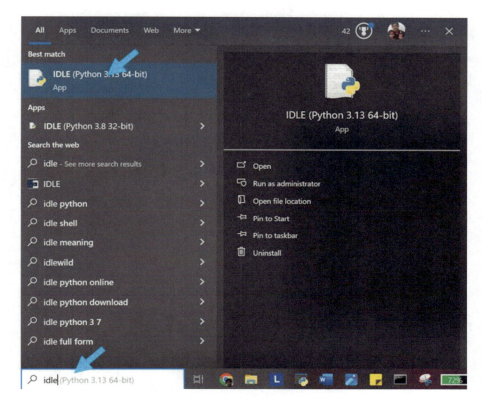

Figure 1-4. *Searching IDLE*

Once you can see the app, click it to launch. You should see the following screen (see Figure 1-5).

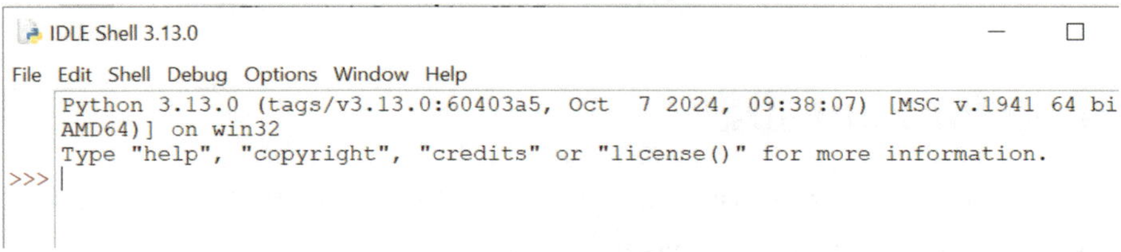

```
IDLE Shell 3.13.0                                              —    □
File Edit Shell Debug Options Window Help
    Python 3.13.0 (tags/v3.13.0:60403a5, Oct  7 2024, 09:38:07) [MSC v.1941 64 bi
    AMD64)] on win32
    Type "help", "copyright", "credits" or "license()" for more information.
>>> |
```

Figure 1-5. *Snapshot of IDLE Shell 3.13.0 where users can execute Python commands*

CHAPTER 1   GETTING READY

This shell waits to get a command from the user, executes the command, and then displays the result. Once this cycle is completed, it waits for the next command to receive from the user.

For example, if you type `print("Hello World!")` after >>> in the shell and press the **Enter** key, you can immediately see the output `Hello World` in the next line. Let us try a few more lines of code and verify the output as follows (see Figure 1-6).

```
IDLE Shell 3.13.0                                         —      □

File  Edit  Shell  Debug  Options  Window  Help
    Python 3.13.0 (tags/v3.13.0:60403a5, Oct  7 2024, 09:38:07) [MSC v.1941 64 b
    AMD64)] on win32
    Type "help", "copyright", "credits" or "license()" for more information.
>>> print("Hello World")
    Hello World
>>> 3+7
    10
>>> 25>19
    True
>>> |
```

Figure 1-6. *Displaying the output in the IDLE shell*

Hopefully, you get an idea! To execute some basic commands or to check whether you are ready for Python programming, this approach is fine.

However, there is a problem: once you exit from the shell, you lose all these commands. This is why you can use a text file to write a Python program and save the file with the **.py** extension. A file with the **.py** extension is called a **Python script**.

Using Popular IDEs

I have shown you the use of simple command prompts to make you aware of the alternative ways to run your Python programs. However, the use of command prompts is not suitable for big programs. Ask any professional about how they write programs. You will come to know that they use specialized text editors or IDEs (**IDE stands for integrated development**

CHAPTER 1 GETTING READY

environment) to write the code. For example, the .NET developers often use the Visual Studio IDE, the Python programmers often use the PyCharm IDE, and the Java developers often use the Eclipse IDE. Let me show you some of the key benefits of using a specialized IDE:

- They help you highlight the syntax error(s).

- They help you organize your files.

- They also support auto-completion for certain functions and phrases, which is extremely helpful.

- You can also set breakpoints to pause at specified lines in your program.

- You find code refactoring very easy.

- There are many IDEs with cross-platform support too.

Q&A Session

Q1.2 What is code refactoring?

It is a process that is often used to improve the existing structure and design of an application without changing its external functionality. You may need to follow this process to make the code more efficient. Normally, once the refactoring is done, the code is cleaner, more readable, and maintainable as well.

Q1.3 It appears to me that we can avoid the process of refactoring by writing better code at the beginning. Is this correct?

It is almost impossible to predict everything in the initial stage of development. Once a product is deployed, you may feel the need for refactoring after a substantial period, more particularly before you add a new functionality to your code.

CHAPTER 1   GETTING READY

I wrote many books on C#. Since the Visual Studio Community Edition is free, I often use this IDE to exercise my C# programs. The good news is that you can run Python programs in this IDE as well. It helps me to switch between C# and Python programs. To give you an example, let me show you a snapshot that shows the presence of both the C# and Python programs in Visual Studio as follows (see Figure 1-7).

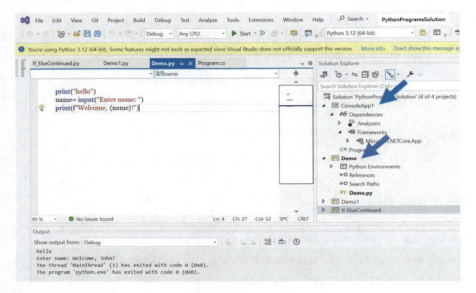

Figure 1-7. *Displaying the presence of a C# project and a Python project in the Visual Studio IDE*

If you also have a C# background and like to exercise the Python scripts (a.k.a. programs) in Visual Studio, you can follow the online link `https://learn.microsoft.com/en-us/visualstudio/python/tutorial-working-with-python-in-visual-studio-step-01-create-project?view=vs-2022`.

CHAPTER 1   GETTING READY

However, I'd like to use the PyCharm IDE to develop my programs for this book. To learn and test simple Python scripts, PyCharm is a pleasant choice for you. The good news is that at the time of this writing, both the Visual Studio Community and PyCharm Community editions are free.

Note   Spyder is another open source and cross-platform IDE, which we often use in Python programming. For my machine learning projects, I use Jupyter Notebook, in which I can test Python scripts. If you install Anaconda distribution on your computer, you can find Spyder IDE, Jupyter Notebook, and many other things. However, as said before, to learn and test simple Python scripts, PyCharm can help you a lot. It helps you to organize your files and identify syntax errors. You can also set breakpoints to pause at specified lines in your program. You find code refactoring very easy when you use PyCharm.

For the following program, I took some screenshots from the PyCharm IDE. These can help you visualize the execution environment. But next time onward, I'll show you the programs and corresponding output only. As said before, to execute the Python scripts, PyCharm is NOT mandatory. You can run these programs in various ways (e.g., using IDLE, Spyder IDE, Jupyter Notebook, etc.). So it makes little sense to take screenshots from PyCharm for each of these programs.

Let me show you the steps. Though you can skip some of these steps, I suggest you not skip them. This is because by following these steps, I organized my code for this book:

Step 1: Open PyCharm.

Step 2: Click **File ➤ New Project**. Now set the project name, location, and the Python version. (You can see that I have named the project *PythonBootcamp*, set the location *E:\MyPrograms,* and chosen the latest version of Python that was available on my computer.) Finally, click the **Create** button (see Figure 1-8).

15

CHAPTER 1 GETTING READY

Figure 1-8. *Creating a project in PyCharm*

Note If you have multiple Python versions installed on your computer, you can see them in the drop-down list, as shown in the previous screenshot (Figure 1-8), and you can pick your preferred Python version from there. I am using the latest version (3.13), which was available at the time of this writing.

Step 3: Once you click the **Create** button, you'll see the following screen (Figure 1-9). Since I have already executed some Python scripts using PyCharm, I get this option. But for the first-time users, you do not see this window.

CHAPTER 1   GETTING READY

Figure 1-9. *Project open options in PyCharm*

Step 3.1: Once I chose the current window, I got the following screen (see Figure 1-10).

Figure 1-10. *The project is opened in a new window*

Step 4: I have organized the code of this book chapter-wise. Right-click the project folder name (PythonBootcamp). Select "**New**" and then choose "**Directory**" (see Figure 1-11).

17

CHAPTER 1　GETTING READY

Figure 1-11. *Adding a new directory under PythonBootcamp*

Step 4.1: Let's name it `chapter1`. Once it is done, you'll see Figure 1-12.

Figure 1-12. *The directory chapter1 is added under PythonBootcamp*

CHAPTER 1 GETTING READY

Step 5: Now create a Python file under the directory named chapter1. To do this, right-click the directory (chapter1), select "**New**," and then choose "**Python file**." Let's name it hello_world for now (see Figure 1-13).

Figure 1-13. *Naming the file hello_world*

Step 5.1: Now press **Enter**. Notice that a new Python file is created for you. See Figure 1-14.

Figure 1-14. *The hello_world.py is ready. You can write the code here*

19

CHAPTER 1   GETTING READY

Congratulations! You are ready to write your first program in PyCharm. Now, I'll show you a simple Python program using PyCharm IDE.

Demonstration 1.1

Let us write a simple Python program. Type the line `print("Hello World!")` in a Python file (refer to the following screen). Now, move the cursor to the next line by pressing the "Enter" key as shown in the following figure (see Figure 1-15).

Figure 1-15. *The hello_world.py file contains a line of code*

Save the file (**File ➤ Save All (Ctrl+S)**).

Now, you can run the program. **Right-click** the file name and click the option **Run 'hello_world'** as shown in the following figure. See Figure 1-16.

CHAPTER 1   GETTING READY

Figure 1-16. *Run hello_world.py in PyCharm*

Output

Congratulation! You have successfully executed your first Python program in PyCharm IDE. You can see the following output: `Hello World!` in the following figure (Figure 1-17).

CHAPTER 1   GETTING READY

Figure 1-17. *The successful execution of the program generates the output*

If you want to run the program again, you can use the following button as pointed by the arrow tip in the following figure. Notice that "`hello_world`" is selected by default before you click the run button. See Figure 1-18.

Figure 1-18. *The alternative option to run hello_world.py*

22

CHAPTER 1   GETTING READY

POINTS TO REMEMBER

- Every time you write a new program, you can follow the same approach.

- Here I have named my file `hello_world.py`. However, once you download the programs from the Apress site, you'll see the script names like ch01_d01_hello_world. py, ch01_d02_comments.py, etc. I followed this structure so that you can easily identify the chapter number and the corresponding demonstration number. For example, ch01_d01 stands for Demonstration 1.1 (in other words, the first demonstration of Chapter 1). In fact, this kind of naming follows the PEP8 guideline (refer to the link `https://www.python.org/dev/peps/pep-0008/`) as well.

Using Comments

It is standard practice to use comments in your program. These comments can help others to understand your code better. Let us consider a real-life scenario. In a software organization, a group of people creates software for its customers. It is possible that after some years, none of them will be available (they may move to a different team, or they may leave the organization). In such a case, someone needs to maintain the software and continue fixing the bugs for its customers. However, it can be difficult to understand the logic if there is no hint or explanation about the program. Comments are useful in such scenarios. In Python, you see the following options for comments:

CHAPTER 1   GETTING READY

Case 1: Single-line comments using # tags. Here is an example:

```
# This is a single-line comment
```

You can use them in line as well. Here is an example:

```
x=5 # Assigning 5 to x
```

However, the official guideline suggests that you should use inline comments only when it makes sense. For example, the previous inline comment was obvious, and this is why it was unnecessary. However, if you write something like the following, it can help you understand the code better:

```
x = x + 2 # Adjusting the border
```

Sometimes, you may work with a block of code that contains multiple lines. In those cases, you can apply # to the beginning of each line of the block, and then you put a single space (unless it is indented text inside the comment).

A block can contain paragraphs. In such cases, those paragraphs are separated by a line containing a single #.

Case 2: Multi-line docstrings as multi-line comments using three double quotations (or single quotations). You can see one-line docstrings as well. Here, I show you the use of docstrings that I used inside a function in Chapter 7. For now, you do not need to understand the code. You only see the texts that begin with triple-double quotations (" " ") and end with triple-double quotations (" " "):

```
def print_details(name, age):
    """

    This function takes two parameters.
    You can supply the name and age of the user
    in this function.
```

24

CHAPTER 1   GETTING READY

```
"""
print(f"Hello {name}! How are you?")
print(f"You are now {age}.")
```

Useful Notes

Before you leave this section, I want you to remember the following points:

- Comments are simple notes or some texts. You use them for human readers but not for the Python interpreter. The Python interpreter ignores the text inside a comment block.

- In the software industry, many technical reviewers review your code. The comments help them understand the program's logic. It is also true that a developer can forget the logic after some months. These comments can help him recollect his logic. However, you need to use comments wisely.

- Experts prefer to use the many single-line comments using # tags.

- In Python programming, functions, modules, and classes should have docstrings. These will make sense when you see them in Chapter 7 or Chapter 11. There, you'll see that I used docstrings to describe a function and class behavior. You'll also know that a docstring becomes the _doc_ attribute of an object. I leave the discussion at this point.

In this chapter, let's learn the use of simple comments that you may see in others' code.

25

CHAPTER 1   GETTING READY

Demonstration 1.2

Let's see a program that has many different comments:

```
# Testing whether 2 is greater than 1
print(2>1)

x=5 # Assigning 5 to x
x = x + 2 # Adjusting the border

'''
I am using multi-line comments using three single quotes.
However, it is not recommended.
These are common in classes, functions, or modules.
'''

"""
I am using multi-line comments using three double quotes.
These are common in classes, functions, or modules.
"""

# Now I'm showing multiple single-line comments
# Multiplying 5 with 25
# And printing the result
print(5*25)
```

Output

Here is the output:

```
True
125
```

26

CHAPTER 1   GETTING READY

Analysis

This program uses different comments, and it is easy to understand. You can see that you have received output for the lines `print(2>1)` and `print(5*25)` only. The remaining portions (comments) are ignored by the interpreter. Since 2 is bigger than 1, the output came as `True`, and when you multiply 5 with 25, the result is `125`.

Q&A Session

Q1.4 I can see that you have used both single quotes and double quotes while describing a multi-line comment. Was this intentional?
The online link `https://peps.python.org/pep-0008/#comments` describes conventions for writing good documentation strings, and there you'll see the use of double quotes but not single quotes. However, I wanted to show you that you'll not receive any errors while using single quotes. I prefer to use double quotes. It is because C# and Java use the same. In the upcoming chapters, you'll become familiar with the `string` data type. There, you'll learn that the online link `https://peps.python.org/pep-0008/#string-quotes` also states the following:

> *For triple-quoted strings, always use double quote characters to be consistent with the docstring convention in PEP 257.*

I know that this chapter was a bit slow, but it is important. These discussions will help you understand upcoming chapters easily.

Summary

This chapter gave a quick overview of the Python programming language. It showed you how to set up your programming environment. It also showed various ways to execute the Python scripts. Finally, it discussed various code comments along with their usage.

CHAPTER 1   GETTING READY

Exercise 1

E1.1 Create a program to print the following structure:

```
*
**
***
```

E1.2 Write a program to print the sum of three numbers: 10, 15, and 25.5.

E1.3 Which one do you prefer – more comments inside your code or fewer comments inside the code?

Keys to Exercise 1

Here is a sample solution set for the exercises in this chapter.

E1.1

Upon executing this program, you can see the intended output:

```
print("*")
print("**")
print("***")
```

E1.2

You can write the following code:

```
print("The sum of 10,15 and 25.5 is as follows:")
print(10+15+25.5)
```

Upon executing this program, you can see the following output:

```
The sum of 10,15 and 25.5 is as follows:
50.5
```

CHAPTER 1   GETTING READY

E1.3

It depends. If a comment helps another developer to understand or review your code, it has significant value. But you need to use your intelligence. You do not want to include too many unnecessary comments to describe a code that is easy to understand.

Additional note:

In the book *Clean Code* (Pearson), Robert C. Martin tells us the following: "Comments are always failures. We must have them because we cannot always figure out how to express ourselves without them, but their use is not a cause for celebration." This book continues, "Every time you express yourself in code, you should pat yourself on the back. Every time you write a comment, you should grimace and feel the failure of your ability of expression." Another great book is *The Pragmatic Programmer* by Andrew Hunt and David Thomas. In this book, the authors tell us: "Programmers are taught to comment their code: good code has lots of comments. Unfortunately, they are never taught why code needs comments: bad code requires lots of comments."

These are good suggestions. However, you may not always agree with these thoughts. You can find developers who can point to pros and cons on both sides of the issue. Even the mentioned books show some examples of both good and bad comments.

There are plenty of examples where the actual code is tricky or difficult to understand. Some good, well-maintained comments can help a first-time reader/developer. For me, comments can be useful because when I hover my mouse over a built-in function in an IDE, the corresponding comment helps me to understand the functionality better.

29

CHAPTER 2

Variables and Operators

In this chapter, you will see some building blocks to help you develop your Python programs. First, it discusses variables. Later, you'll learn how to use operators in your program.

Understanding Variables

In mathematical algebra, you can write something like x=10. Then you say x is a variable to represent the number 10. Python works in a similar way, except that you can represent both numeric and non-numeric values using variables.

Assigning Variables

Assigning a value to a variable is one of the most basic operations in programming. This section discusses the topic in detail.

Assigning a Single Variable

Using an assignment operator, you can assign a value to a variable. For example, you can assign the number 21 to the variable age as follows: age = 21. Similarly, you can assign 5 to another variable, called `students,` as follows: `students = 5.`

© Vaskaran Sarcar 2025

V. Sarcar, *Python Bootcamp*, https://doi.org/10.1007/979-8-8688-1516-4_2

CHAPTER 2   VARIABLES AND OPERATORS

Once the variables are assigned, let's execute the following code:

```
print(age)
print(students)
```

Now you'll see that 21 and 5 are printed on the screen. It shows that the variables are holding the intended values.

Look at the following line again: age = 21. You can see the variable (age) is placed on the left-hand side of the assignment operator (=), and the intended value is placed on the right-hand side of the assignment operator. However, you'll never see a code like

```
21=age   # This is an error
```

If by mistake you do this, you'll receive a syntax error. For your reference, let me execute the code snippets that I just discussed in a Python shell:

```
>>> age=21
>>> students=5
>>> print(age)
21
>>> print(students)
5
>>> 21=age
  File "<python-input-4>", line 1
    21=age
    ^^
SyntaxError: cannot assign to literal here. Maybe you meant
'==' instead of '='?
```

32

CHAPTER 2 VARIABLES AND OPERATORS

If, by mistake, you try to print the value of a variable, say, b, which has not been defined already, you'll see the error as well. Here is a sample:

```
>>> b
Traceback (most recent call last):
  File "<python-input-16>", line 1, in <module>
    b
NameError: name 'b' is not defined
```

Are x=y and y=x the Same?

If you are coding for the first time, you may be confused about the usage of the assignment operator. Let me explain. From a mathematical point of view, it may appear to you that both the statements x=y and y=x have the same meaning, but in programming, they are different.

Demonstration 2.1

To make it clear, you can do a small test using the following code segment in the Python shell:

```
x=25
y=50
print("Initial values of x and y:")
print(x)
print(y)
x=y # assigning the current value of y to x
print("After the assignment, x and y are as follows:")
print(x)
print(y)
```

33

CHAPTER 2 VARIABLES AND OPERATORS

Output

Once you run this code, you'll see the following output:

```
Initial values of x and y:
25
50
After the assignment, x and y are as follows:
50
50
```

Analysis

You can see that initially, x was 25. But once you use the line of code x=y, the current value of y is assigned to x. So, when you print the value of x again, you get 50.

Let's replace the line x=y with the line of code y=x in the previous code segment. Run this code again. You'll see the following output:

```
Initial values of x and y:
25
50
After the assignment, x and y are as follows:
25
25
```

You can see that the statements x=y and y=x can have different meanings in Python programming.

Author's note: Apart from the = operator, there are many other assignment operators. Later, you'll be familiar with them.

34

CHAPTER 2   VARIABLES AND OPERATORS

Assigning Multiple Variables in a Single Line

In Python programming, you can assign multiple variables in one statement. For example, instead of writing the following two lines of code

```
age=21
students=5
```

you can write a single line as follows:

```
age, students=21,5
```

You can see that when you used the line of code age, students = 21, 5, the values 21 and 5 were assigned to age and students variables, respectively. A tuple is a comma-separated list of expressions. So you can say that in the previous example, age and students form one tuple, and 21 and 5 form another tuple. We refer to this assignment process as a ***tuple assignment***.

Note   You will learn more about tuples in Chapter 6.

Assigning the Same Value to Multiple Variables

Now, let us explore another interesting feature in Python programming. You can assign the same value to multiple variables in one statement. For example, using the following code snippet, you can assign all three variables (x, y, and z) the same value (5):

```
x=y=z=5
```

35

CHAPTER 2   VARIABLES AND OPERATORS

This is why the following code

```
x=y=z=5
print(x)
print(y)
print(z)
```

will print the same value 5 three times as follows:

```
5
5
5
```

Is the Print Function Mandatory?

The interactive Python shell can test both expressions and statements. For example, if you type 21, the shell can interpret it as 21. See the following segment:

```
>>> 21
21
```

But when you enter age=21 in the Python shell, it is treated as a correct syntactical statement with no value, and the shell prints nothing. In the next line, when you enter age, the shell can print the corresponding value. This is why it is important to note that in the Python shell, when you print the values, instead of typing print(age), you can simply type age to get the value of age.

By default, you may not observe this behavior when you try to execute this as a program in PyCharm IDE. For example, try to run a program that has the following lines in the PyCharm IDE:

```
age=21
age
```

CHAPTER 2   VARIABLES AND OPERATORS

In this case, you'll not see any output. Here is a sample snapshot after running this program (notice the arrow tips in Figure 2-1).

Figure 2-1. *Executing the program produces no output*

Interestingly, PyCharm has an embedded terminal emulator. It helps you work with the command-line shell from inside the IDE. So, if you like to see the output (as you saw when I executed the code in the interactive shell), you can launch the "Terminal" from **View ➤ Tool Windows ➤ Terminal** in the PyCharm IDE and type your code. Here is a sample screenshot for your reference where the arrow tip shows the terminal location (see Figure 2-2).

37

CHAPTER 2   VARIABLES AND OPERATORS

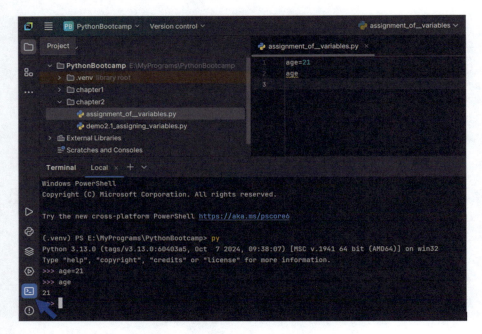

Figure 2-2.   Using PyCharm's terminal emulator

Author's note: To know more about the terminal emulator, visit the link `https://www.jetbrains.com/help/pycharm/terminal-emulator.html`.

Types of Variables

The online link `https://docs.python.org/3/library/stdtypes.html#` mentions the major built-in types in Python. These are numerics, sequences, mappings, classes, instances, and exceptions. As you progress, you'll get to know them. Based on your application, you may need to work with other types as well. You can assign different values to these variables using an assignment operator. For now, let us have a quick look at a set of variables that represent different data types. (I have also pointed their category inside the square bracket.)

CHAPTER 2   VARIABLES AND OPERATORS

```python
# Example of an int variable [Numeric type]
age=21

# Example of floating-point number variable [Numeric type]
book_price=30.5

# Example of a list (of employee names) [Sequence type]
employee_names=["Sam","Bob","Jack"]

# Example of a tuple (these are immutable) [Sequence type]
popular_fruits=("Banana","Apple","Orange","Mango")

# Example of a dictionary (it is a key-value pair)
[Mapping type]
Wimbledon_titles=["Federer":8, "Djokovic": 7]
```

POINT TO NOTE

Do not worry! As you progress, you'll become familiar with them. I believe that in most cases, you'll need strings (you can consider them as sequences of texts), numbers, Booleans, sequences (such as lists, tuples, and range objects), and dictionaries. In the following sections, for your easy understanding, I'll use only the string and number variables. You'll learn more about them in the next chapter (Chapter 3). I'll discuss lists, tuples, and dictionaries in a separate chapter (Chapter 6).

Now I am about to execute a few lines of code. I execute them in PyCharm's terminal emulator. **In fact, now onward when you see >>>, you understand that I am doing the same.** Examine the following code:

```python
>>> number=25
>>> type(number)
<class 'int'>
```

39

CHAPTER 2 VARIABLES AND OPERATORS

You can see that the number 25 is an `int` type.

Now, examine the following code (notice that the `number` has a fractional part now):

```
>>> number=25.0
>>> type(number)
<class 'float'>
```

You can see that number is a `float` now.

You can see that 25 belongs to the `int` type, but 25.0 belongs to the `float` type. **By executing these code segments, you can see that the Python interpreter can determine the type of data that you are working on**.

Q&A Session

Q2.1 I am new to programming. I do not see any difference between 25 and 25.0. However, I see that they belong to different types. So I'd like to know: how does the int type differ from the float type?

The `int` type represents the whole numbers; they do not have fractional parts. We call them integers. An integer can be positive, negative, or 0. For example, 23, -32, 67, -2, 0, and 25 are examples of integers. In Python, we represent integers with the `int` data type.

In contrast, `35.75`, `45.2`, etc. are not integers because they have fractional parts. These are *floating-point numbers*. In Python, you simply call them the `float` data type.

Reassigning Variables

Once you assign a value to a variable, you can reassign it again. To test this, let us see the following code snippet along with the output:

```
>>> age=21
>>> print(age)
```

40

CHAPTER 2   VARIABLES AND OPERATORS

```
21
>>> age=22
>>> print(age)
22
```

You can see that the initial value (21) of the age variable is successfully updated to 22 after the reassignment.

Reassigning Can Change the Type

Note that the type of variable can change if you reassign an expression with a different type. Let's examine the following code along with the output:

```
>>> number=25
>>> type(number)
<class 'int'>
>>> number=25.1
>>> type(number)
<class 'float'>
```

You can see that when I changed the number 25 to 25.1, its type was changed from int to float. This example shows that Python allows you to redeclare a variable with a different type.

Demonstration 2.2

Now you know how to use a variable. You have also learned how to assign a value to a variable and reassign a new value to it. Let us test these understandings by the following program that uses a variable named hello_msg. The hello_msg was assigned an initial value "Hello World!", which is updated later in the program. I also kept the simple comments in this program for your easy understanding. Here is the new program:

```
print("This program shows the use of a variable.")
# hello_msg is holding the value "Hello World!"
```

41

CHAPTER 2   VARIABLES AND OPERATORS

```
hello_msg = "Hello World!"
print(hello_msg)
# Reassigning a new value to hello_msg
hello_msg = "Dear Reader, how are you?"
print(hello_msg)
```

Output

Upon executing this program, you should see the following output:

```
This program shows the use of a variable.
Hello World!
Dear Reader, how are you?
```

Q&A Session

Q2.2 When you use the variable hello_msg, you need to write two lines of code to print: Hello World! However, if I write: print("Hello World!"), I get the same output. Then why should I write more code using variables?

Real-world programming consists of many lines of code. In those cases, variables help you incorporate a change easily. To illustrate, if you execute the following code

```
message="Hello,"
greet_sam= message + "Sam!"
greet_jack= message + "Jack!"
print(greet_sam)
print(greet_jack)
```

you'll see the output

```
Hello,Sam!
Hello,Jack!
```

CHAPTER 2   VARIABLES AND OPERATORS

Now, if you change the message variable in the previous code as follows

```
message="Hi,"
```

you'll see the following output:

```
Hi,Sam!
Hi,Jack!
```

You can see you changed the code in one place, but the intended change is reflected in all the lines in the output. In real-world programming, this type of update is common. It is often useful as well.

Q2.3 "...this type of update is common. It is often useful as well." Can you give me a real-world example?
You can use a variable in your application to display the current date and time. You understand that the value of the variable will keep changing.

Naming Conventions

As you dive deep into Python programming, I recommend you follow the official naming convention. I often visit the online page `https://peps.python.org/pep-0008/` whenever I have a doubt. In this context, I'd like to highlight the following points when you use variables in your program.

In real-world applications, you should try to avoid one-character variable names. Instead, you should use meaningful and descriptive names for your variables. For example, to assign an identification number (say, 5) to an employee in an organization, you can write something like `employee_id=5` instead of `e=5`.

43

CHAPTER 2   VARIABLES AND OPERATORS

Note   Normally, the one-character variable names are used for demonstration purposes, which are easy to understand. In addition, you may see them in loops or functions that you'll learn in later chapters.

The online link `https://peps.python.org/pep-0008/#naming-conventions` also suggests the following:

> *Never use the characters 'l' (lowercase letter el), 'O' (uppercase letter oh), or 'I' (uppercase letter eye) as single character variable names. In some fonts, these characters are indistinguishable from the numerals one and zero. When tempted to use 'l', use 'L' instead.*

Your variable name should not clash with Python keywords. A keyword is a reserved word. So you cannot use them as ordinary identifiers. You can refer to the online link `https://docs.python.org/3/reference/lexical_analysis.html#keywords` to learn about the latest keywords. For your immediate reference, I include them here:

False	await	else	import	pass
None	break	except	in	raise
True	class	finally	is	return
and	continue	for	lambda	try
as	def	from	nonlocal	while
assert	del	global	not	with
async	elif	if	or	yield

Note   The previous link also talks about lexical analysis, tokens, identifiers, soft keywords, and many other things. For now, I am trying to make things as simple as possible for you.

CHAPTER 2   VARIABLES AND OPERATORS

So, if you write for=25, you'll get an error. Here is a sample for you:

```
>>> for=25
  File "<python-input-2>", line 1
    for=25
       ^
SyntaxError: invalid syntax
```

Python has many built-in functions. Your variable name should not clash with those names as well. For example, in Python, you can use the abs function to calculate the absolute value. Here are some examples.

```
>>> abs(25.9)
25.9
>>> abs(-25.9)
25.9
>>> abs(10-2.5)
7.5
```

However, you should not use something like abs=10. However, let's say, by mistake, you used abs=10 earlier in your code. Now, if you call abs(12.7), a Python shell will show you an error. Let's see the following sample:

```
>>> abs=10
>>> abs(12.7)
Traceback (most recent call last):
  File "<python-input-8>", line 1, in <module>
    abs(12.7)
    ~~~^^^^^^
TypeError: 'int' object is not callable
```

45

CHAPTER 2   VARIABLES AND OPERATORS

A similar error may appear if you write something like abs=52.7 and then you try to call abs(12.7). Here is a code fragment:

```
>>> abs=52.7
>>> abs(12.7)
Traceback (most recent call last):
  File "<python-input-10>", line 1, in <module>
    abs(12.7)
    ~~~^^^^^^
TypeError: 'float' object is not callable
```

Both the errors are similar. The only difference is that in the first case, it complains about the int, but in the next case, it complains about a float. It is obvious because you know that 52.7 is a floating-point number, but 10 is an integer. So you understand that this kind of error tries to say that you have used abs before this call. A simple remedy to this is to exit from the shell (or remove the erroneous variable naming practice) and try to use the built-in function again. Let me capture the code fragment from the PyCharm Terminal Window shell for your reference:

```
>>> abs(12.7)
Traceback (most recent call last):
  File "<python-input-8>", line 1, in <module>
    abs(12.7)
TypeError: 'int' object is not callable
>>> abs=52.7
>>> abs(12.7)
Traceback (most recent call last):
  File "<python-input-10>", line 1, in <module>
    abs(12.7)
    ~~~^^^^^^
TypeError: 'float' object is not callable
>>> exit()
```

46

CHAPTER 2 VARIABLES AND OPERATORS

```
(.venv) PS E:\MyPrograms\PythonBootcamp> py
Python 3.13.0 (tags/v3.13.0:60403a5, Oct  7 2024, 09:38:07)
[MSC v.1941 64 bit (AMD64)] on win32
Type "help", "copyright", "credits" or "license" for more
information.
>>> abs(52.7)
52.7
```

You can see that I exited from the shell and then re-entered. This activity deleted the old assignments. This time I did not perform the illegal variable naming practice either. So the built-in function abs() started functioning again.

The online link https://peps.python.org/pep-0008/#naming-conventions mentions the following:

The naming conventions of Python's library are a bit of a mess, so we'll never get this completely consistent – nevertheless, here are the currently recommended naming standards. New modules and packages (including third party frameworks) should be written to these standards, but where an existing library has a different style, internal consistency is preferred.

The previous link talks about several naming conventions, and you can follow any of them. For example, to name a student, you can use your variable name as

studentname (lowercase)

studentName (lower camel case)

StudentName (upper camel case, also known as Pascal case)

student_name (snake style; words are separated by an underscore)

47

CHAPTER 2   VARIABLES AND OPERATORS

Student_name (also a snake style, but the first word starts with a capital letter)

STUDENTNAME (uppercase)

Variable names can be alphanumerical, but the first character must be a letter. For example, student_1 and student1 are both fine, but 1student or 1_student will raise an error. Here is a sample for your reference:

```
SyntaxError: invalid syntax
>>> student_1="John"
>>> student_1
'John'
>>> 1_student="John"
  File "<python-input-4>", line 1
    1_student="John"
     ^
SyntaxError: invalid decimal literal
```

You can use an underscore in your variable name, but other special characters can raise an error in your program. For example, if you use @ inside your variable name, you'll receive an error. Here is an example:

```
>>> student@name="Jack"
  File "<python-input-4>", line 1
    student@name="Jack"
    ^^^^^^^^^^^^
SyntaxError: cannot assign to expression here. Maybe you meant
'==' instead of '='?
```

The variable name should not start or end with an underscore. Though you do not see any error for that, experts strongly discourage this practice. For example, you should not use something like _student = "John" or student_ = "John".

48

CHAPTER 2   VARIABLES AND OPERATORS

Q&A Session

Q2.4 Among these accepted naming conventions, which one is your favorite?

I like to use the form that uses lowercase with underscores, which is something like the following:

```
student_name= "Jack"
```

I recommend the same practice to you.

Q2.5 Can I combine multiple variables?

You can combine two variables if they belong to the same data type. See the following segment:

```
>>> 2+5
7
>>> "Hi,"+ "Jack"
'Hi,Jack'
```

However, you cannot combine variables if they belong to different data types. Let's see the following segment:

```
>>> "2"+5
Traceback (most recent call last):
  File "<python-input-0>", line 1, in <module>
    "2"+5
    ~~~^~
TypeError: can only concatenate str (not "int") to str
```

Or see the following segment:

```
>>> 5+"2"
Traceback (most recent call last):
  File "<python-input-10>", line 1, in <module>
```

49

CHAPTER 2   VARIABLES AND OPERATORS

```
5+"2"
~^~~~
```

TypeError: unsupported operand type(s) for +: 'int' and 'str'

How can you overcome this situation? Let me give you a clue: before combining, you need to ensure that you are working on the same data type. For example, if you want to add two numbers, you need to ensure that both are true numbers. Similarly, if you want to concatenate two strings, make sure that you are working on strings only. The next chapter discusses strings and numbers in more depth, and you'll learn to use built-in functions. For now, let me show you a sample fix for the incorrect code segments that you have just seen:

```
>>> "2"+str(5)
'25'
>>> 5+int("2")
7
```

Operators

Operators are special symbols that are used to carry out some kind of assignment or computations. These operators work on some values, which are termed *operands*. For example, in the expression 2+3, + is an operator, and 2 and 3 are the operands.

Note   In simple terms, a literal value, say 5, or a variable, say empId, is an example of simple expressions. You can combine values, variables, operators, etc. to make a complex expression. If you type an expression at the prompt, you'll see that the Python interpreter evaluates the value of the expression and displays the result.

50

CHAPTER 2   VARIABLES AND OPERATORS

Types

You have seen how to assign a value to a variable using an assignment operator (=). Python supports many other operators such as

- Arithmetic operators

- Assignment operators

- Comparison operators

- Logical operators

- Bitwise operators

- Identity operators

- Membership operators

If you have a strong mathematical background or you are already familiar with a different programming language, you'll find that many of these operators are common and have the usual meaning. I assume that you know them. However, if you'd like to be familiar with them in detail, I recommend you to visit **Appendix A**, which includes examples of various operators.

Precedence of Operators

In programming, you often deal with expressions that contain one or more operators. To evaluate those expressions, you need to understand the order of operations. For the common mathematical operations, you can remember the acronym **PEMDAS**. Let's understand it with examples:

Parentheses have the highest precedence (interestingly, they are not an operator). Using parentheses, you can control the order of executions. Here is a sample:

```
>>> 2*(3+1)
8
```

51

CHAPTER 2   VARIABLES AND OPERATORS

You can see that 3+1 was evaluated first, and then it was multiplied by 2 to produce the value 8. However, without parentheses, the expression will be evaluated to 7. See the following:

```
>>> 2*3+1
7
```

Exponentiation has the next highest precedence. See the following:

```
>>> 3+2**3
11
```

You can see that 3+2**3 evaluates to 11, **but not to** 5**3, i.e., 125.

Then comes **M**ultiplication and **D**ivision. They have higher precedence than **A**ddition and **S**ubtraction. Let's verify this statement by evaluating some expressions:

```
>>> 1+2*3
7
>>> 5-4/2
3.0
```

Now let me show you the precedence of some of the common operators in decreasing order in the following table (see Table 2-1).

52

CHAPTER 2   VARIABLES AND OPERATORS

Table 2-1. *Operator precedence of some of the common operators*

Operator	Symbol/Operation
Parentheses	()
Exponentiation	**
Division, Multiplication, Remainder, Floor Division	/, *, %, //
Addition, Subtraction	+, -
Bitwise AND	&
Bitwise XOR	^
Bitwise OR	|
Relational operators	>, >=, <, <=, = =, !=
Boolean NOT	not x
Boolean AND	and
Boolean OR	or
Conditional expression	if-else

POINT TO NOTE

If interested, you can look into the official documentation (see `https://docs.python.org/3/reference/expressions.html`) to know the precedence of the remaining operators. **Since you can always control the order of execution using parentheses, you do not need to memorize the precedence table.** This official link has a footnote section that discusses some typical corner cases as well. However, I want you to have a basic idea about operator precedence. It can help you avoid any future confusion while evaluating an expression.

CHAPTER 2   VARIABLES AND OPERATORS

Let us verify this table by evaluating some simple expressions. Let's start.

Example 1:

```
>>> 3*4**2+2
50
```

Explanation:

In this expression, ** has the highest precedence. So 4**2 computes first, and we get 16. The resultant expression becomes 3*16+2.

In the previous expression, * has the highest precedence. So 3*16 will compute now, and you get 48.

Now the expression becomes 48+2, which produces the result: 50

Example 2:

```
>>> 3&5
1
>>> 2+(3&5)
3
>>> 2+3&5
5
```

Explanation:

As per the precedence table (see Table 2-1) shown earlier, arithmetic operators have higher precedence than bitwise operators. So the 2+3&5 evaluates as follows:

```
2+3&5
=(2+3)&5
=5&5
=5
```

Author's note: If you're seeing a bitwise operator for the first time, you can read it from the online link: BitwiseOperators - Python Wiki.

54

CHAPTER 2   VARIABLES AND OPERATORS

Operators Associativity

An expression can contain operators that have the same precedence. Most of the operators, except the exponential operator (**), evaluate from left to right. Let's see some examples:

Example 3:

```
>>> 5*8%6
4
```

Explanation:
Here * and % have the same precedence, and they both evaluate from left. So 5*8%6 becomes 40%6, which is 4. Notice that if you evaluate 8%6 first, you'll get the final result as 5*2=10, which is not correct. However, as said before, by using parentheses, you can control the order of evaluation as follows:

```
>>> 5*(8%6)
10
```

Example 4:

```
>>> 10*2//3
6
```

Explanation:
In this expression, * and // have the same precedence. Also, both evaluate from the left. So 10*2//3 becomes 20//3, which is 6. However, 10*(2//3) results in 0.

Example 5:

```
>>> x,y,z = 10,20,30
>>> (x<y) & (y>z)
False
>>> (x<y) | (y>z)
True
```

55

CHAPTER 2   VARIABLES AND OPERATORS

Explanation:
Here I present this example to show that you can apply bitwise operators on conditional statements (that includes comparison operators). Here, x<y is True, but y>z is False. And True & False results False, but True | False results True.

Author's note: It is helpful to note that by using the assignment operator, when you write something like x=5, the expression evaluates from right to left.

Q&A Session

2.6 You often used the word "expression." How does it differ from a statement?
A Python expression is a combination of one or more things, such as values, variables, and operators. In fact, a value itself is an expression. The same is true for a variable as well. For example, in the following sample, I evaluate the expressions x, x+5, and 100:

```
>>> x=7
>>> x
7
>>> x+5
12
>>> 100
100
```

You can see that once these expressions are entered in the terminal, the interpreter evaluates these expressions and finds the value of those expressions.

On the other hand, a statement is something that creates an effect, for example, when you print something on the screen or assign a value to a variable. For example, in the following sample, print("Hello") and x=5 are statements.

56

CHAPTER 2 VARIABLES AND OPERATORS

```
>>> print("Hello")
Hello
>>> x=5
```

In other words, statements are instructions that the Python interpreter can execute. Normally, statements do not have values.

Till now, you have seen the assignment statements. Once you complete this book, you'll be familiar with many different statements such as **if** statements, **while** statements, and **import** statements.

Summary

This chapter discussed the usage of variables and operators in your program. In brief, it answered the following questions:

- How can you assign and reassign a value to a variable?

- How can you launch PyCharm's terminal emulator and work with the command-line shell?

- How should you name your variables?

- What is the difference between an expression and a statement?

- How can you evaluate an expression by controlling the order of execution?

Exercise 2

E2.1 Predict the output:

```
x='10.2'
print('x')
print(x)
```

57

CHAPTER 2   VARIABLES AND OPERATORS

E2.2 Predict the output:

```
x=25
print(x)
print(y)
```

E2.3 Can you assign two different data types in a single line?

E2.4 Identify the invalid statements among the following:

```
i)abc=1
ii)if=2
iii)$fi=3
iv)_public=4
v)abc$=5
vi)bob's=6
vii)emp_id=7
viii)emp id=8
```

E2.5 Predict the output of the following expressions:

```
i)  2+3*(36/9+1)**2-1
ii) 3+2&4|2
```

Keys to Exercise 2

Here is a sample solution set for the exercises in this chapter.

E2.1

You should see the following output:

```
x
10.2
```

CHAPTER 2   VARIABLES AND OPERATORS

E2.2

You should see the following output:

```
25
Traceback (most recent call last):
  File "E:\MyPrograms\PythonBootcamp\chapter2\chapter2_
exercises.py", line 10, in <module>
    print(y) # error
          ^
NameError: name 'y' is not defined
```

E2.3

Yes. Here is a sample where I assigned an integer and a string in a single line, and later, I printed their values:

```
x, y = 1, "hello"
print(x)
print(y)
```

E2.4

The answers are shown using inline comments in bold:

```
abc=1 # OK
# if=2 # Error
# $fi=3 # Error
I = 4 # It will work, but not recommended
# abc$=5 # Error
# bob's=6 # Error
emp_id=7 # OK
# emp id=8 # Error
```

CHAPTER 2   VARIABLES AND OPERATORS

E2.5

Here are the answers with the explanations:

i)

```
>>> 2+3*(36/9+1)**2-1
76.0
```

Explanation:
In this expression, () has the highest precedence. So (36/9+1) computes first. In this sub-expression, / has higher precedence than +. So it results in 4.0+1=5.0, and the resultant expression becomes 2+3*5.0**2-1

In this expression, ** has the highest precedence. So 5.0*2 will compute now. It results in 25.0, and the resultant expression becomes 2+3*25.0-1

In this expression, * has the highest precedence. So 3*25.0 will compute now. It results in 75.0, and the resultant expression becomes 2+75.0-1

Now + and – have the same precedence in the resultant expression. Both these operators are left-associative (evaluates from left to right). So the addition will be done first, and the resultant expression becomes 77.0-1, which produces the final output as 76.0.

ii)

```
>>> 3+2&4|2
6
```

CHAPTER 2   VARIABLES AND OPERATORS

Explanation:

In this expression, + has the highest precedence, then &, and then |. So the expression evaluates as follows:

```
3+2&4|2
=5&4|2
=4|2
=6
```

CHAPTER 3

Simple Data Types

Python has many data types. In Chapter 2, you were introduced to some of them. As a beginner, to proceed further, you need to be very much familiar with strings, numbers (particularly integers and floating-point numbers), and Booleans. These are the primitive data types, and you see them in almost every program. This chapter quickly covers them along with some useful built-in functions.

POINT TO NOTE

In this book, while saying numbers, I mean the numeric types: integers and floating-point numbers collectively. This chapter also shows code snippets using Booleans that are subtypes of integers. Remember that Python supports another numeric type called complex numbers. Students from the mathematical background know that complex numbers have a real and an imaginary part. In addition, the standard library supports additional numeric types, such as **fractions.Fraction**, for rationals, and **decimal.Decimal**, for floating-point numbers with user-definable precision. However, to make things simple, this chapter discusses the code samples that deal with strings, integers, floating-point numbers, and Booleans only.

© Vaskaran Sarcar 2025
V. Sarcar, *Python Bootcamp*, https://doi.org/10.1007/979-8-8688-1516-4_3

CHAPTER 3 SIMPLE DATA TYPES

Strings

Strings can be created with single, double, or triple quotes. These are nothing but a sequence of characters. They can also contain symbols, numbers, whitespace, and even empty space between the quotes. It is also possible to embed one type of quote into another. Let me show you some examples:

- **Using single quotes**: 'This is truly beautiful'

- **Using double quotes**: "This is truly beautiful"

- **Using triple single quotes**: '''This is truly beautiful'''

- **Using triple double quotes**: """This is truly beautiful"""

- **Using double quotes inside single quotes**: 'This is "truly" beautiful'

- **Using single quotes inside double quotes**: "This is 'truly' beautiful"

Playing with Strings

Now, I'll show you some common use cases of strings. Let's go through the following code fragments where the goals are mentioned in the comments.

Note Download **ch03_string_usage_file.py** from the Apress website to verify the code segments. Instead of creating separate files for each of these small code segments, I placed them into a single file. I also keep the comments for your reference. If you want, you can write each segment in separate files, or you can simply execute them in a Python shell. All are fine.

64

CHAPTER 3   SIMPLE DATA TYPES

Code:

```python
# I want to print a character, say hash(#) 10 times.
print("#"*10)
```

Output:

```
##########
```

Additional note:

I use this approach in various examples and projects in this book to decorate top borders and bottom borders. This statement prints the hash symbol (#) ten times. In the same way, you can use print("-"*15) to print the character "–" 15 times. What is the benefit? You can write concise code with less typing.

Code:

```python
# I want to use some control codes (for example, \t and \n)
# within a string.
print("How\tare\you?")
print("Hello\nWorld!")
```

Output:

```
How are you?
Hello
World!
```

Additional note:

Strings can include special characters (often termed **control codes**) preceded by a backslash (\). This example shows you the use of **\t** and **\n**. You can see that when I used \n in the string Hello\nWorld!, the character "n" was escaped, and the text cursor moved down to the next line. Similarly, when I wanted to print a tab between letters, I used \t.

CHAPTER 3   SIMPLE DATA TYPES

The \n and \t are very common in codes. Apart from these, there are other facilities as well. For example, you can use \b for backspace and \a for sounding a beep. But the behavior of \b and \a can vary. To illustrate, let us use a Python command shell first:

```
>>> print("Abc\bd")
Abd
```

Now, execute the same line of code in IDLE. In this case, you see an additional character between 'c' and 'd'

Code:

```
# I want to print the word KFC inside single quotations.
print("'KFC'")
```

Output:

```
'KFC'
```

Code:

```
# I want to print the word: HelloWorld! inside double-quotations
# It is an example that shows the uses of an escape character.
print(" \"Hello World!\"")
```

Output:

```
"Hello World!"
```

Explanation:
Here, you simply tell Python to insert the character (which is a double quotation in this case) after the backslash.

Additional note:
Here is an alternative code to print the same:

```
print(' "Hello World!" ')
```

66

CHAPTER 3   SIMPLE DATA TYPES

However, if you try the following

```
print(""HelloWorld""); # Error
```

you will see a syntax error. Here is a sample:

```
  File "<python-input-11>", line 1
    print(""HelloWorld"")
          ^^^^^^^^^^^^
SyntaxError: invalid syntax. Perhaps you forgot a comma?
```

Code:

```
# I want to print the sentence "Baseball is my favorite game"
# using a string variable.

fav_game = "Baseball is my favorite game"
print(fav_game)
```

Output:

```
Baseball is my favorite game
```

Using Built-In Functions

A function is a reusable block of code that performs a specific task, takes inputs (parameters), processes them, and optionally returns a result. Now, I'll show you the usage of some built-in functions (more specifically, methods). You can write your function(s), or you can use the built-in functions that are already written in Python. By using the words "built-in functions," I mean that they are already available to serve your needs.

Note   You will see a detailed discussion on functions in Chapter 7 of the book.

67

CHAPTER 3 SIMPLE DATA TYPES

Now the obvious question is: how will you know about the available functions? The use of an IDE can help you in this case. You know that I am using the PyCharm IDE for this book. It gives me some special support when I invoke (or call) the functions. Let's assume that you have the following code:

text1= "Python"

Now if you write text1 and then put a **dot(.)**, you can see the available functions. Here is a screenshot for you (see Figure 3-1).

***Figure 3-1.** Showing built-in functions when you type a string variable and put a dot (.)*

Let us use some of these functions.

CHAPTER 3   SIMPLE DATA TYPES

Code:

```python
# I want to concatenate multiple strings following different
# approaches.
text1= "Python"
text2 = "programming language."
print(text1+" is a "+text2) # Using + to concatenate
print(text1,"is a",text2) # Using comma to concatenate
# Using built-in format method
print("{} is a {}".format(text1, text2))
print(f"{text1} is a {text2}") # Using f-strings
```

Output:

```
Python is a programming language.
Python is a programming language.
Python is a programming language.
Python is a programming language.
```

Explanation:
You can concatenate strings in different ways. In this code sample, I have shown you four different approaches. The first two approaches are straightforward where I showed you the use of plus (+) and comma (,).

In earlier days, developers used the built-in **format** method. You can see that I used curly braces {} in a string and created placeholders that the format method filled with the provided values.

Finally, I used the f-strings that were introduced in Python 3.6. In this approach, you put the letter "**f**" in front of a string and then inject a variable into it. To inject a variable inside a string, you need to wrap it inside the curly braces as shown in this example.

69

CHAPTER 3   SIMPLE DATA TYPES

Code:

```
# I want to print the word Cricket in uppercase and lowercase.

game = "Cricket"
print("The original string is:" + game)
# Printing in uppercase
print(game.upper())
# Printing text1 in lowercase
print(game.lower())
```

Output:

```
The original string is: Cricket
CRICKET
cricket
```

Explanation:
You can see the function upper() is converting the original string into uppercase characters, and lower() is doing the opposite.

Code:

```
# I want to use multiple functions together
hello_text = " Hello, Reader!"
print(f"The original string is:{hello_text}")
print(hello_text.upper().islower()) # False
print(hello_text.upper().isupper()) # True
```

Output:

```
The original string is: Hello, Reader!
False
True
```

Explanation:
This fragment of code shows that you can use multiple functions together. For example, hello_text.upper().islower() performed two things:

70

CHAPTER 3 SIMPLE DATA TYPES

At first, it executed hello_text.upper() which converted the string into uppercase characters, and then it invoked the islower() function on the resultant string. The islower() function verified whether the string was in lowercase or not. Since the original string was converted to uppercase characters already, it returned False.

The next line of code verified the reverse scenario. The isupper() function is used to test whether the resultant string is in uppercase or not. Before you invoked this function, you transformed the string to uppercase characters. This is why this time, you see True in the output.

Code:

```
# I want to calculate the length of a string.
text = "Python"
print(f" The length of the string {text} is {len(text)}")
```

Output:

```
The length of the string Python is 6
```

Explanation:
The len function is used to calculate the length of a string.

Code:

```
# I want to examine the index positions of the characters
# inside a string.
fruit = "Mango"
print(f"The fruit name is: {fruit}")
# Printing individual characters inside the string
print(f"Index 0 contains: {fruit[0]}")
print(f"Index 1 contains: {fruit[1]}")
print(f"Index 2 contains: {fruit[2]}")
print(f"Index 3 contains: {fruit[3]}")
print(f"Index 4 contains: {fruit[4]}")
```

CHAPTER 3   SIMPLE DATA TYPES

Output:

```
The fruit name is: Mango
Index 0 contains: M
Index 1 contains: a
Index 2 contains: n
Index 3 contains: g
Index 4 contains: o
```

Explanation:

Here, I have shown you all the index positions from 0 to 4. Notice that the array indexing starts from the 0th position. So M, a, n, g, and n are stored at index positions 0, 1, 2, 3, and 4, respectively. This is why fruit[0] prints the first character M, fruit[1] prints the next character, and so on. You see similar behavior in many other high-level languages, such as Java and C++.

Code:

```
# I want to get the first occurrence of a character (or a word)
# inside a string.
text = "abcABc"
print(f"The text is: {text}")
# Printing individual characters inside the string
print(f"The first occurrence of 'A' is at index: {text.
index("A")}")
print(f"The first occurrence of 'c' is at index: {text.
index("c")}")
print(f"The first occurrence of 'bcA' is at index: {text.
index("bcA")}")
```

Output:

```
The text is: abcABc
The first occurrence of 'A' is at index: 3
The first occurrence of 'c' is at index: 2
The first occurrence of 'bcA' is at index: 1
```

72

CHAPTER 3   SIMPLE DATA TYPES

Explanation:

As shown here, you can use the index() function to retrieve the first occurrence of a particular character inside a string. Notice that inside the string, we had two c's; one is at index 2, and another is at 5. But the function returns the index position 2. Also, I searched for the index position of the combined characters bcA. So you can use the same function to find a particular word inside a string too.

If the particular character (or substring) is not present inside the string, you'll see the error as well. For example, if you try to execute the following line

```
print(text.index("z")) # This line will cause error
```

you'll see the error. Here is a sample:

```
Traceback (most recent call last):
  File "E:\MyPrograms\PythonBootcamp\chapter3\string_usage_
file.py", line 96, in <module>
    print(text.index("z"))
          ~~~~~~~~~~~^^^^^
ValueError: substring not found
```

The error message is self-explanatory. You see this error because the character z is not present inside the string abcABc.

Code:

```
# I want to examine a function that accepts multiple
# parameters. I'm using the replace function in this example.
text = " Hello, John!"
print(f"The initial text is:{text}")
print("Replacing the name 'John' with 'Bob' now.")
text = text.replace("John", "Bob")
print(f"The changed text is:{text}")
```

73

CHAPTER 3   SIMPLE DATA TYPES

Output:

```
The initial text is: Hello, John!
Replacing the name 'John' with 'Bob' now.
The changed text is: Hello, Bob!
```

Explanation:
Notice that the `replace` function takes two arguments. I use the first one for the string that I replace, and the second one I use for the string that reflects the changed value. So, to change the name John to Bob, I have used `text.replace("John", "Bob")`, and I hold this changed value into the same string variable `text`.

Q&A Session

Q3.1 Should I prefer single-quoted strings over double-quoted strings (or vice versa)?
The official documentation (see the online link `https://peps.python. org/pep-0008/#string-quotes`) states the following:

> *In Python, single-quoted strings and double-quoted strings are the same. This PEP does not make a recommendation for this. Pick a rule and stick to it. When a string contains single or double quote characters, however, use the other one to avoid backslashes in the string. It improves readability.*

For triple-quoted strings, always use double quote characters to be consistent with the docstring convention in PEP 257.

Q3.2 You have shown different approaches for string concatenation. Among them, which one is your favorite?
The use of f-strings is my favorite approach. For me, it is easy to read and understand.

CHAPTER 3   SIMPLE DATA TYPES

Numbers

Similar to strings, to print a number without a variable, you can just type the number inside the `print()` function. See the following code segment with inline comments:

```
print(1) # Prints 1
print(5.7) # Prints 5.7
print(-6.789) # Prints -6.789
```

The following code shows how to use the number variables (see that there are no quotes while you assign the numbers to the variables):

```
# Using numeric types
number_of_pens=15
print(number_of_pens) # Prints 15
weight=65.3
print(weight) # Prints 65.3
```

Playing with Numbers

Let us examine some common use cases of numbers. Go through the following code fragments where the goals are mentioned in the comments.

Note   You can download **ch03_numbers_usage_file.py** from the Apress website to verify the code segments.

Code:

```
# Performing some basic arithmetic operations
# The corresponding outputs are shown in comments

print(1+2) # Prints 3
print(100-79) # Prints 21
```

75

CHAPTER 3   SIMPLE DATA TYPES

```
print(25* 3) # Prints 75
print(12.88/4) # Prints 3.22
```

Code:

```
# Performing some complex arithmetic operations
# The corresponding outputs are shown in comments

print(1+2*3) # Prints 7
print((1+2)*3) # Prints 9
print(4/2**3)  # Prints 0.5
print((4/2)**3)  # Prints 8.0
```

Explanation:

In Chapter 2, you learned about the precedence and associativity of operators. There, you learned that * has higher precedence than + and ** has higher precedence than /. However, as shown, the parentheses can be used to control the order of execution.

Code:

```
# Showing the difference between the numbers and strings

string1="10"
string2 = "22"
number1=10
number2=22
print(string1+string2) # Prints 1022
print(number1+number2) # Prints 32
```

Output:

```
1022
32
```

CHAPTER 3   SIMPLE DATA TYPES

Explanation:
The plus (+) operator concatenates the strings, but for numbers, it adds them.

Code:

```
# Improving the readability of big numbers (using underscores)

annual_income=12_000_000
print(annual_income)
```

Output:

```
12000000
```

Explanation:
You can see that the digit is printed without the underscores.

Code:

```
# I want to concatenate a string and a number following
# different approaches.

text1= "Python version:"
version=13.0
print("I'm using",text1, version) # Using comma to concatenate
# Using + to concatenate
print("I'm using "+text1+" "+ str(version))
# Using a built-in method
print("I'm using {} {}".format(text1, version))
print(f"I'm using {text1} {version}") # Using f-strings
```

Output:

```
I'm using Python version: 13.0
I'm using Python version: 13.0
I'm using Python version: 13.0
I'm using Python version: 13.0
```

77

CHAPTER 3 SIMPLE DATA TYPES

Explanation:
Already you have seen different approaches for string concatenation. By following the same approaches, this time you concatenated a string with a number.

Code:

```
# I want to convert strings to integers
# Here I test decimal, binary, and hexadecimal numbers

decimal_number_string="8"
binary_number_string="101"
hexadecimal_number_string="B"
print(int(decimal_number_string)) # Prints 8
print(int(decimal_number_string,10)) # Prints 8
print(int(binary_number_string,2)) # Prints 5
print(int(hexadecimal_number_string,16)) # Prints 11
```

Output:

```
8
8
5
11
```

Explanation:
This example shows you how to convert a string to a number using the int function. You can also see that this function can handle numbers with different bases.

Additional note:
However, not all strings are convertible to an integer. For example, see the following:

```
>>> invalid_number="abc"
>>> print(int(invalid_number, 10))
```

78

CHAPTER 3   SIMPLE DATA TYPES

```
Traceback (most recent call last):
  File "<python-input-5>", line 1, in <module>
    print(int(invalid_number, 10))
          ~~~^^^^^^^^^^^^^^^^^^^^^^
ValueError: invalid literal for int() with base 10: 'abc'
```

Using Built-In Functions

Let's examine some other built-in functions for numbers now.

Code:

```
# Testing whether a given string is a digit string

print(f"Is 25 a valid number? {"25".isdigit()}")
print(f"Is 'abc' a valid number? {"abc".isdigit()}")
```

Output:

```
Is 25 a valid number? True
Is 'abc' a valid number? False
```

Explanation:
You can use the isdigit() function to test whether the string is a digit string. For example, if you execute the following code segment

```
print(f"Is 25 a valid number? {"25".isdigit()}")
print(f"Is 'abc' a valid number? {"abc".isdigit()}")
```

you'll receive the following output:

```
Is 25 a valid number? True
Is 'abc' a valid number? False
```

If you use the PyCharm IDE, when you move your cursor on the function, you can see the function definition easily. For your easy

79

CHAPTER 3 SIMPLE DATA TYPES

reference, let me take the screenshot from this IDE when I move my cursor on the isdigit() function (see Figure 3-2).

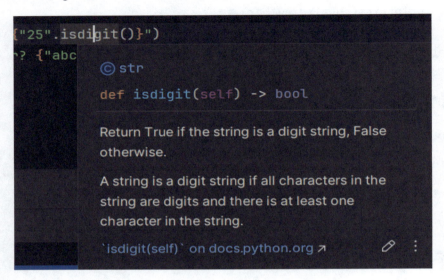

Figure 3-2. *Retrieving the details of the isdigit function from the PyCharm IDE*

Alternatively, you can press the keyboard shortcut **Ctrl+Alt+B** and retrieve the details from the **builtins.py** file as shown in the following figure (see Figure 3-3).

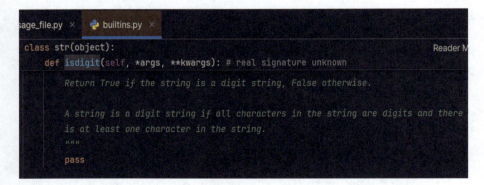

Figure 3-3. *Retrieving the details of the isdigit function using the shortcut keys*

CHAPTER 3   SIMPLE DATA TYPES

This type of simple activity can make your programming life easy. **This is another valid use case, which shows the effectiveness of an IDE over a normal Python shell.** Let us continue our exercises.

Code:

```
# Rounding a few numbers
print(round(2.51))
print(round(5.32))
```

Output:

```
3
5
```

Code:

```
# Finding the maximum number
print(f"Maximum of 1,2,3,4 and 5 is: {max(1,2,3,4,5)}")

# Finding the minimum number
print(f"Minimum of 1,2,3,4 and 5 is: {min(1,2,3,4,5)}")
```

Output:

```
Maximum of 1,2,3,4 and 5 is: 5
Minimum of 1,2,3,4 and 5 is: 1
```

Explanation:
You can see the max function is used to find the greatest among the numbers, and the min function is used to find the smallest among the numbers.

Importing the math Module

In Chapter 7, you'll learn about **modules** and see **import** statements. Using an import statement, you make the previously written codes available in

CHAPTER 3   SIMPLE DATA TYPES

a current file. Since you are seeing the use of some common functions, let me import the mathematical functions and exercise some of those functions. These mathematical functions are available inside the math module. To use those functions, at the top of the exercise file, let's write the following:

```
from math import *
```

You understand that the previous line of code is important. Otherwise, you cannot use (or access) these functions. Let us use some of them in the following code fragments.

Code:

```
# Printing the square root of 25
print(f"The square root of 25 is: {sqrt(25)}")
# Printing the square root of 6.24
print(f"The square root of 6.24 is: {sqrt(6.24)}")
```

Output:

```
The square root of 25 is: 5.0
The square root of 6.24 is: 2.4979991993593593
```

Code:

```
# Finding the ceiling value
# This is the smallest integer that is greater than
# or equal to the given number.

print(f"The ceiling value of 39.3 is: {ceil(39.3)}")

# Finding the floor value
# This is the largest integer that is less than
# or equal to the given number.
print(f"The floor value of 39.3 is: {floor(39.3)}")
```

82

CHAPTER 3   SIMPLE DATA TYPES

Output:

```
The ceiling value of 39.3 is: 40
The floor value of 39.3 is: 39
```

Code:

```python
# Finding the greatest common divisor (gcd) of 4 and 14
print(f"The gcd of 4 and 14 is: {gcd(4,14)}")

# Finding the gcd of 14 and 63
print(f"The gcd of 63 and 14 is: {gcd(63,14)}")
```

Output:

```
The gcd of 4 and 14 is: 2
The gcd of 63 and 14 is: 7
```

Code:

```python
# Finding the factorial of 5
print(f"The factorial of 5 is: {factorial(5)}")

# Finding the factorial of 7
print(f"The factorial of 7 is: {factorial(7)}")
```

Output:

```
The factorial of 5 is: 120
The factorial of 7 is: 5040
```

Explanation:

```
The factorial of 5 is: 5*4*3*2*1=120
The factorial of 7 is: 7*6*5*4*3*2*1=5040
```

83

CHAPTER 3   SIMPLE DATA TYPES

Booleans

The Boolean data type can have either a True or a False value. You can consider it as a switch that is either on or off. Let's have a look at them:

```
>>> a=True
>>> b=False
>>> type(a)
<class 'bool'>
>>> type(b)
<class 'bool'>
```

You can see that both a and b are of bool type that is used to denote the Boolean variables.

Playing with Booleans

Let's begin with the following snippet, which is very easy to understand:

```
>>> a=10
>>> b=5
>>> a>b
True
>>> a<b
False
```

Once you learn about the conditional statements in the next chapter, you can write the following program:

```
a=10
b=5
if a>b:
    print(f"{a} is greater than {b}")
```

CHAPTER 3   SIMPLE DATA TYPES

```
else:
    print(f"{a} is less than or equal to b")
```

Upon executing the program, you'll see the following output:

```
10 is greater than 5
```

It is easy to understand that since the if statement (**a>b**) becomes True, you see this output.

You can directly assign True (or False) to a variable. For example, if you execute the following code

```
a=True
if a:
    print("Hello, reader!")
```

you'll see the output

```
Hello, reader!
```

Now, if you replace the line a=True with the following line **a=False** in the previous code, you'll not see any output.

Q&A Session

Q3.3 Can you discuss some other use cases of the Boolean type?

I already showed you an example where you can use this type. As you progress more, you'll see that the Boolean variables are very useful, and you can use them in many ways. To answer your question, let me give you another example: assume that in a program, you keep incrementing the value of a variable, and you'd like to know when the incremented value is greater than 100. To implement the idea, you can set a flag variable that will become True once the condition is fulfilled.

85

CHAPTER 3   SIMPLE DATA TYPES

Q3.4 I have seen programs where True and False behave like 1 and 0. For example, the following code

```
a=0
if a:
    print("Hello, reader!")
else:
    print("The condition became false!")
```

outputs "The condition became false!" Is this correct behavior?

Don't forget that `bool` is a subtype of `int`. It is true that in some code fragments, you may observe this behavior. However, the official documentation (see Built-in Types – Python 3.13.3 documentation) warns you about this by saying the following:

> *In many numeric contexts, False and True behave like the integers 0 and 1, respectively. However, relying on this is discouraged; explicitly convert using int() instead.*

Making Interactive Programs

Till now, you have seen code segments and programs that do not accept user input. However, real-world applications are much more flexible and capable of processing user inputs. This section will give you an idea of writing that kind of program.

Accepting User Inputs

Python has a built-in function called `input`. You can use this function to pause the program execution and wait for the user's input. Once the input is provided, you can assign it to a variable that is convenient for you.

CHAPTER 3   SIMPLE DATA TYPES

Demonstration 3.1

To examine this, let us write a simple program where the user can supply his name and age. I store these inputs inside some variables. Then, I print the information with some additional messages. Let us type the following lines in your Python file and save the content. Then run the program:

```
# Supply a name
user_name = input("Enter your name: ")
# Enter the age
user_age = input("Enter your age: ")
# Displaying the intended message
print(f"Welcome, {user_name}! You are now {user_age}")
```

Output

Once you start running the program, you'll see the following:

```
Enter your name:
```

Once you supply a name, the program asks for the age as follows:

```
Enter your name: John
Enter your age:
```

Let's enter the age now. Here is a sample output after the user provides the age:

```
Enter your name: John
Enter your age: 21
Welcome, John! You are now 21
```

Author's note: It's a good practice to add a space at the end of your prompts. You can see that I have added a space after the colons to make it clear where to enter the text.

87

CHAPTER 3 SIMPLE DATA TYPES

Analysis

Once the user provides the required information, the input function returns that input as a string. So, if you try to append the following lines in the previous demonstration

```
# Trying to increment the age by 1 as follows:
user_age=user_age + 1 # Error
```

you'll see the following error:

```
user_age=user_age + 1 # Error
            ~~~~~~~~~~^~~
```

```
TypeError: can only concatenate str (not "int") to str
```

To overcome this error, you can convert the string to an integer using the int() function. See the bold lines of code in the following line that can work for you:

```
# Trying to increment the age by 1 as follows:
# user_age=user_age + 1 # Error
user_age=int(user_age)
user_age=user_age + 1 # OK now
```

In the same way, you can use the float function to convert a string variable to a float variable. Here is a sample:

```
user_age=float(user_age)
```

Okay. I assume that you have got an idea of how to process user input in a program.

88

CHAPTER 3   SIMPLE DATA TYPES

Summary

This chapter discussed strings, integers, floating-point numbers, and Booleans. These are the most common primitive data types in programming. It also discussed how to make interactive programs that allow the users to provide inputs.

Exercise 3

POINT TO NOTE

There are some exercises/assignments that ask for input from the user. While developing the solutions, you can assume that the users provide valid inputs only. Once you learn input validations in Chapter 8, you can update these solutions.

E3.1 Can you print the following line?

```
The height of Andrew is 6'9"
```

E3.2 Given the following assignment, x,y=10,2.5, can you predict the output of the following Python statements:

```
print(x+y)
print(x/y)
print("The difference between x and y is:", x-y)
print("x*y=:"+ x*y)
print(x+ "is stored in x.")
```

E3.3 Write a program to calculate the area and perimeter of a circle. Your program should accept the radius from the user.

89

CHAPTER 3   SIMPLE DATA TYPES

Keys to Exercise 3

Here is a sample solution set for the exercises.

E3.1

Any of the following lines of code can produce the intended output:

```
print("The height of Andrew is 6'9\"")
# Alternative solution
print('The height of Andrew is 6\'9"')
```

E3.2

The first three lines are okay. However, the subsequent lines will cause problems. Let's execute each line in a Python shell:

```
>>> x,y=10,2.5
>>> print(x+y)
12.5
>>> print(x/y)
4.0
>>> print("The difference between x and y is:", x-y)
The difference between x and y is: 7.5
>>> print("x*y=:"+ x*y)
Traceback (most recent call last):
  File "<python-input-18>", line 1, in <module>
    print("x*y=:"+ x*y)
          ~~~~~~~^~~~~
TypeError: can only concatenate str (not "float") to str
>>> print(x+ "is stored in x.")
Traceback (most recent call last):
  File "<python-input-19>", line 1, in <module>
```

90

CHAPTER 3   SIMPLE DATA TYPES

```
print(x+ "is stored in x.")
       ~^~~~~~~~~~~~~~~~~~~~
TypeError: unsupported operand type(s) for +: 'int' and 'str'
```

E3.3

Here is a sample program:

```
# Get the radius from the user and convert it into a float
radius = float(input("Enter the radius of the circle: "))
# Area of a circle=(22/7)*r*r where r is the radius
area = (22/7)*radius*radius
perimeter=2*(22/7)*radius
print(f"The area of the circle is: {area} square units.")
print(f"The perimeter of the circle is: {perimeter} units.")
```

Here is a sample output:

```
Enter the radius of the circle: 7.7
The area of the circle is: 186.34 square units.
The perimeter of the circle is: 48.4 units.
```

Case Studies

From this time onward, you'll see case studies (or projects). Before you implement them, I want you to note the following points:

- You'll see the complete code along with the supporting comments at the end of the chapters. I also added some useful information in these projects to help you understand the important segments of code in a better way.

91

CHAPTER 3   SIMPLE DATA TYPES

- I already discussed these codes (or similar codes) in the chapter or a previous chapter. So, if you do not understand a line of code, read the chapter again. This simple activity helps you to refresh your knowledge.

- I showed you the simple solutions at the beginning. It is because your initial aim is to meet the essential requirements. You can ignore the remaining corner cases when you implement them for the first time.

- For example, in Python programming, you often organize the code using functions. You call them to perform the intended job and make your code more Pythonic. In Chapter 7, you'll learn about functions in detail. Once you learn them, you can beautify the initial implementations that I showed you in this book.

- You need to guard your application against unwanted user inputs/scenarios. Chapter 8 shows you how to do that. As a result, you can further improve the previous implementations.

CS3.1 Problem Statement

Welcome to your first project. I want you to develop a company catalog. Assume that this company sells three different dry fruits – apricot, dates, and almond. The seller can sell individual items or a combination of these items. A gift pack is a special combination that contains all three items. Here are some special considerations:

- If a customer purchases individual items, he does not receive any discount.

- If a customer purchases a combo pack with two unique items, he gets a 10% discount.

92

CHAPTER 3   SIMPLE DATA TYPES

- If the customer purchases a gift pack, he gets a 25% discount.

The final output may look like the following (see Figure 3-4).

```
- - - - - - - - - - - - - - - - - - - - - - - - - - - - - - - - - - - - - - - -
ABC Retail
200, Xyz street,
NJ-12345-6789
- - - - - - - - - - - - - - - - - - - - - - - - - - - - - - - - - - - - - - - -
Product(s)   Price (per pack)
Apricot      30
Dates        40
Almond       50
Combo-1      63.0
Combo-2      81.0
Combo-3      72.0
GiftBox      90.0
********************************************************
For free delivery, contact 987-654-321
********************************************************
```

Figure 3-4. *The final output of the CS3.1*

Can you implement this project?

CS3.2 Problem Statement

Consider a restaurant manager who generates bills for his customers. Assume that before generating a final bill, the manager needs to input the service tax amount (in percentage) as well. Here is a sample:

```
Enter the bill amount before tax: $ 150
Enter the service tax percentage: 12
The amount to be paid: $168.0
```

Can you write a program that fulfills this criterion?

93

CHAPTER 3   SIMPLE DATA TYPES

Sample Implementations

Here are the sample implementations for the case studies.

CS3.1 Implementation

Here, I use f-strings to print the seller's name, address, etc. So you see the following codes:

```
print(f"{seller_name}")
print(f"{seller_address}")
```

In this implementation, you do not need these f-strings. I could use hard-coded strings like

```
seller_name = " ABC Retail"
seller_address = " 200, Xyz street,\n NJ-12345-6789"
```

But the problem is that when you need to update the seller information, you need to reflect the change in every place. So I suggest that you use variables in similar places for better maintenance. In that case, once you can update the variable in one place, the effect will be reflected in the remaining place. Now, go through the complete implementation:

```
# Seller information
seller_name = " ABC Retail"
seller_address = " 200, Xyz street,\n NJ-12345-6789"
seller_contact = "987-654-321"

# Decorating the top segment
print("-" * 50)
print(f"{seller_name}")
print(f"{seller_address}")
print("-" * 50)
```

CHAPTER 3   SIMPLE DATA TYPES

```python
apricot_pack = 30
dates_pack = 40
almonds_pack = 50
apricot_dates_combo = (apricot_pack + dates_pack) * .9
dates_almond_combo = (dates_pack + almonds_pack) * .9
almond_apricot_combo = (almonds_pack+ apricot_pack) * .9
gift_pack = (apricot_pack + dates_pack + almonds_pack) * .75
print("Product(s) \tPrice (per pack)")
print(f"Apricot\t\t{apricot_pack}")
print(f"Dates\t\t{dates_pack}")
print(f"Almond\t\t{almonds_pack}")
print(f"Combo-1\t\t{apricot_dates_combo}")
print(f"Combo-2\t\t{dates_almond_combo}")
print(f"Combo-3\t\t{almond_apricot_combo}")
print(f"GiftBox\t\t{gift_pack}")

# Decorating the bottom segment.
# It contains the contact information.
print("*" * 50)
print(f"For free delivery, contact {seller_contact} ")
print("*" * 50)
```

CS3.2 Implementation

```python
bill_before_tax=float(input("Enter the bill amount before
  tax:$ "))
service_tax=float(input("Enter the service tax percentage: "))
amount_to_be_paid = bill_before_tax + bill_before_tax *
  service_tax/100
print(f"The amount to be paid: ${amount_to_be_paid}")
```

PART II

Building Smart Programs

I found a very interesting quote in the book *The Almanack of Naval Ravikant*:

> *The really smart thinkers are clear thinkers. They understand the basics at a very, very fundamental level. I would rather understand the basics really well than memorize all kinds of complicated concepts I can't stitch together and can't rederive from the basics. If you can't rederive concepts from the basics as you need them, you're lost. You're just memorizing.*

I also believe the same. Part II is designed to help you learn about loops, decision-making, file handling, functions, and modules with exception-handling mechanisms. This part will also familiarize you with advanced data types such as lists, tuples, and dictionaries. Upon completion of this part, you'll be confident about Python programming.

CHAPTER 4

Decision-Making

Decision-making is an integral part of programming. You often need to examine certain conditions in a program. Based on those conditions, you control the flow of the program execution. This chapter teaches how to respond based on the state of your program.

Understanding Conditional Structures

A real-world program often checks different values and executes code based on those values. That is where conditional logic comes into play. We often perform conditional tests using various `if` statements. For example, you may see a simple `if` statement, an `if-else` chain, or an `if-elif-else` chain in a program. The choice depends on how many conditions you want to test at a specific point. To test various conditions, you'll use the comparison operators. This chapter uses those operators to verify these conditions.

Using an if Statement

Let us begin with a program that uses an `if` statement.

CHAPTER 4   DECISION-MAKING

Demonstration 4.1

The following program asks the user to supply a valid integer. If the user provides a value that is less than 5, the program will print the supplied value that is less than 5:

REMINDER

Exception handling will be discussed in Chapter 8. For now, let us assume that the users are providing valid inputs only.

```
user_input=int(input("Enter an integer: "))
# Skipping the validation of the user's input
if user_input < 5:
    print(f"{user_input} is less than 5")
```

Output

Here is a sample output:

```
Enter an integer: 3
3 is less than 5
```

Analysis

There is a potential drawback in this program: if the user provides a value that is 5 or more, it will NOT print that information.

Using the `if-else` Statements

Let's add a few more lines to the previous demonstration. This time, you'll see the use of an else statement.

CHAPTER 4   DECISION-MAKING

Demonstration 4.2

Here is a sample program with the key changes in bold:

```
# Skipping the validation of the user's input user_
input=int(input("Enter an integer: "))
if user_input < 5:
    print(f"{user_input} is less than 5")
else:
    print(f"{user_input} is greater than or equal to 5")
```

Output

Let me show you two outputs from two valid inputs. These outputs cover two possible branches of execution:

Sample output 1:

```
Enter an integer: 4
4 is less than 5
```

Sample output 2:

```
Enter an integer: 20
20 is greater than or equal to 5
```

Analysis

Now you can get an output if the user provides a value that is greater than or equal to 5 as well. However, notice that the output shows that 20 is greater than or equal to 5. We all know that 20 is certainly greater than 5. So, instead of saying "greater than or equal to," you can segregate the cases – "greater than" and "equal to." Let's try to implement the idea.

101

CHAPTER 4   DECISION-MAKING

Using the `if-elif-else` Statements

Whenever a program needs to check three or more conditions, you can use an if-elif-else chain. The following program demonstrates a usage.

Demonstration 4.3

In this program, the `elif` part uses the double equal to (==) operator, which is nothing but the comparison operator to test the equality of both sides. It returns True if the values of both sides of the operator match; otherwise, it returns False.

POINT TO NOTE

We use a single equal to (=) sign to assign a value to a variable. For example, you can read the code a=5 as "Set the value 5 to the variable a." You have seen this kind of usage several times. However, we use double equal to (==) for the equality operator. It returns True if the values of both sides of the operator match; otherwise, it returns False. So, while running the following program, if the user enters 5, the program can detect that it is neither greater nor less than 5.

The `!=` operator does exactly the opposite of ==. (The exclamation sign is for "not"; so you pronounce "!=" as "not equal to.") You may also see similar syntaxes in many other programming languages such as Java and C#.

Let us execute the following code:

```python
# Skipping the validation of the user's input
user_input=int(input("Enter an integer: "))
if user_input < 5:
    print(f"{user_input} is less than 5")
```

102

```
elif user_input == 5:
    print(f"The user-provided value is equal to 5")
else:
    print(f"{user_input} is greater than 5")
```

Output

Here are some sample outputs:

Case 1: The user supplies 12.

```
Enter an integer: 12
12 is greater than 5
```

Case 2: The user supplies 4.

```
Enter an integer: 4
4 is less than 5
```

Case 3: The user supplies 5.

```
Enter an integer: 5
The user-provided value is equal to 5
```

Q&A Session

Q4.1 How can you handle a scenario that considers more than three cases?

You can add more elif statements. For example, consider the following program (Demonstration 4.4) that first checks whether a user input is less than 5, equal to 5, or less than 7. Otherwise, it can detect that the input is greater than or equal to 7.

CHAPTER 4 DECISION-MAKING

Demonstration 4.4

Here is a sample program that uses multiple elif statements:

```python
# Skipping the validation of the user's input
user_input=int(input("Enter an integer: "))
if user_input < 5:
    print(f"{user_input} is less than 5")
elif user_input == 5:
    print(f"The user-provided value is equal to 5")
elif user_input <7:
    print(f"{user_input} more than 5 but less than 7")
else:
    print(f"{user_input} is greater than or equal to 7")
```

Output

Here are some sample outputs:

Case 1: The user supplies 3.

```
Enter an integer: 3
3 is less than 5
```

Case 2: The user supplies 5.

```
Enter an integer: 5
The user-provided value is equal to 5
```

Case 3: The user supplies 6.

```
Enter an integer: 6
6 more than 5 but less than 7
```

Case 4: The user supplies 15.

```
Enter an integer: 15
15 is greater than or equal to 7
```

CHAPTER 4   DECISION-MAKING

POINTS TO REMEMBER

Python executes only one block from an `if-else` or `if-elif-else` chain. The control flows in the sequential order until one condition becomes `True`. You may see many indented lines of code under any of these blocks (`if`, `elif`, or `else`). When a condition becomes `True`, all the indented lines inside the block will execute.

You can also note that the `else` block is not mandatory. In Demonstration 4.1, you have seen that you can write a program with an `if` block only. In that program, the `else` block was not present.

So far, I used only one statement inside an **if** block, **elif** block, or **else** block. However, if needed, you can place multiple statements in any of these blocks.

Q&A Session

Q4.2 It appears to me that to avoid the use of an if-elif-else chain, I can always use an if-else chain. Is this correct?

You can solve a mathematical problem in various ways. The same is true for programming as well. If the program logic is correct, you'll see the expected output. However, to evaluate multiple conditions, I prefer the `if-elif-else` chain over the `if-else` chain. Why? Let's analyze the following program.

Demonstration 4.5

Here is an alternative implementation of the previous demonstration (Demonstration 4.4) that uses only the `if-else` chains as follows:

```
# Skipping the validation of the user's input
user_input=int(input("Enter an integer: "))
if user_input < 5:
```

105

CHAPTER 4   DECISION-MAKING

```
    print(f"{user_input} is less than 5")
else:
    if user_input == 5:
        print(f"The user provided value is equal to 5")
    else:
        if user_input < 7:
            print(f"{user_input} more than 5 but less than 7")
        else:
            print(f"{user_input} is greater than or equal to 7")
```

Output

You can test this program against the same inputs that I used in Demonstration 4.4. Since you'll receive the same output, I do not show them again.

Analysis

Now compare Demonstration 4.4 with Demonstration 4.5. Notice that in Demonstration 4.5, as the number of conditions grows, the texts are drifting to the right side. And this pattern will continue if you need to evaluate more conditions. This is why rather than using the if-else chains, I'd prefer to use the if-elif-else chain in a similar context. For me, it is a better option and more manageable.

Note   The previous code segment shows you can write nested if (or else) statements too.

106

CHAPTER 4   DECISION-MAKING

Alternative Designs

Demonstration 4.5 was an alternative implementation of Demonstration 4.4. Still, you may see many other designs in a similar context, and Python does not complain if you follow them. Let's see such an example.

Demonstration 4.6

The following program shows another way of using an **if** statement to check a condition. Normally, I prefer the approach that you saw in the first four demonstrations. However, I am showing you this for one reason: you should not be surprised if you see a similar construct in other people's code. At the same time, I also acknowledge that in some cases, it helps you write more concise code compared with the other approach. We refer to this as `inline-if`. You can summarize the concept as follows:

```
Do task-1 if the condition is True else do task-2
```

To demonstrate, let me rewrite Demonstration 4.2. Before you see this, I want you to note the following points:

- I kept the old code in the comments for your immediate reference.

- I created three new variables, named `msg1`, `msg2`, and `result`. This new approach is demonstrated when I assign the `result` variable.

- The variables `msg1` and `msg2` help me avoid writing a long line of code while assigning the `result` variable.

107

CHAPTER 4 DECISION-MAKING

POINT TO NOTE

The official link (see `https://peps.python.org/pep-0008/#maximum-line-length`) suggests limiting all lines to a maximum of 79 characters. However, this link also informs

- Some teams strongly prefer a longer line length. For code maintained exclusively or primarily by a team that can reach agreement on this issue, it is okay to increase the line length limit up to 99 characters, provided that comments and docstrings are still wrapped at 72 characters.

- The Python standard library is conservative and requires limiting lines to 79 characters (and docstrings/comments to 72).

```python
# Skipping the validation of the user's input
user_input=int(input("Enter an integer: "))
# if user_input < 5:
#     print(f"{user_input} is less than 5")
# else:
#     print(f"{user_input} is greater than or equal to 5")

msg1 = f"{user_input} is less than 5"
msg2 = f"{user_input} is greater than or equal to 5"
result= msg1 if user_input< 5 else msg2
print(result)
```

Output

You can test this program against the same inputs that I used in Demonstration 4.2. Since you'll receive the same output, I do not show them again.

108

CHAPTER 4   DECISION-MAKING

Pattern Matching Using the match Statement

Python 3.10 introduced **match** statements. The online link https://docs.
python.org/3/tutorial/controlflow.html#match-statements states the
following:

> *A match statement takes an expression and compares its value
> to successive patterns given as one or more case blocks. This is
> superficially similar to a switch statement in C, Java or
> JavaScript (and many other languages), but it's more similar
> to pattern matching in languages like Rust or Haskell. Only
> the first pattern that matches gets executed and it can also
> extract components (sequence elements or object attributes)
> from the value into variables.*

Demonstration 4.7

The official statements are self-explanatory. Let's confirm this with the
following program that can classify only three different types of errors:

```python
user_input=input("Enter an HTTP error code (400,404 or 408): ")
# Converting it to an int( Skipping the validation of the
# user's input)
value=int(user_input)
msg="n/a"
match value:
    case 400:
        msg=msg.replace("n/a","bad request")
    case 404:
        msg= msg.replace("n/a","not found")
    case 408:
        msg= msg.replace("n/a","request timeout")
    case _:
        msg= msg.replace(  "n/a","unknown")
print(f"The code {value} represents the '{msg}' error.")
```

CHAPTER 4   DECISION-MAKING

Output

Here are some sample outputs:

Case 1: The user enters 404.

```
Enter an HTTP error code (400,404 or 408): 404
The code 404 represents the 'not found' error.
```

Case 2: The user enters 401.

```
Enter an HTTP error code (400,404 or 408): 401
The code 401 represents the 'unknown' error.
```

Q&A Session

Q4.3 What will happen if an exact match is not found?
The previous output confirms that in that case, the last case, a wildcard_,
if provided, will be used as the matching case. The online link https://
docs.python.org/3/whatsnew/3.10.html also confirms that if an exact
match is not confirmed and a wildcard case does not exist, the entire
match block is a no-op.

**Q4.4 Does this mean that while pattern matching, the wildcard case is
mandatory?**
No. However, I'd like to include this in my program because it never fails to
match. You can understand that if no case matches, none of the branches
will be executed. For example, if the wildcard_ case is absent in this
program and the user provides the input 401, you'll notice the initial value
of the msg variable in the final output that is as follows:

```
Enter an HTTP error code (400,404 or 408): 401
The code 401 represents the 'n/a' error.
```

110

CHAPTER 4   DECISION-MAKING

Q4.5 Can I match multiple possible values?

Yes. Let me show you a sample program in which I highlight the important portion in bold:

```
user_input=input("Enter the HTTP error code (such as 4xx): ")
# Converting it to an int( Skipping the validation of the
user's input)
value=int(user_input)
```

```
match value:
    case 400:
        msg="Bad request"
    case 404|408:
        msg= "Not found or request timeout"
    case _:
        msg= "Error excluding bad request, not found or request
        timeout"
print(f"The error code {value} is for: {msg}")
```

Here is a possible output from this program:

```
Enter the HTTP error code (such as 4xx): 404
The error code 404 is for: Not found or request timeout
```

Tautology and Contradictions

You should be careful about your logic. Sometimes the result of the compound expressions is always False. For example, if you write

```
if a < 5 and a > 7:  # This condition cannot be satisfied.
    print("The if condition is satisfied.")
```

111

CHAPTER 4   DECISION-MAKING

think now. Is it possible that a variable is less than 5 but greater than 7 at the same time? The answer is no. We term these as `contradictions`. We term the opposite scenario as a `tautology,` where the resultant value of the compound expressions is always `True`.

Summary

This chapter discussed the conditional structures in Python programming. Upon completion of this chapter, you can answer the following questions:

- How can you use an **if** statement?

- How can you use an **if-else** chain?

- How can you use an **if-elif-else** chain?

- How can you use **inline if** statements?

- How can you use the **match** statements?

- What do you mean by **tautology** (and **contradiction**)?

Exercise 4

E4.1 Do you find any issue with the following code (assume that the user provides the valid inputs only)?

```
# Skipping the validation of the user's input
user_input=float(input("Enter a number: "))
if user_input > 10:
    result= "The number is greater than 10."
print(result)
```

112

CHAPTER 4   DECISION-MAKING

E4.2 Predict the output:

```
user_input=float(input("Enter a number: "))
if 7 > user_input > 9:
    print("The condition is satisfied.")
else:
    print("The condition will never be satisfied.")
```

E4.3 Predict the output:

```
number = 0
if number:
    print(f"The condition is satisfied with {number}")
else:
    print(f"The condition is not satisfied with {number}")
```

E4.4 Give an example of a tautology.

E4.5 Can you predict the output of the following program?

```
value = 408
match value:

    case 408:
        msg= "Request timeout"
    case _:
        msg= "Error excluding request timeout or bad request"
    case 400:
        msg = "Bad request"
print(f"The error code {value} represents {msg}")
```

113

CHAPTER 4   DECISION-MAKING

Keys to Exercise 4

E4.1

If you supply a number that is greater than 10, you'll see the output. Here is a sample:

```
Enter a number: 11.5
The number is greater than 10.
```

Otherwise, you'll encounter an error. Here is a sample:

```
Enter a number: 5
Traceback (most recent call last):
  File "E:\MyPrograms\PythonBootcamp\chapter4\chapter4_
exercises.py", line 6, in <module>
    print(result)
          ^^^^^^
NameError: name 'result' is not defined
```

It is because the result variable could not be initialized because the if condition was not satisfied. So you need to figure out a way when the if condition is not satisfied. How can you do that? Obviously, you can use an else block and initialize the result variable. I assume that you can do this. So let me show you another easy way where I can initialize the result variable before the if statement as follows (shown in bold):

```
# Skipping the validation of the user's input
user_input=float(input("Enter a number: "))
result = "The number is not more than 10"
if user_input > 10:
    result= "The number is greater than 10."
print(result)
```

114

CHAPTER 4   DECISION-MAKING

This modified program can handle an input that is less than or equal to 10. Here is a sample:

```
Enter a number: 5.5
The number is not more than 10
```

E4.2

For any input, you'll see the following:

```
The condition will never be satisfied.
```

Explanation:
This is because the result of the compound expressions is always False in this case. It is an example of a contradiction.

E4.3

You should see the following output:

```
The condition is not satisfied with 0
```

Explanation:
In Python 3.x programming, when you convert int to bool, except 0, Python evaluates all to True. For example, if you try a non-zero number such as -2.5, you'll see the following:

```
The condition is satisfied with -2.5
```

E4.4

Let us say that the flag is a number variable. Now consider the following expression: flag>0 or flag<=0, which is always true. So it is an example of tautology.

115

CHAPTER 4   DECISION-MAKING

E4.5

You'll see the following syntax error. Here is a sample:

```
File "E:\MyPrograms\PythonBootcamp\chapter04\ch04_e04.py",
line 7
  case _:
       ^
SyntaxError: wildcard makes remaining patterns unreachable
```

Case Study

It's time to analyze the following case studies.

CS4.1 Problem Statement

Let us assume you are about to launch a product that asks for different donation amounts for various age groups are as follows:

- Kids up to age 10 can use the product for free.

- If the user is above 10 years but less than 20 years, he needs to pay 1$.

- If the user is between the age of 20 years and less than 30 years, he needs to pay 2$.

- If the user is between the age of 30 years and less than 40 years, he needs to pay 3$.

- Users from 40 and above need to pay 4$.

So you can write a program that will ask the age of a user. Based on this user's input, the program should display the expected donation amount from the user. Can you implement the idea?

CHAPTER 4 DECISION-MAKING

CS4.2 Problem Statement

Would you like to take a test? The test is simple. You need to predict the value of an expression by seeing it. You can take this test as many times as you want, but there is a twist. The computer can show you a unique expression each time you play the game. Are you ready?

For a better understanding, let me show you some sample output:

Case 1: Wrong prediction

```
Predict the value of the following expression: 12*8%3
Enter your answer:5
Your answer is wrong.
The correct answer is:0
```

Case 2: Correct prediction

```
Predict the value of the following expression: 12+(2*3)/4
Enter your answer:13.5
Correct answer.
```

Author's comment:

To implement the idea, you can consider only one expression and change the data inside it. But I want you to make an improved solution. A better application can test you with different expressions using varying data. So I placed this project in this chapter, but not in Chapter 3.

Sample Implementations

Here are the sample implementations for the case studies.

117

CHAPTER 4   DECISION-MAKING

CS4.1 Implementation

You can handle this scenario using an `if-elif-else` chain (or match statements). Here is a sample program for you. For the sake of simplicity, I skipped the validation of user inputs:

```python
user_input = input("Enter your age: ")
# Skipping the validation of the user's input
age = float(user_input)
if age < 10:
    print("Hi Dear. You can use the product for free.")
elif 10 <= age < 20:
    print("Please donate $1 for the product.")
elif 20 <= age < 30:
    print("Please donate $2 for the product.")
elif 30 <= age < 40:
    print("Please donate $3 for the product.")
else:
    print("Please donate $4 for the product.")
```

Let me show you some sample outputs.

Case 1:

```
Enter your age: 9.2
Hi Dear. You can use the product for free.
```

Case 2:

```
Enter your age: 12.5
Please donate $1 for the product.
```

Case 3:

```
Enter your age: 25
Please donate $2 for the product.
```

118

CHAPTER 4   DECISION-MAKING

Case 4:

```
Enter your age: 37
Please donate $3 for the product.
```

Case 5:

```
Enter your age: 57.3
Please donate $4 for the product.
```

CS4.2 Implementation

I started with three unique expressions in this project. When you run this application, you get a unique expression in each run. For example, in the sample output you can see that in one run, you get an expression 12*8%3. But in a different run, you get a new expression: 12+(2*3)/4. To give it more ***dynamic behavior, I change the data in a particular type of expression too. For example, in one run, you may see the expression*** 12*8%3, ***but in a different run, you may see*** 11*8%3. It is because I replace some data in these initial expressions with random data in each run. To do this, I import the randint() function. The randint(a,b) can return a random integer in the range [a, b] including both endpoints.

The following code segment with supporting comments can explain it:

```
x = randint(10, 12)
question1 = "2*3-4"
# Replacing 2 in question1 with x
question1 = question1.replace("2", str(x))
question2 = "1+(2*3)/4"
# Replacing 1 in question2 with x
question2 = question2.replace("1", str(x))
question3 = "5*8%3"
# Replacing 5 in question3 with x
question3 = question3.replace("5", str(x))
```

119

CHAPTER 4   DECISION-MAKING

I use another important function eval() in this implementation. This function has three parameters; the first one is mandatory and the last two are optional. I do not need these optional parameters now. We can pass a string to eval() that can evaluate it as a Python expression. To show how it works, I present you the following code segment:

```
>>> eval("1+2+3")
6
>>> eval("2*5+2")
12
```

You should not find any difficulties in understanding the complete implementation now. Here is the complete code:

```
from random import randint

x = randint(10, 12)
#First question with initial data
question1 = "2*3-4"
# Replacing 2 in question1 with x
question1 = question1.replace("2", str(x))

#Second question with initial data
question2 = "1+(2*3)/4"
# Replacing 1 in question2 with x
question2 = question2.replace("1", str(x))

#Third question with initial data
question3 = "5*8%3"
# Replacing 5 in question3 with x
question3 = question3.replace("5", str(x))

# The randint(1,3) function returns a number
# between 1 and 3 (both included)
pick_question = randint(1,3)
```

120

CHAPTER 4   DECISION-MAKING

```python
if pick_question == 1:
    quiz = question1
elif pick_question == 2:
    quiz = question2
else:
    quiz = question3

print(f"Predict the value of the following expression:{quiz}")
# User's input
user_input = input("Enter your answer:")
# Converting it to float
predicted_value = float(user_input)
actual_value = eval(quiz)
if predicted_value == actual_value:
    print("Correct answer.")
else:
    print("Your answer is wrong.")
    print(f"The correct answer is:{actual_value}")
```

CHAPTER 5

Loops

The popular programming languages allow you to execute a code segment repeatedly via a construct called a loop. This chapter discusses different loop statements in Python. Once you finish this chapter, you'll understand that these are essential parts of programming.

The Purpose of Iteration

Developers often use the term *iteration* to denote repetition. The first question that may come into your mind is: why do I need loop statements (or iterations)? To understand the answer, let's look at the following code snippet:

```python
print("Printing 1 to 5:")
print(1)
print(2)
print(3)
print(4)
print(5)
```

CHAPTER 5   LOOPS

There is no surprise that upon executing this code, you'll see the following output:

```
Printing 1 to 5:
1
2
3
4
5
```

It is a simple program, and the output is obvious. Now, I give you a task: I want you to write a program that can print up to 5000 or 50000 in the same way. If you follow the previous approach, how many print statements are required? Can you imagine this? Even if you use a simple copy/paste technique, there is a substantial amount of work. This is why it is an impractical and tedious approach. Is there any alternative? You guessed it right! Loop statements are ready to help you in similar situations.

POINTS TO NOTE

When you write a program or implement an algorithm, you may need to iterate over a certain part of the code until a specific condition meets. You can use the loop statements along with the conditional statements to make concise and smarter programs.

However, while implementing a loop, you need to be careful. It is because an incorrect logic can cause an infinite loop that you must avoid.

There are different loop statements. You can use them at your convenience. For now, let's start with while loops.

124

CHAPTER 5   LOOPS

The `while` Loop

The while loop continues executing as long as a certain condition is true. It has the following form:

```
while "Your specified condition(s)":
  statement-1
  statement-2
  ....
```

Notable Characteristics

Here are the notable characteristics of the while loop:

- It starts with a reserved keyword `while`.

- There is a colon (:) after the condition(s) you mentioned.

- There can be many statements inside the while loop. You indent these lines. (Notice that these lines have the same number of spaces from the left.) This correct indentation is important. It is because indentations tell you which statements are inside the `while` loop and which are not.

- You check the condition before you enter this block of statements. If the condition is true, the control can enter the block and execute these statements. You repeat this block of statements as long as the condition is true.

125

CHAPTER 5   LOOPS

- To come out from a `while` loop, the condition needs to be false. Otherwise, the block of statements inside the loop will continue executing. If the condition is false initially, you cannot enter the loop at all.

- If you enter a loop but do not satisfy the exit criteria, you fall into the trap of an infinite loop.

Demonstration 5.1

In the following example, I used a variable called `current_number`. Initially, I set its value to 1. Then I introduced the while loop that keeps printing the number if the `current_number` is less than or equal to 5. The following flowchart can depict the scenario (see Figure 5-1).

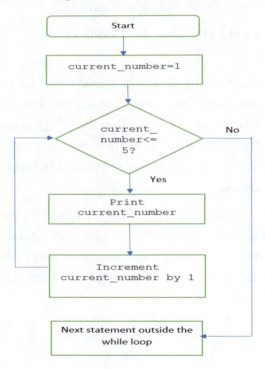

Figure 5-1. *Flowchart of a while loop*

CHAPTER 5   LOOPS

You can see that once you enter the loop, the program prints the current value of this variable, increments the value of the variable by 1, and repeats this process. Let us see the sample demonstration that is as follows:

```
print("Printing 1 to 5 using a while loop:")
current_value = 1
while current_value <= 5:
    print(current_value)
    # incrementing the value
    current_value += 1
# The following statement is placed outside the while loop
print("Completed. The control exits from the loop.")
```

Author's note: The statement current_value += 1 is a shortcut for the statement current_value = current_value + 1.

Output

When you run this program, you'll see the following output:

```
Printing 1 to 5 using a while loop:
1
2
3
4
5
Completed. The control exits from the loop.
```

You may note that I chose the number 5 arbitrarily. However, you can choose any number you want. For example, if you want a print till 500 or 5000, you can replace 5 with the intended number in this program.

CHAPTER 5 LOOPS

Q&A Session

Q5.1 You said that while implementing a loop, I need to be careful because incorrect logic can cause an infinite loop. Can you give an example?

If you comment out the line `current_value += 1` in the previous program, you'll fall into an infinite loop. Here is a sample output:

```
Printing 1 to 5 using a while loop:
1
1
...
```

You can see that the control inside the while loop cannot come out now. So you need to apply the logic accordingly.

Author's note: In PyCharm, to interrupt this infinite loop, you can click the stop button as shown in the following figure (see Figure 5-2).

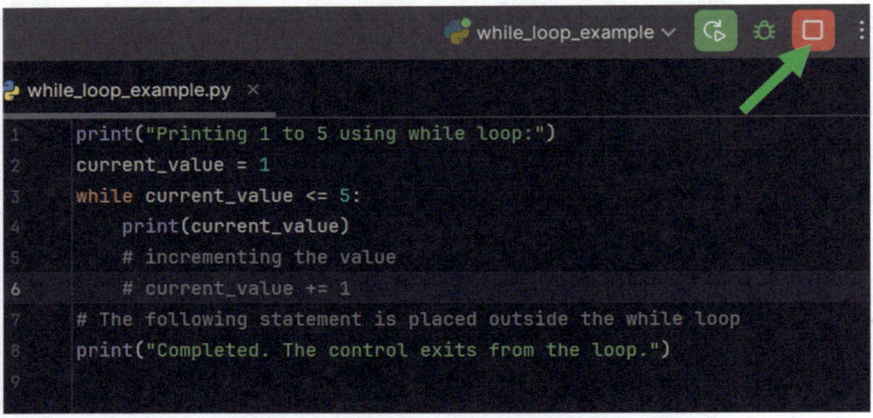

Figure 5-2. *Click the stop button to interrupt the execution of the infinite loop*

128

CHAPTER 5   LOOPS

The **for** Loop

There is another loop called the for loop. Before I discuss it, I suggest you investigate the construction and usage of the while loop again. Notice that there were three major parts as follows:

- **Initialization**: You use it before the control enters the while loop. For example, the previous program initialized the current_value to 1 before entering the while loop.

- **Condition**: This is important because it decides whether the control should enter the loop, keep executing the loop, or exit the loop. Notice that in Demonstration 5.1, current_value <= 5 was the condition for the while loop.

- **Update**: You must implement the proper logic to update your intended variable (which you use in the condition of the while loop). This helps you to come out of the loop and process the next statement, if any. This is why the statement current_value += 1 was placed inside the while loop. If the control cannot exit from the loop, you fall into an infinite loop. You have seen an example of an infinite loop in Q&A 5.1.

The for loop provides a convenient way to express the steps of a while loop. In support of this statement, let me show you the following code snippet:

```
for current_value in range(1,6,1):
    print(current_value)
```

129

CHAPTER 5   LOOPS

Upon executing this code snippet, you'll see the following output:

```
1
2
3
4
5
```

In the previous code snippet, I used the range function that generates a sequence of numbers. The general form of this function is range(start, stop, step) where

- You use the start parameter for the first value. The default value is 0.

- You use the stop parameter for the one past the last value.

- You use the step parameter to denote the increment or decrement value.

Is range a Function or a Type?

The online link Built-in Functions – Python 3.13.2 documentation lists the built-in functions, and you'll find the presence of range in that list. However, once you dig further, you'll see that the official documentation (see Built-in Functions – Python 3.13.2 documentation) further says the following:

Rather than being a function, range is actually an immutable sequence type...

From this link, you can also see the following two forms:

```
class range(stop)
class range(start, stop, step=1)
```

130

CHAPTER 5 LOOPS

It indicates that while using it, you need to pass at least one argument. However, you can pass a maximum of three arguments. To illustrate, if you use the following code

```
for current_value in range(6):
    print(current_value)
```

you'll see that numbers from 0 to 5 (6 – 1) are printed. It is because, by default, the sequence starts at 0, increments by 1, and stops before the specified number.

Since the step parameter is optional for you, Python will not complain if you pass only two arguments. For example, in the previous code segment, if you replace range(6) with **range(1,6)**, you'll see that the numbers from 1 to 5 are printed again.

You can use the step parameter wisely. For example, if you run the following code

```
# Printing 0,3,6,9 using for loop
for i in range(0, 11, 3):
    print(i)
```

you'll see the following output:

```
0
3
6
9
```

You can see that the program prints the values as follows: 0, 0+3=**3**, 3+3=**6**, 6+3=**9**. The next value, 9+3=12, is beyond the limit/range (11-1=10). So you do not see 12 in this output.

131

CHAPTER 5   LOOPS

You can use the for loop to print these values from the reverse direction. Here is the code segment for your reference:

```python
# Printing 0,3,6,9 using for loop
for current_value in range(9, -1, -3):
    print(current_value)
```

Notice that this code segment prints the values in the following order:

```
9
6 (since 9-3=6)
3 (since 6-3=3)
0 (since 3-3=0)
```

The next value 0-3=-3 is beyond the limit/range. So you do not see -3 in this output.

PYTHON VERSUS C# (AND JAVA)

Many other programming languages such as C# and Java use a different structure to describe the traditional/ general-purpose "for" loop. Let's see the equivalent code in some of those languages.

In Java, you can use the following code to print the numbers 1–5 (in Java's code convention, the opening brace should be at the end of the line):

```java
for (int i=0; i<6; i++) {
    System.out.println(i);
}
```

You can get an equivalent output if you exercise the following code in C# as well:

```csharp
for (int i=0; i<6; i++)
{
    Console.WriteLine(i);
}
```

132

CHAPTER 5   LOOPS

You can see that these programming languages use the concept of an index variable that counts the number of iterations. In Python programming, the for loop structure is different from them. However, it is also true that Python's **for** loop is similar to C#'s **foreach** loop. For example, the following code snippet in C# can print the numbers 1 through 5 as well:

```
int[] numbers={1,2,3,4,5};
foreach(int i in numbers)
{
   Console.WriteLine(i);
}
```

Demonstration 5.2

I hope you have got the idea of using the range function in a for loop. Let us make an equivalent program of Demonstration 5.1 that is as follows:

```
print("Printing 1 to 5 using a 'for' loop:")
# The range(1,6) function prints values from 1 to 6-1=5
for current_value in range(1, 6):
    print(current_value)
# The following statement is placed outside the for loop
print("Completed. The control exits from the loop.")
```

Output

If you run this program, you get the following output:

```
Printing 1 to 5 using a 'for' loop:
1
2
3
```

133

CHAPTER 5   LOOPS

```
4
5
Completed. The control exits from the loop.
```

This demonstration has given an overview of the for loop. Let us examine one more use case using this loop.

Introducing Lists

In the next chapter, you'll see some advanced data types, including lists, tuples, and dictionaries. To understand the upcoming example, it will be enough for you to know that a list can store a sequence of elements that can be of the same data type or different data types. You can define a list something like

```
list_name=[value1,value2,value3,..]
```

You often use the for loop when you traverse an iterable element like a list, tuple, string, etc. What is an iterable element? In simple terms, an iterable element is an element that can be looped over. The general syntax to traverse and print the content of an iterable element is as follows:

```
for element in iterable_element:
    print(element)
```

Demonstration 5.3

Assume you have a list of employee names as follows:

```
employee_names = ["Sam", "Bob", "George", "Kate", "Julie"]
```

134

CHAPTER 5   LOOPS

Can you print these names using a for loop? Yes, you can. See the following code:

```python
employee_names = ["Sam", "Bob", "George", "Kate", "Julie"]
for employee in employee_names:
    print(employee)
```

Output

Upon executing this program, you can see the following output:

```
Sam
Bob
George
Kate
Julie
```

Analysis

Let us understand: how did the loop work in this demonstration? The first time you passed through the for loop, the first element of the list, "Sam", was assigned to the variable employee. Next time, the second element in the list, "Bob", was assigned to the variable employee. And it continued like this until you reached the end of the list.

Q&A Session

Q5.2 It appears to me that you could print the list elements without using a for loop. Is this a correct understanding?

Yes. However, consider a scenario where your list contains many names or when the list changes very often. In these cases, to access the list elements, the for loop can provide the best potential support to you.

135

CHAPTER 5   LOOPS

Q5.3 It will be helpful if you summarize the difference between a for loop and a while loop.

Apart from the structure and individual developers' preferences, you can summarize the difference as follows: A while loop runs as long as the specified condition is true. In contrast, a for loop is suitable for a collection of items where you want to execute a block of code for each item in the collection.

Q5.4 How does a list differ from a string?

Both are indeed sequences. However, a string contains a sequence of characters, whereas a list element can be of any type.

Use of the break Statement

Sometimes, you may need to exit from a loop based on a certain condition(s). The break statement can help you in those contexts. To illustrate, if you execute the following code snippet

```
for number in range(1,6):
    print(number)
```

you will see that the numbers from 1 to 5 are printed. Let us assume that you do not want to go to the end of the loop. Instead, you have decided that you'll exit from this loop when the number becomes 3. In this case, you need to incorporate some changes in the loop. Let us understand the changes in the following demonstration.

Demonstration 5.4

Since you want to come out from the loop based on a condition, you can insert an if block that contains a break statement (break is a keyword in Python) as follows (notice the bold segment):

136

```
for num in range(1,6):
    if(num==3):
        print("Exiting the loop.")
        break
    print(num)
```

Author's note: While using the if statement, I used parentheses for better readability. However, it was not required in this example.

Output

Execute the code now. You'll see the following output:

```
1
2
Exiting the loop.
```

You can see that a break statement allows the loop to terminate prematurely.

Q&A Session

5.5 It appears to me that you could simplify the program. For example, if I know that I'll exit at 3, why should I write a program that can continue till 5?

This simple demonstration was made to show you how to come out of a loop. You can use this concept as per your need. In addition, it is not always possible to know in advance when you should break a loop. For example, consider a case when you generate some random numbers inside a loop, and you design the application in such a way that for a particular random number inside a loop, you do not process further. In a case like this, the break statement can help you come out of the loop.

CHAPTER 5   LOOPS

Use of the continue Statement

You have seen the use of a break statement. There is another interesting keyword in Python called continue. Using this keyword, you can skip some statements inside a loop in an iteration. You place those statements after the keyword continue.

There is a reason for this. When a specific condition is met, you may not want to exit entirely from a loop. Instead, in this iteration, you may want to skip the remaining statements of the loop and go back to the beginning of the loop. The continue keyword is made for this purpose. To help you understand the usage, I use a similar example that you saw in Demonstration 5.4. The only difference is that this time, I use continue instead of break. I also make some meaningful changes before I print the message. Let us follow the next demonstration.

Demonstration 5.5

Here is a program that uses the continue statement:

```
for num in range(1,6):
    if(num==3):
        print("Skipping the remaining part of the iteration.")
        continue
    print(num)
```

Output

When you run this program, you'll see the following output:

```
1
2
Skipping the remaining part of the iteration.
4
5
```

138

CHAPTER 5   LOOPS

Analysis

Notice that I placed the last print statement after the continue statement. When the program sees the continue statement, it skips the remaining part of the loop for that particular iteration. This is why you do not see the number 3 in this output. The output also reflects that the loop continued even after the num variable became 3. This is why you can see the numbers 4 and 5 in the output. However, in case of a break, the control jumped out from the loop, and this is the reason the numbers 4 and 5 were absent when you used the break statement in the previous demonstration **(Demonstration 5.4).**

POINTS TO NOTE

The concepts of the while loop, break, and continue statements are very similar when you practice programming C, C++, Java, or C#.

Using Built-In Functionalities

Chapter 3 showed you how to use the built-in functions. This chapter also gave you a quick introduction to lists. These two concepts will help you use some more helpful functions that are often used with conditional statements and loops.

The iter and next Functions

I have used the word *iterable* previously. If you investigate further, you'll know that an iterable object has a function called iter(). You can use it to get an iterator. For example, given the following list, employees = ["Sam",

139

CHAPTER 5   LOOPS

"Bob", "George"], you can print the values inside the list using the iter()
and next() methods. To illustrate, let us examine a few code snippets.
First, execute the following snippet:

```
employees = ["Sam", "Bob", "George"]
iterator=iter(employees)
next(iterator)
```

You will see the output 'Sam'. If you execute the next(iterator)
again, you will see the output 'Bob'. If you execute the next(iterator)
one more time, you will see the output 'George'.

Q&A Session

**Q5.6 What will happen if you execute the same code next(iterator) one
more time?**
It's an easy guess. You know that you have reached the end. So you'll see
the error. Let me show you the same by executing the code repeatedly in a
terminal:

```
>>> employees = ["Sam", "Bob", "George"]
>>> iterator=iter(employees)
>>> next(iterator)
'Sam'
>>> next(iterator)
'Bob'
>>> next(iterator)
'George'
>>> next(iterator)
Traceback (most recent call last):
  File "<python-input-5>", line 1, in <module>
    next(iterator)
    ~~~~^^^^^^^^^^
StopIteration
```

140

CHAPTER 5   LOOPS

The enumerate Function

You have seen that in general, Python's for loop does not use an index variable. In other words, loop counters are absent in the for loops in Python. However, if you need such a counter, you can get it.

Demonstration 5.6

To illustrate, look into the following code snippet in which using the enumerate function, I print the index value along with the employee's name:

```
employees = ["Sam", "Bob", "George"]
for index,emp in enumerate(employees):
    print(index, emp)
```

Once you execute this code, you'll see the following output:

```
0 Sam
1 Bob
2 George
```

You can see that the enumerate function iterates over the collection and it returns the value of the item along with the index of the item.

Nested Loop

In the previous chapter (Chapter 4), you have seen that a program can contain an if statement inside another if statement. We call it a **nested** if statement. Similarly, you can have nested loops, which means you can have a loop that is contained in another loop. It is useful when you want to repeat an iterative process.

141

CHAPTER 5   LOOPS

To demonstrate, let me show you the following program that uses two for loops. For each iteration of the "outer" for loop, the "inner" for loop executes completely.

Demonstration 5.7

Here is a sample program for you:

```
print("*** Nested loop example.***")
colors = ["Red","Green","Yellow"]
fruits = ["Mango","Banana"]
for color in colors:
    for fruit in fruits:
        print(color, fruit)
```

Output

Here is the output:

```
*** Nested loop example.***
Red Mango
Red Banana
Green Mango
Green Banana
Yellow Mango
Yellow Banana
```

Analysis

By default, the print function ends with a new line (in other words, it has the default parameter "\n"). However, you can pass any other character. To illustrate, to organize the output differently, replace the previous loop statements with the following block of code (the key change is shown in bold):

142

CHAPTER 5   LOOPS

```
// There is no change in the previous code
for color in colors:
    for fruit in fruits:
        print(color, fruit, end="  ")
    print()
```

If you execute this modified program, you'll see the following output:

```
*** Nested loop example.***
Red Mango  Red Banana
Green Mango  Green Banana
Yellow Mango  Yellow Banana
```

Summary

Loops are very common in computer programming. This chapter discussed different loops along with their usage in Python programming. Upon completion of this chapter, you can answer the following questions:

- What is a loop and why is it essential in programming?

- How can you use a while loop?

- How can you use a for loop?

- How does the break statement differ from the continue statement?

- How can you use the iter, next, and enumerate functions while using loops?

- How can you use a nested loop?

143

CHAPTER 5   LOOPS

Exercise 5

E5.1 You have learned nested loops in this chapter. Using the concept, can you print the first five multiples of 7 and 8?

E5.2 Can you print the following shape using the for loop(s)?

```
*
* *
* * *
* * * *
* * * * *
```

E5.3 Can you print the previous shape using the while loop(s)?
E5.4 How many asterisks do you expect to see by executing the following code?

```python
for i in range(20,9,-5):
    print(i)
```

E5.5 Can you predict the output of the following code?

```python
for index, i in enumerate(range(10,15,2)):
    print(index,i*5)
```

Keys to Exercise 5

E5.1

Here is a sample program:

```python
for i in range(7,9):
    for j in range(1,6):
        print(f"{i}*{j}={i*j}")
    print("-"*10)
```

144

Here is the output:

```
7*1=7
7*2=14
7*3=21
7*4=28
7*5=35
----------
8*1=8
8*2=16
8*3=24
8*4=32
8*5=40
----------
```

E5.2

Here is a sample program:

```python
for i in range(1,6):
    for j in range(1,i+1):
        print("*",end=" ")
    print()
```

E5.3

Here is a sample program:

```python
i=1
while i<6:
    j=0
    while j<i:
        print("*",end=" ")
```

CHAPTER 5   LOOPS

```
        j+=1
    print()
    i+=1
```

E5.4

You should see three asterisks that should appear for the index locations 20, 15, and 10.

E5.5

Here is the output:

```
0  50
1  60
2  70
```

Case Study

Let's make solutions for the following case studies.

CS5.1 Problem Statement

Assume that there is an application where users supply some valid numbers (so that you do not need to write extra code to validate the input). Now write a Python program where a user can keep supplying the numbers, and for each input, it can print whether it is a positive number or not. The program will end when the user types quit.

146

CHAPTER 5   LOOPS

CS5.2 Problem Statement

Would you like to play a game? It is simple but interesting. The computer will pick a number between 1 and 15 for you. You need to guess the number. But here is the challenge. To win the game, you need to make a correct guess within three attempts. Note another point: each time you play the game, the computer can pick a different number for you. Are you ready?

For a better understanding, let me show you some sample output:

Case 1: You have lost the game.

```
The computer has picked a random number for you.
Clue: It is between 1 and 15 (both inclusive).
Can you guess it within 3 attempts? Give it a try.
Enter your answer: 12
It is high. Try again!
Enter your answer: 10
It is high. Try again!
Enter your answer: 8
It is high. Try again!
The computer picked the number: 3.
You have lost the game now!
```

Case 2: You have won the game.

```
The computer has picked a random number for you.
Clue: It is between 1 and 15 (both inclusive).
Can you guess it within 3 attempts? Give it a try.
Enter your answer: 5
It is high. Try again!
Enter your answer: 3
It is low. Try again!
```

147

CHAPTER 5 LOOPS

```
Enter your answer: 4
Excellent. You have guessed it right.
You've taken 3 attempt(s).
```

Author's comment:
For a simple illustration, the computer picks a number between 1 and 15. The game will be more challenging when it picks the number from a broader range. Similarly, it becomes easy if it picks the number from a narrow range. Once you see the solution, I encourage you to vary the range through user input.

Sample Implementations

Here are the sample implementations for the case studies.

CS5.1 Implementation

Here is a sample implementation:

```
# Initially flag contains an empty string.
# We need a string other than quit to enter
# into the while loop to proceed further.
flag = ""
while flag != 'quit':
    user_input = input("Enter a valid number(type quit to end): ")
    # If the user does not type 'quit'
    # We can convert the valid user input to float
    if user_input != 'quit':
        user_input = float(user_input)
    else:
        flag = 'quit'
        break
```

148

CHAPTER 5   LOOPS

```python
if user_input > 0:
    print("You have supplied a positive number.")
elif user_input < 0:
    print("The supplied number is negative.")
else:
    print("You've entered 0.")

print("Thank you. It is the end of the program.")
```

Here is a sample output:

```
Enter a valid number(type quit to end): -12.5
The supplied number is negative.
Enter a valid number(type quit to end): 3.7
You have supplied a positive number.
Enter a valid number(type quit to end): 0
You've entered 0.
Enter a valid number(type quit to end): quit
Thank you. It is the end of the program.
```

Author's note: You may think: can I use a number (an integer or a float) flag to exit from the program? I suggest you not to do so. It is because, in that case, your program can suffer from a potential drawback (known as an anti-pattern called **Zero Means Null).** To illustrate, let's assume that when a user presses -999, you'll end the program. However, if you use -999 to exit from the loop, what will you do if you need this number at a later stage? Therefore, you should choose the exit criterion wisely.

CS5.2 Implementation

I made this implementation using the randint() function, the if-elif-else chain, and the while loop. You have seen the discussion of the if-elif-else chain in Chapter 4, the use of the randint() function

149

CHAPTER 5   LOOPS

in CS4.2 implementation, and the discussion of the while loop in this chapter. Refer to the supporting comments and strings that I used in the print() functions. Those can help you understand the code easily. Let's see the implementation:

```python
from random import randint

picked_number = randint(1, 15)
print("The computer has picked a random number for you.")
print("Clue: It is between 1 and 15 (both inclusive).")
print("Can you guess it within 3 attempts? Give it a try.")
no_of_attempt = 0
guess = False
user_input = 0  # an initial value
while no_of_attempt < 3:
    # User's input
    user_input = int(input("Enter your answer:"))
    no_of_attempt += 1
    if user_input == picked_number:
        guess = True
        break
    elif user_input > picked_number:
        print("It is high. Try again!")
    else:
        print("It is low. Try again!")
if guess:
    print("Excellent. You have guessed it right.")
    print(f"You've taken {no_of_attempt} attempt(s).")
else:
    print(f"The computer picked the number: {picked_number}.")
    print("You have lost the game now!")
```

150

CHAPTER 6

Advanced Data Types

Lists, tuples, and dictionaries are three advanced data types. While using them, some of the fundamental concepts in programming will be crystal clear to you. This is why this chapter primarily focuses on them.

Lists

I believe that apart from the strings, integers, floating-point numbers, and Booleans, you'll mostly use lists in your programs. In the previous chapter, I gave you a quick overview of lists. There, you learned that you can define a list by separating the values inside the square brackets as follows: `list_name=[value1,value2,value3,..]`. This kind of arrangement can help you to store multiple values in a single variable. You also learned that list elements can be any type. Let me show you some other common use cases of lists as well.

Playing with Lists

Let's go through the following code fragments where the goals and supportive notes are mentioned in the comments.

Code:

```python
# I want to display the content of a list
numbers = [1,2.5,3,5.7,9.1]
print(f"The contents of the list are: {numbers}")
```

© Vaskaran Sarcar 2025
V. Sarcar, *Python Bootcamp*, https://doi.org/10.1007/979-8-8688-1516-4_6

151

CHAPTER 6   ADVANCED DATA TYPES

Output:

```
The contents of the list are: [1, 2.5, 3, 5.7, 9.1]
```

Additional note:
You can see that a list can contain different data types.

Code:

```
# Printing the elements of a list using an index. The
# indexing starts with 0 from the extreme left. (The usage is
# similar to strings.)
names = ["John", "Sam", "Kate"]
print(names[0])
print(names[1])
print(names[2])
# Error: List index out of range
# print(names[3])
```

Output:

```
John
Sam
Kate
```

Explanation:
Notice that the line print(name[3]) is commented. There is currently no element at index position 3 in names. So you'll receive an error if you try to use names[3] now. This error is similar to the following:

```
Traceback (most recent call last):
  File "E:\MyPrograms\PythonBootcamp\chapter6\lists_usage.py",
    line 13, in <module>
      print(names[3])
          ~~~~~^^^
IndexError: list index out of range
```

152

CHAPTER 6   ADVANCED DATA TYPES

I placed several code segments in the same file. So, in the previous segment, line number 13 indicates the error location in my file, which may differ in your case. **The same comment applies to similar error messages in this book.**

Code:

```python
# Printing the elements of a list from the extreme right.
# In this case, it starts from -1
names = ["John", "Sam", "Kate"]
print(names[-1])
print(names[-2])
print(names[-3])
```

Output:

```
Kate
Sam
John
```

Code:

```python
# Let me show you some ways to reverse a list
contents = ["John", 12, "Sam", True, 50.7]
print(f"The original list:{contents}")
print("Reversing the list.")
contents.reverse()
print(f"The modified list is:{contents}")
print("Reversing the list again using the reversed function")
rev_contents=list(reversed(contents))
print(f"Now the list is:{rev_contents}")
print("-"*10)
```

153

CHAPTER 6   ADVANCED DATA TYPES

Output:

```
The original list:['John', 12, 'Sam', True, 50.7]
Reversing the list.
The modified list is:[50.7, True, 'Sam', 12, 'John']
Reversing the list again using the reversed function
Now the list is:['John', 12, 'Sam', True, 50.7]
```

Explanation:

There are many different ways to reverse a list. This code segment shows you two different ways to print the list elements in reverse order.

Code:

```
# Demonstrating the slicing of a list
contents = ["John", 12, "Sam", True, 50.7]
print(f"The original list is: {contents}")
print("Printing the elements from index position 2 to end:")
print(contents[2:])
print("Printing the elements from index position 1 to 3(i.e.4-1):")
print(contents[1:4])
```

Output:

```
The original list is: ['John', 12, 'Sam', True, 50.7]
Printing the elements from index position 2 to end:
['Sam', True, 50.7]
Printing the elements from index position 1 to 3(i.e.4-1):
[12, 'Sam', True]
```

Explanation:

This code segment shows you examples of slicing. When you use contents[2:], you consider elements starting from index 2 to the end of the list. When you use contents[1:4], you consider elements starting from index 1 to index 4-1, i.e., 3.

154

CHAPTER 6   ADVANCED DATA TYPES

Code:

```
# Showing some more slicing examples
contents = ["John", 12, "Sam", True, 50.7]
print("Omitting the first index to start slicing at the
   beginning.")
print(contents[:4])
print("Omitting both indexes is allowed as well.")
print(contents[:])
print("Printing the first element while skipping every
   second one.")
print(contents[0::2])
print("The reverse list is as follows:")
print(contents[::-1])
```

Output:

```
Omitting the first index to start slicing at the beginning.
['John', 12, 'Sam', True]
Omitting both indexes is allowed as well.
['John', 12, 'Sam', True, 50.7]
Printing the first element while skipping every second one.
['John', 'Sam', 50.7]
The reverse list is as follows:
[50.7, True, 'Sam', 12, 'John']
```

Explanation:

You can see that omitting the first index is allowed. In this case, the slice starts at the beginning. When you omit both indexes, the slice is a copy of the whole list. The next segment in this output shows that by using a step value (2), you can skip every second element from a list. The final segment is interesting: **it shows one more technique to reverse a list**.

155

CHAPTER 6   ADVANCED DATA TYPES

Code:

```python
# You can reassign a new value inside the list
list_contents = ["John", 12, "Sam", True, 50.7]
print(f"The original list: {list_contents}")
print("Changing the element at index 2.")
list_contents [2] = "Bob"
print(f"Now the list is: {list_contents}")
```

Output:

```
The original list: ['John', 12, 'Sam', True, 50.7]
Changing the element at index 2.
Now the list is: ['John', 12, 'Bob', True, 50.7]
```

Explanation:

Lists are mutable. You can see that I've set a new value at index position 2. So, instead of 'Sam', you see 'Bob' inside this modified list.

Code:

```python
# Concatenation example
contents1 = ["John", 12, 50.7]
contents2 = ["Sam", 25, "John", False, 100.2]
print("Original lists are:")
print(contents1)
print(contents2)
print("After concatenating the lists, you get the following list:")
print(contents1 + contents2)
```

Output:

```
Original lists are:
['John', 12, 50.7]
['Sam', 25, 'John', False, 100.2]
```

156

CHAPTER 6   ADVANCED DATA TYPES

After concatenating the lists, you get the following list:
['John', 12, 50.7, 'Sam', 25, 'John', False, 100.2]

Explanation:

There are various ways to concatenate multiple lists. The simplest among them is to use the "+" operator. One sample usage of this is shown in the example.

The concatenated list can have duplicates; for example, once you concatenate the lists, notice that 'John' from both lists is present in the new list.

Code:

```python
# Printing a specific number of elements of a list from the end.
sample_list = ["John", 12, "Sam", True, 50.7]
print(f"The original list is: {sample_list}")
print(f"The last 3 elements of the list are: {sample_list[-3:]}")
print(f"The last 2 elements of the list are: {sample_list[-2:]}")
print(f"The last element of the list is: {sample_list[-1]}")
```

Output:

```
The original list is: ['John', 12, 'Sam', True, 50.7]
The last 3 elements of the list are: ['Sam', True, 50.7]
The last 2 elements of the list are: [True, 50.7]
The last element of the list is: 50.7
```

Code:

```python
# Removing list elements using three different approaches
contents = ["John", 12, "Sam", True, 50.7,12]
print(f"The original list is: {contents}")
print("Removing the element at index 2 using the del function.")
del(contents[2])
```

157

CHAPTER 6   ADVANCED DATA TYPES

```
print(f"Now the list is: {contents}")
print("Removing the element at index 3 using the pop function.")
contents.pop(3)
print(f"Now the list is: {contents}")
print("Removing the first occurrence of 12 using the remove
  function.")
contents.remove(12)
print(f"Now the list is: {contents}")
```

Output:

```
The original list is: ['John', 12, 'Sam', True, 50.7, 12]
Removing the element at index 2 using the del function.
Now the list is: ['John', 12, True, 50.7, 12]
Removing the element at index 3 using the pop function.
Now the list is: ['John', 12, True, 12]
Removing the first occurrence of 12 using the remove function.
Now the list is: ['John', True, 12]
```

Additional note:

This example shows the use of the del, pop, and remove functions to modify a list. Initially, the number 12 was present twice in the list. You can see that the remove function removed the first occurrence of 12. Notice that another occurrence of 12 is still present in this modified list.

Code:

```
# Checking whether an element is present inside a list
names = ["John", "Sam","Bob", "Ester"]
print(f"Is 'Sam' present on the list? {'Sam' in names} ")
print(f"Is 'sam' present on the list? {'sam' in names} ")
# Checking whether an element is absent in this list
print(f"Is 'Jeniffer' missing from the list? {'Jennifer' not in
  names}")
```

158

CHAPTER 6   ADVANCED DATA TYPES

Output:

```
Is 'Sam' present on the list? True
Is 'sam' present on the list? False
Is 'Jeniffer' missing from the list? True
```

Explanation:

List elements are case-sensitive. So the element 'Sam' is different from the element 'sam'. You can also see that "**not in**" was used to perform the reverse check. This is why the statement print('Jennifer' not in names) outputs True.

Code:

```
# Finding the maximum and minimum from a number list
numbers = [1, 23, 56.2, -3.7, 999]
print("The original list is:")
print(numbers)
print(f"The largest number is: {max(numbers)}")
print(f"The smallest number is: {min(numbers)}")
```

Output:

```
The original list is:
[1, 23, 56.2, -3.7, 999]
The largest number is: 999
The smallest number is: -3.7
```

Additional note:

The max() and min() functions will NOT work if the list contains a mix of numbers and strings. For example, if you try to execute the following code segment

159

CHAPTER 6   ADVANCED DATA TYPES

```
# The max function cannot work on the following list
contents = [1, 23, -3.7, 999, "abc", "bob"]
print("The original list is:")
print(contents)
print(f"The largest number is: {max(contents)}")
```

you'll see the error TypeError: '>' not supported between instances of 'str' and 'int'.

Code:

```
# Testing booleans with max() and min()
contents = [0.75, True, False, 0.5, 0.6, 1, 0]
print(f"The original list: {contents}")
print(f"The largest number: {max(contents)}")
print(f"The smallest number: {min(contents)}")
```

Output:

```
The original list: [0.75, True, False, 0.5, 0.6, 1, 0]
The largest number: True
The smallest number: False
```

Explanation:

By design, if you use these Boolean values in a numerical context, there is no error; True is treated as 1, and False is treated as 0. So, in this case, you can see the largest number is True and the smallest number is False.

To test this fact, let's consider the following list: contents = [0.75, 1, 0, 0.5, 0.6, True, False]. Notice that I have interchanged the positions of True and 1 in this list. Also, I have interchanged the positions of False and 0 here.

160

CHAPTER 6   ADVANCED DATA TYPES

Once you run this modified segment, you can see the following output:

```
The original list: [0.75, 1, 0, 0.5, 0.6, True, False]
The largest number: 1
The smallest number: 0
```

You can see that False and True behave like 0 and 1. However, the official link Built-in Types – Python 3.13.3 documentation discourages you from relying on this. In Chapter 3, I already mentioned that the online link wants you explicitly convert using int(), if required.

Code:

```python
# You can add an element or a list of elements at the end
# of a list
contents = ["John", 12, "Sam"]
print(f"The original list is:{contents}")
print("Appending 25 at the end of the list.")
contents.append(25)
print(f"After adding 25, the list is: {contents}")
print("Appending a list of elements ['Kate', 20] at the end of
    the list.")
contents.append(['kate',20])
print(f"Now the list is: {contents}")
# contents.append(10,20) # error
```

Output:

```
The original list is:['John', 12, 'Sam']
Appending 25 at the end of the list.
After adding 25, the list is: ['John', 12, 'Sam', 25]
Appending a list of elements ['Kate', 20] at the end of
    the list.
Now the list is: ['John', 12, 'Sam', 25, ['Kate', 20]]
```

161

CHAPTER 6   ADVANCED DATA TYPES

Additional note:
Using append(), you can add one element at a time. If you try to append multiple elements like contents.append(10,20), you can see an error that states the following: TypeError: list.append() takes exactly one argument (2 given). However, you can use this function to add a list that contains multiple elements.

Author's note: Shortly, you'll see me comparing the append() and extend() functions in Q6.2.

Code:

```
# Using the insert function, you can add an element to a
# particular position
contents = ["John", 12, "Sam", True, 50.7]
print("The original list is:")
print(contents)
print("Inserting the element 'Jack' at index 3.")
contents.insert(3, "Jack")
print(f"Now the list is:{contents}")
```

Output:

```
The original list is:
['John', 12, 'Sam', True, 50.7]
Inserting the element 'Jack' at index 3.
Now the list is:['John', 12, 'Sam', 'Jack', True, 50.7]
```

Code:

```
# Sorting a list
numbers = [33, 11, 555, 77, 111, 333]
print(f"The original list is: {numbers}")
numbers.sort()
```

162

CHAPTER 6   ADVANCED DATA TYPES

```
print(f"The sorted list in ascending order: {numbers}")
print("Now sorting the list in descending order.")
numbers.sort(reverse = True)
print(f"Now the list is: {numbers}")
```

Output:

```
The original list is: [33, 11, 555, 77, 111, 333]
The sorted list in ascending order: [11, 33, 77, 111, 333, 555]
Now sorting the list in descending order.
Now the list is: [555, 333, 111, 77, 33, 11]
```

Additional note:

Remember the following information while you use the sort() function:

It changes the original list. If you want to avoid modifying the original list, you can refer to the sorted() function, which I'll discuss next.

You can sort a list if all the elements are of the same data type. If you have mixed data types in your list and you apply sort() on those elements, you'll encounter errors. For example, if you execute the following code segment

```
contents = ["John", 12, "Sam", True, 50.7]
contents.sort() # Error now
```

you'll see the following error: TypeError: '<' not supported between instances of 'int' and 'str'.

Q&A Session

Q6.1 I understand that lists are mutable. I also recognize that sorting can be helpful in certain scenarios. However, while sorting a list, is there any way to prevent the modification of the original list?

163

CHAPTER 6   ADVANCED DATA TYPES

Programmatically, you can always have a backup. However, let me also tell you that by using the sorted function, you can prevent modification to the original list. Let's examine the following code:

```
numbers = [33, 11, 555, 77, 111, 333]
print(f"The list of numbers are: {numbers}")
print(f"The sorted list: {sorted(numbers)}")
print(f"The current list of numbers is: {numbers}")
```

Upon executing this code, you can get the following output:

```
The list of numbers are: [33, 11, 555, 77, 111, 333]
The sorted list: [11, 33, 77, 111, 333, 555]
The current list of numbers is: [33, 11, 555, 77, 111, 333]
```

In short, you may note the following points from the official documentation (see Sorting Techniques – Python 3.13.3 documentation):

- The list.sort() method modifies the list in place (and returns None to avoid confusion). Usually, it's less convenient than sorted() - but if you don't need the original list, it's slightly more efficient.

- In addition, the list.sort() method is only defined for lists. In contrast, the sorted() function accepts any iterable.

Finally, remember that you should use this function on the same data types.

Q6.2 When you used the append function, you got the modified list as ['John', 12, 'Sam', 25, ['Kate', 20]], where the last element is itself a list. However, I'd like to know whether I could append the elements in such a way that I make a plain list.

CHAPTER 6   ADVANCED DATA TYPES

You can add multiple elements to a list using the extend function:

```
contents = ["John", 12, "Sam"]
print(f"The original list is:{contents}")
print("Adding 25,'Kate', and 100.2 at the list end.")
contents.extend([25, 'Kate', 20])
print(f"Now the list is:{contents}")
```

Upon executing this code, you can get the following output:

```
The original list is:['John', 12, 'Sam']
Adding 25,'Kate', and 20 at the list end.
Now the list is:['John', 12, 'Sam', 25, 'Kate', 20]
```

You can see that when you used the append function, you got the modified list as `['John', 12, 'Sam', 25, ['Kate', 20]]` where the last element is itself a list. However, after using the extend function, you got a plain list: `['John', 12, 'Sam', 25, 'Kate', 20]`.

Tuples

Tuples are another important data type and are similar to lists. But there are some noticeable differences. Let's see them:

First, **tuples are immutable**. This means that once created, you cannot incorporate changes in them. However, you have seen that lists can be modified. For example, you reassigned a value in a list, you extended a list, etc. So lists are mutable.

Next, declaring a tuple is similar to a list, but this time, you'd put elements inside the **round brackets** (but not the square brackets) as follows:

```
contents = ("John", 12, "Sam", True, 50.7)
```

165

CHAPTER 6   ADVANCED DATA TYPES

However, you may note that while creating a tuple, the use of parentheses is optional. To verify this, let us see the following segment and the associated output:

```
>>> contents="Sam",1,"Bob"
>>> type(contents)
<class 'tuple'>
```

Finally, **all the functions that are available for lists are not available for tuples**. For example, if you write the following

```
contents = ("John", 12, "Sam", True, 50.7)
contents.remove(12) # error
```

you can notice the error saying

```
AttributeError: 'tuple' object has no attribute 'remove'
```

Or if you write the following

```
contents.append("Jack") # error
```

you can notice the error saying

```
AttributeError: 'tuple' object has no attribute 'append'
```

However, there are also some similarities with lists. For example, see the following code:

```
>>> contents = ("John", 12, "Sam", True, 50.7)
>>> contents[1]
12
```

Or use the slice operator as follows:

```
>>> contents[0:3]
('John', 12, 'Sam')
```

You can also convert a list to a tuple.

166

CHAPTER 6   ADVANCED DATA TYPES

Playing with Tuples

Let's examine some built-in functions for tuples.

Code:

```
# Creating a tuple and printing the elements inside it.
contents = ("John", 12, "Sam", True, 50.7)
print(f"The content of the tuple is: {contents}")
```

Output:

```
The content of the tuple is: ('John', 12, 'Sam', True, 50.7)
```

Code:

```
# Accessing the tuple elements (indexing is similar to the lists)
contents = ("John", 12, "Sam", True, 50.7)
print(f"The content of the tuple is: {contents}")
print(f"The first element is: {contents[0]}")
print(f"The last element is: {contents[-1]}")
print(f"Elements from index 1 to 3: {contents[1:4]}")
print(f"Elements from index 2 to end: {contents[2:]}")
```

Output:

```
The content of the tuple is: ('John', 12, 'Sam', True, 50.7)
The first element is: John
The last element is: 50.7
Elements from index 1 to 3: (12, 'Sam', True)
Elements from index 2 to end: ('Sam', True, 50.7)
```

Code:

```
# You cannot reassign the value inside a tuple.
my_tuple = ("John", 12, "Sam", True, 50.7)
print("The content of my_tuple is:")
```

167

CHAPTER 6   ADVANCED DATA TYPES

```
print(my_tuple)
print("Trying to replace 'Sam' with 'Bob':")
my_tuple[2]= 'Bob' # Error
```

Output:

The last line of this code segment will raise the following error:

```
TypeError: 'tuple' object does not support item assignment
```

Explanation:

Tuples are immutable by design. This is why you cannot modify them.

Code:

```
# Converting a list to a tuple by using the built-in tuple()
function
list_sample = ["John", 12, "Sam", True, 50.7]
print(f"The contents of the list are:{list_sample}")
# Converting the list to a tuple
tuple_sample = tuple(list_sample)
print(f"The contents of the tuple are:{tuple_sample}")
```

Output:

```
The contents of the list are:['John', 12, 'Sam', True, 50.7]
The contents of the tuple are:('John', 12, 'Sam', True, 50.7)
```

Explanation:

You can use the built-in tuple() function to convert a list to a tuple. In fact, you can use this function to create an empty tuple. Here is a sample:

```
>>> sample_tuple=tuple()
>>> sample_tuple
()
>>> type(sample_tuple)
<class 'tuple'>
```

CHAPTER 6   ADVANCED DATA TYPES

Code:

```
# Reversing the tuple elements
sample_tuple = (1, 2, 3, 4, 5)
print(f"The contents of the tuple are: {sample_tuple}")
print("Reversing the tuple now.")
rev_tuple = tuple(reversed(sample_tuple))
print(f"The contents of rev_tuple are: {rev_tuple}")
```

Output:

```
The contents of the tuple are: (1, 2, 3, 4, 5)
Reversing the tuple now.
The contents of rev_tuple are: (5, 4, 3, 2, 1)
```

Code:

```
# Replacing one tuple with another
sample_tuple = (1, 2, 3, 4, 5)
print(f"The contents of sample_tuple are: {sample_tuple}")
sample_tuple = ("a","b") + sample_tuple[2:]
print(f"The contents of sample_tuple are: {sample_tuple}")
```

Output:

```
The contents of sample_tuple are: (1, 2, 3, 4, 5)
The contents of sample_tuple are: ('a', 'b', 3, 4, 5)
```

Explanation:

Since tuples are immutable, you cannot modify elements. However, this example demonstrates that you can replace one tuple with another. In this case, you made a new tuple, and sample_tuple now refers to this new tuple.

169

CHAPTER 6 ADVANCED DATA TYPES

Code:

```
# Testing relational operators
tuple_sample1 = (1, 2, 3)
tuple_sample2 = (1,1,250)
tuple_sample3 = (0,50,500)
print(f"The contents of tuple_sample1 are: {tuple_sample1}")
print(f"The contents of tuple_sample2 are: {tuple_sample2}")
print(f"The contents of tuple_sample3 are: {tuple_sample3}")
print(f"tuple_sample1 < tuple_sample2 ? {tuple_sample1 <
    tuple_sample2}")
print(f"tuple_sample2 > tuple_sample3 ? {tuple_sample2 >
    tuple_sample3}")
```

Output:

```
The contents of tuple_sample1 are: (1, 2, 3)
The contents of tuple_sample2 are: (1, 1, 250)
The contents of tuple_sample3 are: (0, 50, 500)
tuple_sample1 < tuple_sample2 ? False
tuple_sample2 > tuple_sample3 ? True
```

Explanation:
You can use relational operators to compare tuples (and other sequences). Here, the comparison starts with the first element of each sequence. If they are equal, it checks the next element and so on, until it finds the difference. Once the difference is found, the subsequent elements are not considered (even if they are big).

CHAPTER 6   ADVANCED DATA TYPES

Q&A Session

Q6.3 You said that while creating a tuple, the use of parentheses is optional. However, if I write content="a", the terminal shows that it is a string type. Here is a sample:

```
>>> content="a"
>>> type(content)
<class 'str'>
```

I also see that a value in parentheses is not a tuple. See the following:

```
>>> content=("a")
>>> type(content)
<class 'str'>
```

Am I noticing the correct behavior?

Yes, you are seeing the correct behavior.

Q6.4 If the previous codes show the correct behavior, I'd like to know how to make a tuple with a single element.

You need to use a final comma. Let's see the following code:

```
>>> content="a",
>>> type(content)
<class 'tuple'>
```

In the same way, you can validate the other code:

```
>>> content=("a"),
>>> type(content)
<class 'tuple'>
```

171

CHAPTER 6   ADVANCED DATA TYPES

Q6.5 When should I prefer tuples over lists?

You should prefer tuples to represent constants like

```
days_of_week = ("Monday", "Tuesday", "Wednesday", "Thursday",
"Friday", "Saturday", "Sunday")
```

Since they are immutable, they offer faster performance.

Dictionaries

Now, you see the use of another important data type called the dictionary. These are some noticeable characteristics of this data type:

- It is a collection of key–value pair(s). These keys and values can be of any type.

- The keys are unique.

- Dictionaries are indexed through their keys.

- When you create a dictionary, you wrap the key–value pairs in braces as follows: `dictionary_sample = {1: "John", 2: 12, 3: "Sam"}`.

Playing with Dictionaries

Let us examine them now.

Code:

```
# Printing the details of a dictionary that has three key-
# value pairs
dictionary_sample = {1: "John", 2: 12, 3: "Sam"}
print(f"The dictionary contains: {dictionary_sample}")
```

172

CHAPTER 6   ADVANCED DATA TYPES

Output:

```
The dictionary contains: {1: 'John', 2: 12, 3: 'Sam'}
```

Code:

```python
# A dictionary can have keys and values of different types
dictionary_sample  = {1: "John", 2: 12, "third": "Sam", }
print(f"The dictionary contains: {dictionary_sample}")
```

Output:

```
The dictionary contains: {1: 'John', 2: 12, 'third': 'Sam'}
```

Code:

```python
# I want to print values for particular keys
dictionary_sample = {1: "John", 2: 12, "three": "Sam"}
print(f"The dictionary contains: {dictionary_sample}")
print("Value at key 1:", dictionary_sample[1])
print("Value at key 2:", dictionary_sample[2])
print("Value at key three:", dictionary_sample["three"])
```

Output:

```
The dictionary contains: {1: 'John', 2: 12, 'three': 'Sam'}
Value at key 1: John
Value at key 2: 12
Value at key three: Sam
```

Code:

```python
# Finding the total number of elements in your dictionary.
dictionary_sample = {1: "John", 2: 12}
print(f"The dictionary contains: {dictionary_sample}")
print(f"Number of items: {len(dictionary_sample)}")
```

CHAPTER 6   ADVANCED DATA TYPES

Output:

```
The dictionary contains: {1: 'Bob', 2: 12}
Number of contents: 2
```

Explanation:
The output shows that you can use the len() function to determine the total number of elements in your dictionary.

Q&A Session

Q6.6 Can I reassign a different value to the key of a dictionary?
Yes. However, in that case, the dictionary will keep the last assigned value. For example, if you execute the following code

```
dictionary_sample = {1: "John", 2: 12, 1: "Bob"}
print(f"The dictionary contains: {dictionary_sample}")
print("Value at key 1:", dictionary_sample[1])
```

you'll see the following output:

```
The dictionary contains: {1: 'Bob', 2: 12}
Value at key 1: Bob
```

You can see that the dictionary holds the last assigned value Bob, for key 1.

Summary

This chapter discussed lists, tuples, and dictionaries using various code segments, useful built-in functions, and associated outputs. In Chapter 3, you learned strings, numbers, and Booleans. These are the most common data types in Python programming.

CHAPTER 6   ADVANCED DATA TYPES

Exercise 6

E6.1 Create a list that contains at least three elements. Then, remove the last two elements from the list.

E6.2 Is there any problem in the following code?

```
sample_tuple = (1, 2, 3, "Sam", 5)
print(sample_tuple[2:6])
```

E6.3 Predict the output of the following code:

```
sample_tuple = (1, 2, 3, 4, 5)
first=sample_tuple[0]
print(f"Got first: {first}")
last=sample_tuple[-1]
print(f"Got last: {last}")
print(f"first+last: {first+last}")
```

E6.4 Predict the output of the following code:

```
sample_tuple = (1, 2, 3, 4, 5)
first=sample_tuple[:1]
print(f"Got first: {first}")
last=sample_tuple[-1:]
print(f"Got last: {last}")
print(f"first+last: {first+last}")
```

E6.5 Consider the following dictionary:

```
sample_dictionary = {1:"One", 5:"Five", 3:"Three", 2:"Two"}
```

Can you traverse the keys in sorted order and display the corresponding values?

175

CHAPTER 6   ADVANCED DATA TYPES

E6.6 Predict the output of the following code:

```
dictionary_sample = {1: "John", 2: 12, 1:"Bob"}
print(f"The dictionary contains: {dictionary_sample}")
print(f"Number of items: {len(dictionary_sample)}")
```

Keys to Exercise 6

Here is a sample solution set.

E6.1

```
contents = ["John", 12, 25,"Sam", True, 50.7]
print(f"The original list is: {contents}")
# Removing the last two elements from the list
del(contents[-2:])
print(f"Now the list is: {contents}")
```

Here is the output:

```
The original list is: ['John', 12, 25,'Sam', True, 50.7]
Now the list is: ['John', 12, 25,'Sam']
```

E6.2

Interestingly, this code will not raise any error, and you'll see the following output:

```
(3, 'Sam', 5)
```

However, remember that when you use a single index, you cannot go beyond the bounds. For example, the following code

```
# print(sample_tuple[5]) # Error
```

176

CHAPTER 6   ADVANCED DATA TYPES

will raise an error saying `IndexError: tuple index out of range`. So you can see that Python is more forgiving if you try to retrieve a slice.

E6.3

You should see the following output:

```
Got first: 1
Got last: 5
first+last: 6
```

E6.4

You'd see the following output:

```
Got first: (1,)
Got last: (5,)
first+last: (1, 5)
```

Additional note: Compare the outputs of E6.3 and E6.4. Can you see the difference? When you perform slicing, you get back the same type. For example, slicing a list will give you a list, slicing a tuple will give you a tuple, and so on. However, if you retrieve an individual element from the sequence, you'll get whatever was stored in that location – it does not guarantee the sequence type.

E6.5

Here is a sample solution:

```
sample_dictionary={1:"One", 5:"Five", 3:"Three", 2:"Two"}
print(f"The given dictionary is: {sample_dictionary}")
keys_sorted=sorted(sample_dictionary)
print(f"Traversing the keys in the sorted order.")
for key in keys_sorted:
    print(key,sample_dictionary[key])
```

177

CHAPTER 6   ADVANCED DATA TYPES

Here is a sample output:

```
The given dictionary is: {1: 'One', 5: 'Five', 3: 'Three', 2: 'Two'}
Traversing the keys in the sorted order.
1 One
2 Two
3 Three
5 Five
```

E6.6

You should see the following output:

```
The dictionary contains: {1: 'Bob', 2: 12}
Number of items: 2
```

Author's note: Since you reassigned a value ('Bob') for the same key (1), the number of items in the dictionary is 2, not 3.

Case Study

Let's focus on the following case studies.

CS6.1 Problem Statement

Make an application where a user can keep entering his favorite names. Once the user enters "quit," the application will display names that have at least four characters.

178

CHAPTER 6   ADVANCED DATA TYPES

CS6.2 Problem Statement

Let us design a multiple-choice question bank. Each question has four options. The user needs to pick the correct answer among these options. Once the test is over, he can see the score.

For a better understanding, let me supply some sample output for you:

```
Welcome to the MCQ test.
==========================
Q1.What is the value of the expression:2*3-4?
(a)1
(b)2
(c)3
(d)None.
Type your answer(a/b/c/d): b

Q2.What is the value of the expression:1+(2*3)/4?
(a)1.5
(b)3
(c)2.5
(d)None.
Type your answer(a/b/c/d): d

Q3.The list data type can hold duplicate values. The
statement is:
(a)True
(b)False
(c)Partially correct.
(d)None.
Type your answer(a/b/c/d): a

Your Score: 2 out of 3
```

179

CHAPTER 6   ADVANCED DATA TYPES

Author's comment: Once you get the idea, you can add more questions to this test. The test is more challenging when you do not pick a fixed set of questions. Instead, you can select a specific number of questions at random from an extensive set of questions. At this stage, you can work with a fixed number of questions only. You can also avoid input validations now.

Sample Implementations

Let's see the sample implementations for the case studies.

CS6.1 Implementation

Here is a sample implementation:

```
flag = ""
long_names=[]
while flag != 'quit':
    user_input = input("Enter a name (type quit to end): ")
    if user_input =='quit':
        flag = 'quit'
        break
    elif len(user_input) > 3:
        long_names.append(user_input)
print(f"The names with at least four characters: {long_names}")
```

Here is a sample output:

```
Enter a name (type quit to end): Sam
Enter a name (type quit to end): Jack
Enter a name (type quit to end): Shyam
Enter a name (type quit to end): Jo
Enter a name (type quit to end): Jennifer
```

180

CHAPTER 6   ADVANCED DATA TYPES

```
Enter a name (type quit to end): Ron
Enter a name (type quit to end): quit
The names with at least four characters: ['Jack','Shyam',
  'Jennifer']
```

CS6.2 Implementation

I used a dictionary to store answers to the questions. I also used the len()
function to get the total number of questions in this question bank. To
beautify the output, I print the questions and corresponding options on
new lines. Here is a sample implementation for you:

```
# All questions
question1 = "Q1.What is the value of the expression:2*3-4?" \
            "\n(a)1" \
            "\n(b)2" \
            "\n(c)3" \
            "\n(d)None."
question2 = "\nQ2.What is the value of the
expression:1+(2*3)/4?" \
            "\n(a)1.5" \
            "\n(b)3" \
            "\n(c)2.5" \
            "\n(d)None."
question3 = "\nQ3.The list data type can hold duplicate
values." \
            "The statement is:" \
            "\n(a)True" \
            "\n(b)False" \
            "\n(c)Partially correct." \
            "\n(d)None."
```

181

CHAPTER 6　ADVANCED DATA TYPES

```python
# Storing the questions with answer keys
# inside the following dictionary.
question_bank = {question1: "b",
                 question2: "c",
                 question3: "a"}
print("Welcome to the MCQ test.")
print("="*25)
score = 0  # initial value
for key in question_bank:
    print(key)
    user_input = input("Type your answer(a/b/c/d): ")
    if user_input == question_bank[key]:
        score += 1
print(f"\nYour Score: {score} out of {len(question_bank)}")
```

Possible Improvements

To improve the implementation, you can use a function to make a better implementation. In Chapter 7, you'll learn about functions. At the end of Chapter 7, you'll see a better solution.

To improve the project, you can consider storing more questions and picking a subset of these questions at random. You may also note that CS4.2 implementation showed you how to dynamically change data in an expression. You can bring that concept here as well.

CHAPTER 7

Functions and Modules

This chapter covers user-defined functions, lambda functions, and modules. Using them, you can organize your code in a better way.

Function Overview

You can consider a function as a logical set of statements that perform a specific task. Using them, you can divide your code into manageable pieces, which in turn help you optimize and reuse the code. When you see a function usage in someone's code, you notice the following things:

- They define the function to describe a behavior.

- They call the function single or multiple times.

Characteristics

An ordinary function has a name and a body. Before I discuss more about functions, let me cover the following points:

© Vaskaran Sarcar 2025
V. Sarcar, *Python Bootcamp*, https://doi.org/10.1007/979-8-8688-1516-4_7

CHAPTER 7   FUNCTIONS AND MODULES

A function definition begins with the def **keyword**. Then, you type the function name with the parameters (if any). Finally, a def statement ends with a colon. Let me show you a simple function that is as follows:

```
def print_hello():
    print("Hello")
```

You can invoke this function using the following code: print_hello(). Once you invoke this function, it'll print Hello. You'll see the complete demonstration shortly.

The statements of the body of the function are indented. This format is used to show that all these statements belong to the function.

POINTS TO REMEMBER

If you use the PyCharm IDE, once you press Enter to go to the next line, this indentation is automatic. However, it's up to you how many spaces you want to indent your code. For example, you can use a tab or space, but you should not mix both.

Previously, you've seen a function that does not accept any parameter. However, **a *function can* have zero, one, or more parameters**. For example, consider the following function, called print_details, which takes two parameters – the first one is for a name, and the second one is for an age:

```
def print_details(name,age):
    print(f"Hello {name}! How are you?")
    print(f"You are now {age}.")
```

To invoke this function, you can use the following line of code:

```
print_details("Bob",20)
```

184

CHAPTER 7   FUNCTIONS AND MODULES

Upon executing this code, you can see the following output:

```
Hello Bob! How are you?
You are now 20.
```

You can have function documentation. Function documentation helps others to understand *what the function does*. You can also print this documentation using **<your_function_name>.__doc__**. Note that you're seeing the use of double underscores here. To understand this, let me add some documentation to the previous function as follows:

```
def print_details(name,age):
    """
    This function takes two parameters.
    You can supply the name and age of the user
    in this function.
    """
    print(f"Hello {name}!How are you?")
    print(f"You are now {age}.")
```

Now, if you want, you can print this documentation using the following line of code: print(print_details.__doc__).

Demonstration 7.1

Go through the following demonstration. It contains all the functions and associated codes that I have discussed so far:

```
# The following function does not take any argument
def print_hello():
    print("Hello")

# The following function has two parameters.
```

185

CHAPTER 7   FUNCTIONS AND MODULES

```
def print_details(name, age):
    """
    This function takes two parameters.
    You can supply the name and age of the user
    in this function.
    """
    print(f"Hello {name}! How are you?")
    print(f"You are now {age}.")

print("Calling the function that has no parameter.")
print_hello()
print("Now, calling the function that has two parameters.")
print_details("Bob", 20)
```

Output

Here is the output:

```
Calling the function that has no parameter.
Hello
Now, calling the function that has two parameters.
Hello Bob! How are you?
You are now 20.
```

Analysis

Notice that when I call print_details("Bob", 20), I pass two arguments in the function call. The first one is a string, and the second is a number. This demonstrates that a function can have multiple parameters that can be of different types.

You can repeat function calls, and you can vary the arguments. In Demonstration 7.1, you have seen the following line:

```
print_details("Bob",20)
```

186

CHAPTER 7   FUNCTIONS AND MODULES

You can repeat the line as many times as you want. You can also vary the arguments of your function. So the following segment of code

```python
def print_details(name,age):
    """
    This function takes two parameters.
    You can supply the name and age of the user
    in this function.
    """
    print(f"Hello {name}! How are you?")
    print(f"You are now {age}.")

print_details("Bob", 20)
# You can repeat function calls.
print_details("Bob", 20)
# You can vary the arguments of the functions
print_details("Sam", 35)
```

can produce the following output:

```
Hello Bob! How are you?
You are now 20.
Hello Bob! How are you?
You are now 20.
Hello Sam! How are you?
You are now 35.
```

Q&A Session

Q7.1 You are using the words *parameters* and *arguments*. Is there any difference?

Developers often use the words *arguments* and *parameters* interchangeably. However, expert programmers are particular about this. The variables in a function definition are called the function's parameters. For example, when you see the following function definition

187

CHAPTER 7   FUNCTIONS AND MODULES

```
def print_details(name,age):
    # some code
```

the name and age are called parameters (or **formal parameters**) of the function print_details. But, when you invoke the function using the code print_details("Bob",20), we say that "Bob" and 20 are the arguments that you've passed to this function. Similarly, in the line print_details("Sam",30), "Sam" and 30 are arguments. Many developers refer to them as **actual parameters** as well.

You can say that we pass the arguments to a function. These values are assigned to the function parameters. However, I already mentioned that some programmers do not emphasize these terms too much. So they interchangeably use these terms.

Discussion on Function Arguments

You are now familiar with function arguments and parameters. These are essential to understand the upcoming section. Let us take a deeper look at a function argument now.

Positional Argument

In the previous segment of code, instead of writing the code print_details("Bob",20), if you write

```
print_details(20,"Bob") # Unexpected outcome
```

you'll receive the following output:

```
Hello 20! How are you?
You are now  Bob
```

188

CHAPTER 7 FUNCTIONS AND MODULES

Oh ...no! How is this possible? Yeah, you've guessed it right. You needed to pass the arguments in the correct order. For example, in this case, 20 is assigned for the name parameter (as it is in the first position in the function definition), and "Bob" is assigned for the age parameter (which is in the second position in the function definition). Unless you specify these differently, by default, Python expects that you pass the arguments following the order of the parameters that are defined in the function definition. When the values are matched in this way, you say that you are following **positional arguments.**

Keyword Arguments

Let us invoke the function differently. This time, I use the following lines:

```
print_details(age=20,name="Bob") # Expected outcome
print_details(name="Bob", age=20) # Again expected outcome
```

As mentioned in the comments, in both cases, you get the expected result. You can verify the result when you execute the code. For example, in the previous demonstration, execute the following two lines of code. You'll see the following output:

```
Hello Bob! How are you?
You are now 20
Hello Bob! How are you?
You are now 20
```

So what we see now is that when you pass arguments in this name-value pair, you will always see the expected result. Programmatically, these are called **keyword arguments**.

189

CHAPTER 7   FUNCTIONS AND MODULES

Use of Default Values

Instead of supplying values for each of the parameters, you can pass some default values to them. To demonstrate, let's modify the previous function definition as follows:

```
# Using default values in a function
def print_details(name="Sam",age=35):
    """

    This function takes two parameters.
    You can supply the name and age of the user
    in this function.
    By default, the name is 'Sam' and the age is 35.
    """
    print(f"Hello {name}! How are you?")
    print(f"You are now {age}.")
```

Notice the presence of (name="Sam",age="35") in the updated function. You can see that I've added the following line in the function documentation as well:

```
By default, the name is 'Sam' and the age is 35.
```

You know that it is a documentation comment, and it is **optional** for you. But the changes in the modified function definition tell us that from now onward, you can invoke the function with or without parameters. It is because you have supplied default values for all these parameters.

Demonstration 7.2

Let us verify the understanding by executing the following program (I have kept the supportive comments for your easy understanding):

```
# Using default values in a function
def print_details(name="Sam",age=35):
```

190

CHAPTER 7   FUNCTIONS AND MODULES

```
"""
This function takes two parameters.
You can supply the name and age of the user
in this function.
By default, the name is 'Sam' and the age is 35.
"""
print(f"Hello {name}! How are you?")
print(f"You are now {age}.")

print_details()  # Will take both the default values
print_details(name="Jack")  # Will take age=35 as default
print_details(age=45)  # Will take name="Sam" as default
# None of the default values are considered in the
following line
print_details("Bob", 20)
```

Output

Upon executing the program, you'll see the following output:

```
Hello Sam! How are you?
You are now 35.
Hello Jack! How are you?
You are now 35.
Hello Sam! How are you?
You are now 45.
Hello Bob! How are you?
You are now 20.
```

191

CHAPTER 7   FUNCTIONS AND MODULES

Warning

In Python, a function parameter without a default value cannot follow a function parameter with a default value. To illustrate, if you write something like

```
def print_details(name="Sam",age): # Incorrect
    # The function body
```

you'll see the following error:

```
def print_details(name="Sam",age):
                              ^^^
```

SyntaxError: parameter without a default follows parameter with a default

To overcome this error, you need to alter their positions in the function definition. For example, the following segment displays the correct order:

```
def print_details(age, name="Sam"): # Correct
    # The function body
```

Q&A Session

Q7.2 What are the benefits of using default values in a function?
Here are some typical benefits:

- Sometimes, you may not wish to pass all values in your function invocation, and you can type less.

- You may discover that in some specific function calls, a particular argument does not vary.

- You are not sure what to pass when a function is executing.

192

CHAPTER 7   FUNCTIONS AND MODULES

Variable Arguments

Till now, you have seen functions that do not return any value. However, most often, you'll use functions that return values. For example, if you execute the following code

```
def calculate_sum(x, y):
    return x + y

total = calculate_sum(12, 15)
print(f"The sum of 12 and 15 is: {total}")
```

you'll see the following output:

```
The sum of 12 and 15 is: 27
```

You can see that the calculate_sum function calculated the sum of the two numbers without any issue. However, if you try to compute the sum of three numbers as follows

```
total = calculate_sum(12, 15, 25) # Error
```

you'll see the error saying

```
TypeError: calculate_sum() takes 2 positional arguments but 3
were given
```

The error is self-explanatory: this function can handle two valid arguments only. In this context, it is interesting to note that you can supply a variable number of arguments to a function. However, **in that case, you need to mention your intention by supplying a star character before the argument**. Let's see the following demonstration.

193

CHAPTER 7 FUNCTIONS AND MODULES

Demonstration 7.3

The following demonstration uses a function named repeat_sum that accepts a variable number of arguments:

```python
def repeat_sum(*args):
    current_total=0
    for num in args:
        current_total=current_total+num
    return current_total

total = repeat_sum(12, 15)
print(f"The sum of 12 and 15 is: {total}")

total = repeat_sum(20.5, 37,100)
print(f"The sum of 20.5, 37, and 100 is: {total}")
```

Output

Here is the output:

```
The sum of 12 and 15 is: 27
The sum of 20.5, 37, and 100 is: 157.5
```

Analysis

This program shows some typical characteristics. Let's look into them:

First, you can see that I have used repeat_sum to calculate the sum of 12 and 15. Using the same function, I calculated the total of 20.5, 37, and 100. You can see that I did not need to write the programming logic repeatedly. **This program also demonstrates the concept of code reuse using functions.**

Next, I draw your attention to the following lines:

```python
total = repeat_sum(12, 15)
print(f"The sum of 12 and 15 is: {total}")
```

CHAPTER 7   FUNCTIONS AND MODULES

This code segment shows that the repeat_sum function took two numbers as arguments, added them, and stored the result into another variable called total. Later, I displayed the value inside the total variable. **It describes the fact that when you use a function, you do not need to print the result immediately. Instead, you can store the value that comes out from a function in another variable.** This value is called the **return value** of a function.

Q&A Session

Q7.3 Can a function return multiple values?
You often see that a function returns only one value. However, using a smart program, you can return multiple values from a function as well. Let's see the following demonstration.

Demonstration 7.4

In this example, you'll see a simple list called initial_list that contains the numbers 1, 2, 3, 4, and 5. I also have a function called make_double(). This function takes a list as an argument and makes the elements double. Finally, it appends the result into another list called resultant_list, which was initially empty. Let's see the program now:

```
def make_double(input_list):
    """

    It is a function that can return multiple values.
    Each element in the list will be doubled
    by this function.
    """

    for element in input_list:
        resultant_list.append(2 * element)

initial_list=[1,2,3,4,5]
resultant_list=[]
```

195

CHAPTER 7 FUNCTIONS AND MODULES

```
print(f"The initial_list is: {initial_list}")
print("Calling the function make_double now.")
make_double(initial_list)
print(f"The resultant list is: {resultant_list}")
print(f"The initial_list is: {initial_list}")
```

Output

Here is the output:

```
The initial_list is: [1, 2, 3, 4, 5]
Calling the function make_double now.
The resultant list is: [2, 4, 6, 8, 10]
The initial_list is: [1, 2, 3, 4, 5]
```

Analysis

The content of resultant_list shows all the double values of the original integers that I initially supplied through a list. However, you must note that the make_double function should work on numbers only. You can easily assume that to make the program short and simple, the input validations are ignored here.

Q&A Session

Q7.4 In the previous demonstration, you did not modify the initial list. Was this intended?
Nice catch. It is safe to keep the original list as it is. If you do not want to maintain it, you can directly update the list as well. However, this can be risky. In this chapter, I have given you an exercise (E7.6) in which, while creating a new list, you'll update the original list as well.

CHAPTER 7 FUNCTIONS AND MODULES

Lambda Functions

Now let me give you a quick overview of anonymous functions (a.k.a. lambda functions). In simple words, a lambda function is a short inline function without a name. This function can take one or multiple arguments but can have a single expression.

How to Use?

A common function starts with the def keyword. A lambda function starts with a lambda keyword. You may also note that while using a lambda function, you do not see the return statement. This is because the value of the expression is automatically returned. Let's see a demonstration.

Demonstration 7.5

The following demonstration uses two lambda functions. The first one does not take any argument. It simply prints Hello, Reader! The next one takes one argument and can be used to double a number. Here is a complete program:

```
print("Lambda function example and uses-1.")
say_hello = lambda: print("Hello, Reader!")
say_hello()

print("Lambda function example and uses-2.")
make_double = lambda x: x * 2
print(f"Double of 10 is: {make_double(10)}")
print(f"Double of 25.35 is: {make_double(25.35)}")
```

Output

Here is the output:

```
Lambda function example and uses-1.
Hello, Reader!
```

197

CHAPTER 7   FUNCTIONS AND MODULES

```
Lambda function example and uses-2.
Double of 10 is: 20
Double of 25.35 is: 50.7
```

Q&A Session

Q7.5 I understand that lambda functions are short. However, I'd like to know the primary benefits of using them.

First, let me tell you that the examples shown are used only for simple illustration purposes. However, you'd like to use lambda functions as typical tiny throwaway functions that are often passed as function arguments to other functions to organize other complex operations. In fact, it is beneficial to use a lambda function rather than creating a whole new function when you need to perform a simple task only once. It helps you avoid unnecessary function declaration and improves readability.

Author's note: Although lambda functions are a popular choice, you must analyze the scenario before using them. If the function logic is complex and spans over multiple lines, I recommend that you use a docstring for an explanation of the function usage.

Q7.6 Can you demonstrate an example where you pass a lambda function as an argument?

In the following example, I used the built-in map function. This map function requires a function object and any number of iterables, such as a list or a dictionary. So here I pass a lambda function and a list as arguments. The initial list contains some numbers. I use the lambda function to increment each number by 100 in the list.

Demonstration 7.6

Now go through the following demonstration:

```
numbers = [1, 2, 3, 4, 5]
# Adds 100 to each item in the list
```

CHAPTER 7   FUNCTIONS AND MODULES

```
new_numbers= list(map(lambda x: x + 100, numbers))
print(f"The original list: {numbers}")
print(f"The updated list: {new_numbers}")
```

Output

Here is the output:

```
The original list: [1, 2, 3, 4, 5]
The updated list: [101, 102, 103, 104, 105]
```

Modules

Modules are used to organize big projects. Upon investigation, you'll know that the Python standard library is also divided into modules. Modules help you reuse the code as well.

For a small application, you may not need to use modules. However, instead of putting everything in a file and making it big, it's better to organize your code into modules. Now the question is: what is a module? Let's retrieve the definition from the official documentation (see 6. Modules – Python 3.13.3 documentation):

> *A module is a file containing Python definitions and statements. The file name is the module name with the suffix .py appended.*

Now you understand that a module is nothing but a file that contains some code, such as variables, functions, and classes. Once the module is ready, you can use an import statement to access these codes from the current file.

CHAPTER 7   FUNCTIONS AND MODULES

Creating a Module

Let's begin our discussion with a simple module that contains some Python variables and functions only. First, create a file called **bootcamp_library.py** and place the following codes into it. You can see that this file contains a list, a dictionary, and two functions:

Note   I've organized the codes chapter-wise in this book. For example, I stored all programs of Chapter 7 inside a directory named chapter07. I placed the library file in this directory as well.

```
# A simple list
numbers = [1, 2.2, 3.3, 4, 5.5]

# A simple dictionary
employees = {1: "Jack", 2: "Kate", 3: "Bob"}

def double_the_total(first, second):
    """
    This function takes two numbers, adds them
    and doubles the result
    """
    total = first + second
    return total * 2

def make_average(first, second, third=0):
    """
    This function takes three numbers and returns
    the average. The third number is optional.
    """
    total = first + second + third
    return total / 3
```

200

CHAPTER 7   FUNCTIONS AND MODULES

Importing Partial Contents

Now create another file inside the chapter07 directory and write the following lines of code:

Note   The following code is available in ch07_d07_partial_import.py.

```
from bootcamp_library import numbers, employees

print(f"Available numbers are:{numbers}")
print(f"The third number is: {numbers[2]}")
print(f"The working employees are: {employees}")
```

If you run this code, you see the following output:

```
Available numbers are:[1, 2.2, 3.3, 4, 5.5]
The third number is: 3.3
The working employees are: {1: 'Jack', 2: 'Kate', 3: 'Bob'}
```

You can see that I can access the list and dictionary elements from this file (**ch07_d07_partial_import**), though these elements are placed in a separate file (**bootcamp_library.py**). I could access them because I used the import statement at the beginning of the file. In the same way, you can access the function double_the_total that was defined in bootcamp_library.py.

Let us revisit and verify all these points in the following demonstration.

Demonstration 7.7

Here is the content of ch07_d07_partial_import.py for you:

```
from bootcamp_library import numbers, employees, double_the_total

# Using the list from the library.
print(f"Available numbers are:{numbers}")
```

201

CHAPTER 7   FUNCTIONS AND MODULES

```python
print(f"The third number is: {numbers[2]}")

# Using the dictionary from the library.
print(f"The working employees are: {employees}")
print(f"The employee with ID 2 is: {employees[2]}")

# Using the double_the_total function from the library now.
result = double_the_total(20, 30.5)
print(f"Two times of 20 + 30.5 is: {result}")
```

Output

Here is the output:

```
Available numbers are:[1, 2.2, 3.3, 4, 5.5]
The third number is: 3.3
The working employees are: {1: 'Jack', 2: 'Kate', 3: 'Bob'}
The employee with ID 2 is: Kate
Two times of 20 + 30.5 is: 101.0
```

Importing Entire Contents

In the previous demonstration, using the following line

```python
from bootcamp_library import numbers, employees, double_the_total
```

I made numbers, employees, and the double_the_total function
available in the current program file. Already, this line of code is long. You
have seen that the bootcamp_library.py contains one more function (in fact,
it could contain many more functions and variables). Following the same
approach, if you want to access those additional contents, the line of import
statement will be longer as well. So let us see an alternative approach.

202

CHAPTER 7   FUNCTIONS AND MODULES

Python allows you to import the entire content (except a few stuff) from the file into your current program in an alternative way. For example, the following line of code will import the whole content of the bootcamp_library.py:

```
import bootcamp_library
```

However, this time, you need to prepend the name of the module before you access the module contents to guarantee the "**name safety.**" Here is a sample code fragment with the inline comments for your immediate reference:

```
print(f"Available numbers are: {numbers}") # Error now
print(f"Available numbers are:{bootcamp_library.numbers}") # OK
```

Demonstration 7.8

Let us see an alternative version of the previous program with the key changes in bold:

```
import bootcamp_library

# Using the list from the library.
print(f"Available numbers are:{bootcamp_library.numbers}")
print(f"The third number is: {bootcamp_library.numbers[2]}")

# Using the dictionary from the library.
print(f"The working employees are: {bootcamp_library.employees}")
print(f"The employee with ID 2 is: {bootcamp_
    library.employees[2]}")

# Using the double_the_total function from the library now.
result = bootcamp_library.double_the_total(20, 30.5)
print(f"Two times of 20 + 30.5 is: {result}")
```

203

CHAPTER 7 FUNCTIONS AND MODULES

If you run this program, you'll see the same output that you saw in the previous demonstration.

POINT TO REMEMBER

You can import the whole module, or you can import a particular function from a module. I have shown you both approaches. If you import the whole module, you need to use the syntax `module_name.function_name()` to access a function from the module. The same comment applies to variables and classes of the module. Chapter 11 includes more discussion on modules.

Q&A Session

Q7.7 In the previous demonstration, importing the whole content was easy. However, I needed to prepend the module name whenever I used a function or a variable of the module. Is there any specific thought behind this design?

A program can import multiple modules. Consider that there are two modules and each of them has a variable named `flag`. Let us also assume that you have imported both modules into your current program. Now if you refer flag, it's impossible to point out which flag you are referring to. However, if you write <module_name>.flag, there will be no name collision; it is pretty clear that you are referring to the `flag` variable from that particular module. So you understand that by prepending the module name, Python ensures the name safety.

Q7.8 Does a module contain the Python code only?

Most often, the answer is yes. However, there are exceptions. For example, apart from the Python source code, a module can contain compiled C/C++ object files as well.

204

CHAPTER 7   FUNCTIONS AND MODULES

Q7.9 It'll be helpful if you highlight the primary advantages of using a module.

Read the following bullet points:

- You make the current program file small and focus on the high-level logic in this file.

- The inner working logic is in a separate file that is not immediately visible to the user.

- Once you create a module, you can reuse the code.

Alias

Typing a big module name repeatedly is a boring activity. To avoid such a situation, you can use an alias. You can consider the alias as a short name for your function or module.

Let us test a function alias. In the following demonstration, I make an alias for the function double_the_total. Taking the first character from each of the individual words, I have chosen the alias name as dtt. This is why you'll see the following line of code:

```
from bootcamp_library import double_the_total as dtt
```

The remaining program is easy to understand. Go through it.

Demonstration 7.9

Here is the complete program:

```
from bootcamp_library import double_the_total as dtt

# Using the double_the_total function from the library now.
result = dtt(20, 30.5)
print(f"Two times of 20 + 30.5 is: {result}")
```

205

CHAPTER 7   FUNCTIONS AND MODULES

Output

Upon executing the program, you should see the following output:

```
Two times of 20 + 30.5 is: 101.0
```

You can test a module alias as well. I want you to try it yourself. Otherwise, you can download the file **ch07_d10_module_alias.py**, in which I have shown you an alternative version of Demonstration 7.8 using module alias.

Additional Notes

This section will draw your attention to two useful notes. Let's see them.

General Form of Import

In Demonstration 7.7, if you replace the following line

```
from bootcamp_library import numbers, employees, double_
  the_total
```

with the following one

```
from bootcamp_library import *
```

you'll see the same output. It is a general form of the import statement. However, I did not use it for the following reasons:

- You need to be careful. If you import multiple modules using this kind of statement, there is a possibility of name collisions.

- It is difficult for readers to identify the source.

- This kind of import does not import objects whose names start with an underscore.

206

CHAPTER 7   FUNCTIONS AND MODULES

Executing a Program as the Main Program

If you are like me, who comes from a C# or Java background, let me tell you that Python does not automatically look for a specific function when the program starts. So you may be surprised by seeing the output in some specific situations. Let me give you an example.

When you download the source code, you'll see that the code of Demonstration 7.1 is contained in the file named ch07_d01_basic_functions.py. Let's try to reuse the code in another file, named **ch07_reusing_demo1.py**, as follows:

```
import ch07_d01_basic_functions as demo1
print("Reusing the code of demonstration 7.1")
demo1.print_hello()
```

Upon executing this code, you will see the following output:

```
Calling the function that has no parameter.
Hello
Now calling the function that has two parameters.
Hello Bob! How are you?
You are now 20.
Reusing the code of demonstration 7.1
Hello
```

Probably, you were expected to see the last two lines of this output. Instead, you are seeing the additional lines at the beginning. Why? They appeared due to the execution of Demonstration 7.1 (the imported program) as well. However, you may not intend to see the additional output. To prevent executing the imported program unnecessarily, you may restructure Demonstration 7.1 as follows (see the key changes in bold):

207

CHAPTER 7 FUNCTIONS AND MODULES

```python
# There is no change in the function definitions
def main():
    print("Calling the function that has no parameter.")
    print_hello()
    print("Now calling the function that has two parameters.")
    print_details("Bob", 20)

if __name__ == "__main__":
    main()
```

If you execute Demonstration 7.1 now, you'll see the same output that you saw earlier at the beginning of the chapter. However, this time, upon executing **ch07_reusing_demo1.py**, you'll see the following output:

```
Reusing the code of demonstration 7.1
Hello
```

How did this work? Let me pick two important lines from the official documentation (https://docs.python.org/3/library/__main__.html):

- When a Python module or package is imported, __name__ is set to the module's name. Usually, this is the name of the Python file itself without the .py extension.

- However, if the module is executed in the top-level code environment, its __name__ is set to the string '__main__'.

In the previous code segment, I used this if statement to verify whether, after loading the module, the interpreter assigned the __ **name**__ variable to the value __**main**__. So you can see that the **if** block helped me distinguish between the following cases:

208

CHAPTER 7   FUNCTIONS AND MODULES

- Whether a Python file was being included in another program

- Whether the Python code was being executed as its own program

For example, when you executed Demonstration 7.1, it was executed as the main program. However, when you executed `ch07_reusing_demo1.py`, the imported file did not execute as the main program.

I hope that you have got the idea! **Now onward, if needed, you can restructure all the previous demonstrations as well. In fact, I recommend this practice.** If interested, you can learn more on this topic from the official documentation: __main__ – Top-level code environment – Python 3.13.3 documentation.

Summary

This chapter covered functions and modules with different code samples. Upon completion of this chapter, you will know the answer to the following questions:

- How can you use functions in your program?

- How can you use the positional arguments, keyword arguments, default values, and return values of a function?

- How can you use the lambda functions? How does it help?

- How can you use modules? What are the associated benefits of using a module?

- How can you use a function alias or a module alias in your program?

209

CHAPTER 7   FUNCTIONS AND MODULES

Exercise 7

It's time for the exercises. You can assume that all these programs were executed as the main programs.

E7.1 Can you predict the output of the following code segment?

```python
def print_x(x):
    print(int(x)+5)

def main():
    print_x('25')

main()
```

E7.2 Can you predict the output of the following code segment?

```python
def print_me(x):
    print(x+2)

def print_me(x):
    print(x+3)

print_me(5)
```

E7.3 Can you predict the output of the following code segment?

```python
def make_total(type, *args):
    """

    This function can take multiple arguments.
    However, it considers only the integers, floating-
    point numbers and string data types.
    """

    if type=='strings':
        total=' '
```

210

CHAPTER 7   FUNCTIONS AND MODULES

```python
    elif type == 'numbers':
        total = 0.0
    # Traversing the arguments
    for item in args:
        total= total + item
    return total

result = make_total("numbers",2.5,3)
print(result)
result = make_total("strings","2.75","3")
print(result)
```

E7.4 Can you predict the output of the following code segment?

```python
x = 10
print(f"x = {x}")

def print_me(x):
    x += 2
    print(f"Now x is: {x}")

print_me(x)
print(f"Here x is: {x}")
```

E7.5 Can you predict the output of the following code segment?

```python
def print_me(x):
    print(x)

def print_me(x,y):
    print(x+y)

print_me(5)
print_me(5,7)
```

211

CHAPTER 7   FUNCTIONS AND MODULES

E7.6 Demonstration 7.4 doubled each number in the given list and placed those numbers into a new list. However, you did not alter the original list. Now, I want you to modify the program where you remove the elements from the initial list, make them double, and place them into a new list. So, in the end, when you examine the original list, you should see that it is empty. Can you write the program?

E7.7 Suppose you have a list of numbers. Using a lambda function, can you increase each number by 5%?

Keys to Exercise 7

Here is a sample solution set.

E7.1

You'll see the following output:

30

Explanation: This is straightforward. The main function invoked the other function, print_x, which transforms the input string '25' to an integer and adds 5 to it.

E7.2

You'll see the following output:

8

Explanation: Python does not show you any error if you use the same name for two functions, but it calls the latest one. In this exercise, Python assumes that you redeclared the print_me function, in which the function increments the value of x by 3. This is why print_me(5) results in 5 + 3 = 8.

212

CHAPTER 7   FUNCTIONS AND MODULES

E7.3

Here is the output:

```
5.5
2.753
```

Explanation: This example gives you an idea about how a function can behave differently. If you are familiar with method overloading in Java or C#, you are already familiar with this kind of behavior. Python does not support method overloading by default. However, there are different ways to achieve this concept in Python. This example demonstrates one of those approaches (though it is not the most efficient).

E7.4

Here is the output:

```
x = 10
Now x is: 12
Here x is: 10
```

Explanation: The initial value of x was 10. Then I called the print_me function, which incremented the value to 12. However, this change happened inside the function body. It means that I worked on a local copy of x. So, when I came out from the function body, I again got the value 10 for x. In other words, I lost the value of a local variable between function invocations.

You can use the same local variable for different functions too. In simple terms, the memory of a local variable is used when it is in the scope. When you leave the scope, you free the memory.

Sometimes, you may want to a have variable that does not die before your program ends. In such a case, you can use a global variable. Since global variables are not for any specific functions, you place them outside

213

CHAPTER 7 FUNCTIONS AND MODULES

of all functions. In Python, global is a reserved word. To illustrate, let me modify E7.4 as follows (see the presence of the global keyword inside the print_me function that does not accept any argument now):

Note I placed the following code in **ch07_use_of_global_variable. py**, which you can download from the Apress website.

```
print("Example of a global variable.")
x = 10
print(f"x = {x}")

def print_me():
    global x
    x += 2
    print(f"Now x is: {x}")

print_me()
print(f"Here x is: {x}")
```

Now you can get the following output:

```
Example of a global variable.
x=10
Now x=12
Here x=12
```

E7.5

Upon executing the program, you'll see the following error:

```
TypeError: print_me() missing 1 required positional
argument: 'y'
```

214

CHAPTER 7   FUNCTIONS AND MODULES

Explanation: Exercise E7.2 explained that if you have multiple functions with the same name, Python considers the latest one. So, in this case, you were supposed to supply two arguments because the latest definition of the print_me function had two parameters.

E7.6

Here is a sample program:

```python
def transform_lists():
    """
    It is a function that can return multiple values.
    Each element in the initial_list will be doubled
    by this function.
    """
    global initial_list
    global resultant_list
    # First, reversing the list before calling pop()
    initial_list.reverse()
    #print(f"The list becomes:{input_list}")
    while initial_list:
      for element in initial_list:
        element = initial_list.pop()
        # print(element)
        resultant_list.append(2 * element)

initial_list = [1,2,3,4,5]
resultant_list=[]
print(f"The initial_list is: {initial_list}")
print("Calling the function transform_lists now.")
transform_lists()
print(f"The initial_list is: {initial_list}")
print(f"The resultant list is: {resultant_list}")
```

215

CHAPTER 7   FUNCTIONS AND MODULES

Here is the output:

```
The initial_list is: [1, 2, 3, 4, 5]
Calling the function transform_lists now.
The initial_list is: []
The resultant list is: [2, 4, 6, 8, 10]
```

E7.7

```
initial_numbers= [100, 200, 300, 400, 500]
print(f"The original numbers are {initial_numbers}")
# Incrementing each item in the list by 5%
new_numbers = list(map(lambda x: x * 1.05, initial_numbers))
print(f"The updated numbers are {new_numbers}")
```

Here is the output:

```
The original numbers are [100, 200, 300, 400, 500]
The updated numbers are [105.0, 210.0, 315.0, 420.0, 525.0]
```

Case Study

Let's make solutions for the following case studies.

CS7.1 Problem Statement

This time, I want you to make a calculator. Using the calculator, you should be able to perform the basic operations: addition, subtraction, multiplication, and division. Here, I provide you a sample output when the user supplies the valid inputs:

```
==========================
This is a simple calculator.
It supports the following operations:
```

216

CHAPTER 7   FUNCTIONS AND MODULES

```
i) Addition
ii) Subtraction
iii) Multiplication and
iv) Division.
========================
Enter the first number: 12.5
Enter the next number: 3
Enter an operator(+,-,*,/): *
The final result is:37.5
```

Author's comment:

Chapter 8 can help you evaluate all the valid inputs. In this project, you can add one simple validation that checks whether a user supplies an invalid operator. In this case, your application should inform the user about this error. Here is a sample output for this negative scenario:

```
========================
This is a simple calculator.
It supports the following operations:
i) Addition
ii) Subtraction
iii) Multiplication and
iv) Division.
========================
Enter the first number: 2
Enter the next number: 5
Enter an operator(+,-,*,/): >
Invalid operator. Cannot compute the result.
```

217

CHAPTER 7   FUNCTIONS AND MODULES

CS7.2 Problem Statement

You can organize the CS6.2 implementation in a better way. Your guess is correct. I want you to use functions in your implementation.

Sample Implementations

Let's see the sample implementations for the case studies.

CS7.1 Implementation

I use many small functions in this implementation. I convert a valid operand into a float before I calculate the result. So you'll find codes like

```
usr_input1 = input("Enter first number:")
first_number = float(usr_input1)
```

I store valid operators in a list. Here is the code:

```
valid_operators = ["+", "-", "*", "/"]
```

If the operator is not included in this list, I report an error. I use an if-else chain to do this task:

```
if usr_opr in valid_operators:
    compute(first_number, usr_opr, second_number)
else:
    print("Invalid operator. Cannot compute the result.")
```

The remaining code is easy to understand. Refer to the supporting comments if you need them. Here is the complete implementation:

```
print("=" * 25)
print("This is a simple calculator.")
print("It supports the following operations:")
```

218

CHAPTER 7   FUNCTIONS AND MODULES

```python
print("i) Addition"
      "\nii) Subtraction"
      "\niii) Multiplication and "
      "\niv) Division.")
print("=" * 25)
valid_operators = ["+", "-", "*", "/"]

def add_numbers(num1, num2):
    """
    Adds the numbers.
    """
    return num1 + num2

def subtract_numbers(num1, num2):
    """
    Subtracts the numbers.
    """
    return num1 - num2

def multiply_numbers(num1, num2):
    """
    Multiplies the numbers.
    """
    return num1 * num2

def divide_numbers(num1, num2):
    """
    Divide num1 by num2.
    """
    return num1 / num2
```

219

CHAPTER 7   FUNCTIONS AND MODULES

```python
def compute(num1, operator, num2):
    """
    This function computes the final result.
    """
    result = 0   # the default value

    if operator == '+':
        result = add_numbers(num1,num2)
    elif operator == '-':
        result = subtract_numbers(num1,num2)
    elif operator == '*':
        result = multiply_numbers(num1,num2)
    else:
        result = divide_numbers(num1, num2)
    print(f"The final result is:{result}")

def main():
    """
    This is the top-level function.
    It calls the compute() function.
    """
    usr_input1 = input("Enter the first number:")
    first_number = float(usr_input1)
    usr_input2 = input("Enter the next number:")
    second_number = float(usr_input2)
    usr_opr = input("Enter an operator(+,-,*,/): ")
    if usr_opr in valid_operators:
        compute(first_number, usr_opr, second_number)
    else:
        print("Invalid operator. Cannot compute the result.")

if __name__ == "__main__":
    main()
```

CHAPTER 7 FUNCTIONS AND MODULES

Possible Improvements

To improve the implementation, you can try to validate all the user inputs when you learn the exception-handling mechanism. You'll see a sample implementation at the end of Chapter 8.

To improve the project, you can support more operations in your calculator.

CS7.2 Implementation

Here is an improved and organized solution for CS6.2 using functions:

```python
# The initial part is not shown to avoid repetitions.
# i.e. there is no change in the
# question1, question2, question3 and question_bank variables

def run_test(questions):
    """
        This function takes the question bank as a parameter.
        You can supply the question bank with answer keys
        in this function.
    """
    print("Welcome to the MCQ test.")
    print("=" * 25)
    score = 0  # initial value
    for key in questions:
        print(key)
        user_input = input("Type your answer(a/b/c/d):")
        if user_input == question_bank[key]:
            score += 1
    print(f"\nYour Score:{score} out of {len(questions)}")

if __name__ == "__main__":
    run_test(question_bank)
```

CHAPTER 7   FUNCTIONS AND MODULES

> **Note**   You can download the file ch07_cs02.py to see the complete program.

Possible Improvements

To improve the implementation, you can validate all the user inputs when you learn the exception-handling mechanism in Chapter 8.

CHAPTER 8

Exception Management

Coding is fun. You face continuous challenges and encounter sudden surprises during your program execution. Some problems are visible before executing the program. For example, if you write `print("Hello)`, the PyCharm IDE will immediately help you discover the syntax error by highlighting that you're missing the closing quotes. This type of error is common but sometimes hard to find with human eyes at the very beginning. So the parser or an IDE like `PyCharm` can help you in these situations. Finding this kind of error is easy.

There is another category of problems that you find during the execution of a program. Here are some typical examples:

- Dividing an integer by 0.

- Trying to convert an invalid string to an integer.

- An expected file is not found, or it doesn't exist at all, and so forth.

Programmers term these unusual situations as *exceptions*. Handling these exceptions is a challenging activity. The core concept is not new. In fact, it has been around for some time. Python has its own set of exceptions. These are available for your immediate use. You can also write a custom exception to handle a specific situation. This chapter discusses the topic.

© Vaskaran Sarcar 2025
V. Sarcar, *Python Bootcamp*, https://doi.org/10.1007/979-8-8688-1516-4_8

223

CHAPTER 8   EXCEPTION MANAGEMENT

General Philosophy

You can define an exception as an event that breaks the normal execution flow of the program during the runtime of the program. So the primary purpose of exception handling is to handle those errors. However, consider the case when you have a big application with many small functions. If you need to consider all possible errors in every code segment, the task can be boring as well as repetitive.

Let me give you a simple example. Suppose your application computes something, and you periodically store the result on a disk. These operations can be interrupted in various ways. Here are some possibilities:

- A user provides one or more invalid inputs.

- At some stage, you encounter something unwanted, say a division by zero operation.

- The disk does not have enough space.

- The disk is not fully functional. So you cannot save the result.

You understand that handling these unwanted situations (a.k.a. exceptions) is important. Otherwise, any of these unwanted situations is sufficient to break the normal flow of the execution. You'll see an example shortly in Demonstration 8.1.

To secure an application, let's assume that you check all possible error conditions in advance. Under this method, the error-detecting and error-handling code becomes a significant portion of the entire program. This code can be repetitive and scattered as well. So it is not desirable. Exception-handling mechanisms can act as a bridge between these possibilities.

To illustrate, for the discussed example, at a high level, you can consider two imaginable types of errors – one to detect a computational

224

CHAPTER 8   EXCEPTION MANAGEMENT

error and another one to detect disk errors. Now, you use two handlers to handle these situations. Then, you organize your code in such a way that if any of these errors occur, you refer to the corresponding error handler.

POINT TO REMEMBER

Usually, the problems that can cause an exception are different. For example, an arithmetic problem such as division by 0 differs completely from a memory shortage problem in a disk. Therefore, you need to use specific handlers to manage the corresponding types of problems.

Common Terms

Python creates some special objects called exceptions to manage runtime errors. Before diving into Python-specific terms, let me use some general terms that you'll often hear while discussing exceptions.

We say that a particular block of code *raises* (or throws) an exception. We call the act of responding to an exception *catching* an exception. We refer to the code that handles the exception as an *exception handler*. You can see multiple exception handlers in a program. They help you catch different types of exceptions in the code. It is also possible that different handlers handle the same exception, but in general, they do not live in the same place.

If you have the correct exception handlers, your program continues to run. **Otherwise, the program may halt and die prematurely**. In these cases, follow the traceback, which includes a detailed report about the situation.

225

CHAPTER 8   EXCEPTION MANAGEMENT

Exception Handling in Python

Python generates an exception object with a `raise` statement. Once it is raised, Python follows the common exception-handling mechanism, i.e., instead of proceeding with the next statement, the current calling chain searches for the handler that can handle the situation. If it finds such a handler, it can access the exception object for more information. Otherwise, the program aborts with an error message.

Python's exception-handling philosophy differs slightly from some traditional programming languages, such as C. To illustrate, developers may try to check all possible errors before performing a critical action to avoid runtime exceptions. We call this style ***look before you leap*** (LBYL). Python likes to deal with exceptions after they occur. Yes, it is risky. But they encourage you to write code, which is less cumbersome and easily readable. We call this approach ***Easier to Ask for Forgiveness than Permission*** (EAFP).

> *It is often easier to ask for forgiveness than to ask for permission.*
>
> —Grace Hopper, American computer scientist

Hierarchical Structure

Python has its own set of exceptions. It has a hierarchical structure. At the time of this writing, Python 3.13 has just been released. So you can get the latest list from the link `http://bit.ly/python-exceptions`. Instead of filling the pages with the complete list of exceptions, I prefer to show a subset of it to give you an idea:

```
BaseException
     SystemExit
     ...
```

226

CHAPTER 8   EXCEPTION MANAGEMENT

```
Exception
        ArithmeticError
                FloatingPointError
                ZeroDivisionError
        AssertionError
        ...
        ValueError
                UnicodeError
                ...
        ...
```

Notice the indentation. It is deliberate. Each exception type is a class. These classes follow the inheritance hierarchy. The hierarchical structure helps us to determine the parent–child relationship. Class, objects, and inheritance make the heart of object-oriented programming (OOP). You may be unfamiliar with OOP. Do not worry, it's okay. I have included a discussion about them in the last part of the book.

POINT TO REMEMBER

Python's exception-handling mechanism follows the object-oriented programming (OOP) style. Chapters 10 and 11 in this book discuss the OOP. You do not need to learn the OOP in detail to understand the material in this chapter.

Following the list, it's enough for you to know that a ZeroDivisionError is one type of ArithmeticError, which is again one type of Exception. But SystemExit is not an Exception type; it is a BaseException type. You can get the full meaning of each type from the Python documentation. You can become familiar with them as you continue reading this chapter and writing programs.

227

CHAPTER 8   EXCEPTION MANAGEMENT

It can be easier for you to relate this hierarchy with some real-world examples. For example, you can think of a vehicle as the base class for both buses and trains. So, when we talk about a bus or train, we know that a bus is nothing but a specific type of vehicle. Similarly, a train is nothing but a specific type of vehicle. Similarly, the `ZeroDivisionError` is nothing but a specific type of `ArithmeticError`.

Demonstration 8.1

Let us examine the case when you do not handle an exceptional situation. Instead, you leave the decision to Python to manage the error.

The following program expects you to supply two valid integers. Then, it displays the result of the division. Everything seems to be fine at the beginning because you do not see any syntax errors. Let's see the program:

```python
a = input("Enter the dividend: ")
b = input("Enter the divisor: ")
c = int(a)/int(b)
print(f"The result of a/b is {c}")
print("The program completes successfully.")
```

Output

Now, analyze the program against some valid and invalid inputs. If you supply 7 and 2, everything seems to work fine. Here is the output.

```
Enter the dividend: 7
Enter the divisor: 2
The result of a/b is 3.5
The program completes successfully.
```

228

CHAPTER 8   EXCEPTION MANAGEMENT

Now, analyze the program with some different inputs. If you supply 7 as dividend and 0 as divisor, the application raises a runtime error as follows:

```
Enter the dividend: 7
Enter the divisor: 0
Traceback (most recent call last):
  File "E:\MyPrograms\PythonBootcamp\chapter8\ch08_d01_
exception_demo.py", line 3, in <module>
    c = int(a)/int(b)
        ~~~~~~~^~~~~~~~

ZeroDivisionError: division by zero
```

Notice that Python generates a traceback for you. Following this report, you can identify that in line 3, you have encountered the problem. It is because there is an attempt of a division by zero. Once this error is raised, Python does not execute the next statement anymore. So you do not see the line "The program completes successfully." in this output. As shown in the output, Python names this kind of error as ZeroDivisionError.

Now, analyze the program again when you pass an invalid dividend. Let's supply abc and 2. Since you cannot convert abc to a valid integer, the application produces a different runtime error as follows:

```
Enter the dividend: abc
Enter the divisor: 2
Traceback (most recent call last):
  File "E:\MyPrograms\PythonBootcamp\chapter8\ch08_d01_
exception_demo.py", line 3, in <module>
    c = int(a)/int(b)
        ~~~^^^

ValueError: invalid literal for int() with base 10: 'abc'
```

229

CHAPTER 8   EXCEPTION MANAGEMENT

Notice that this time, you see a ValueError. Again, once this error is raised, Python does not execute the next statement anymore. So you do not see the line "The program completes successfully." in this output.

Q&A Session

Q8.1 Why do we see exceptions?
This kind of problem may occur due to various reasons, such as implementing an incorrect program logic or bypassing a typical loophole in the code.

Q8.2 Why do you believe that exception handling is a challenging activity?
Since you do not see the syntax (or parsing) errors, everything appears to be fine. Still, you find problems during the program execution.

Author's note: Sometimes, you do not see syntax errors or exceptions. However, the program may still produce an incorrect output. This type of error is known as a semantic error. Identifying semantic errors can be tricky. In this case, to figure out the problem, you need to work backward by looking at the output of the program. Examples of semantic errors include passing a numeric variable where a character value was intended or encountering a race condition. Some developers also treat this type of error as exceptions.

Q8.3 Can built-in functions raise exceptions?
Yes. For example, see the following code:

```
>>> mylist=[1,2,3,4]
>>> mylist
[1, 2, 3, 4]
>>> mylist[5]
Traceback (most recent call last):
  File "<python-input-2>", line 1, in <module>
```

230

CHAPTER 8   EXCEPTION MANAGEMENT

```
mylist[5]
~~~~~~~^^^
```

```
IndexError: list index out of range
```

Q8.4 Is it possible to force an exception to occur?
Yes, you can use the `raise` statement to force a specified exception to occur. For example, the following code segment raises an exception if the sum of two variables (x and y) is greater than 5:

```
x,y = 2,4
if x+y > 5:
    raise ArithmeticError("The total is greater than 5")
else:
    print(f"x+y is {x+y}")
```

Author's note: You can download `ch08_raising_exception.py` from the Apress website to verify this program.

Key Points

In this section, I highlight some key points about the exception-handling mechanism. You can revisit these points as per your need:

- An exception object is created when a runtime error occurs. It is used to describe an erroneous situation.

- Exceptions are raised during the program execution. Whenever such a situation occurs, in programming terminology, you say that the application has raised (or thrown) an exception.

- You can guard an exception using a `try-except` block. You place the code that may raise an exception inside a `try` block. You handle an exceptional situation inside an except block.

231

CHAPTER 8   EXCEPTION MANAGEMENT

- Demonstration 8.1 shows that the same program can generate a variety of exceptions. So you may notice the presence of multiple except blocks with a try block in a program.

- If the codes inside the try block execute without an exception, the program control bypasses the except block(s).

- When a particular except block handles an exception, we often say that the except block has caught the exception.

- You need to be prepared for all possible exceptions. For example, let's say that in a program, you may have a code segment to handle the ZeroDivisionError, but you do not have an except block to handle ValueError. In this case, if the ValueError occurs inside the try block, your program ends prematurely.

- When an exception occurs, Python shows you an error report. You can use this report to know the error location and the details of it.

- The **try...except** statement can have an optional **else** clause. If this is present, it must follow all except clauses. Typically, it is useful to make a concise try block.

- However, if you are coming from a C# or Java background, there is good news for you! You can have a finally block as well to perform cleanup operations.

Do not worry! We'll examine all these possibilities.

232

CHAPTER 8   EXCEPTION MANAGEMENT

Q&A Session

Q8.5 How does the else block help me in exception handling?
As said before, it helps you make a concise try block. Shortly, you'll see
an implementation. For now, you can refer to the official documentation
(see 8. Handling Exceptions – Python 3.13.3 documentation) that states the
following:

> *The use of the else clause is better than adding additional code
> to the try clause because it avoids accidentally catching an
> exception that wasn't raised by the code being protected by the
> try ... except statement.*

Using try-catch-finally

In the upcoming demonstration, you'll see the use of try, except, and
finally blocks. **This program is a modified version of Demonstration
8.1.** So it expects you to supply two valid integers before it displays the
result of the division. Again, we'll discuss the program by supplying valid
and invalid inputs.

Demonstration 8.2

Here is the complete program for you:

```python
print("The following program can handle two different errors.")
a = input("Enter the dividend: ")
b = input("Enter the divisor: ")

try:
    result = int(a) / int(b)
    print(f"The result of the division is: {result}")
except ZeroDivisionError as e:
    print("Invalid input! Your divisor becomes zero!")
    print(f"Error details: {e}")
```

233

CHAPTER 8   EXCEPTION MANAGEMENT

```
except ValueError as e:
    print("Invalid input! Provide a correct input next time!")
    print(f"Error details: {e}")
finally:
    print("The program completes successfully.")
```

Output

If you supply valid inputs such as 7 and 2, everything seems to work fine. Here is the output:

```
The following program can handle two different errors.
Enter the dividend: 7
Enter the divisor: 2
The result of the division is: 3.5
The program completes successfully.
```

Let's supply 7 and 0 now. Since the divisor is 0 before the division operation, the application raises an exception (ZeroDivisionError), but you have handled the situation using an except block. Here is the output:

```
The following program can handle two different errors.
Enter the dividend: 7
Enter the divisor: 0
Invalid input! Your divisor becomes zero!
Error details: division by zero
The program completes successfully.
```

Notice that this time, the program ends gracefully. You also see the line "The program completes successfully." in this output. **It is because this line was supposed to be executed under all situations.** This is why the finally block typically contains the cleanup operations, application closing messages, etc.

234

CHAPTER 8   EXCEPTION MANAGEMENT

POINT TO NOTE

You may also note that instead of showing a detailed error report, you can use the except block to print some custom messages. When you do this, you provide better security to your application. It is because you do not disclose important details like your program file name, file location, etc. A skilled hacker can do illegal activities using this information.

Now analyze the program again when you pass an invalid divisor, say 'abc'. This causes the ValueError to be raised. However, the situation is managed in another except block. Here is the output:

```
The following program can handle two different errors.
Enter the dividend: 5
Enter the divisor: abc
Invalid input! Provide a correct input next time!
Error details: invalid literal for int() with base 10: 'abc'
The program completes successfully.
```

Once again, since the program ended gracefully, so you can see the line "The program completes successfully." in this output. Again, you have done an excellent job to prevent the skilled attacker by not disclosing the important details of the file.

Q&A Session

Q8.6 I understand that you are hiding the error detail using the except block. However, in this demonstration, if I'd like to see the traceback, how can I see that?

In this demonstration, if you do not handle the exceptional situation, you'll see the traceback. For example, if you do not handle the ZeroDivisionError and you pass the divisor 0, you'll see the traceback.

235

CHAPTER 8   EXCEPTION MANAGEMENT

However, while using the except block, you can display the same. For example, let's import the **traceback** module and modify the except block as follows:

```
except ZeroDivisionError as e:
    print("Invalid input! Your divisor becomes zero!")
    print(f"Error details: {e}")
    print(traceback.print_exc())
```

This time, if you pass 0 as a divisor, you can see the traceback again. Here is a sample:

```
The following program can handle two different errors.
Enter the dividend: 7
Enter the divisor: 0
Invalid input! Your divisor becomes zero!
Error details: division by zero
Traceback (most recent call last):
  File "E:\MyPrograms\PythonBootcamp\chapter8\ch08_d02_
modified_demo1.py", line
    6, in <module>
    result = int(a) / int(b)
             ~~~~~~~^~~~~~~~
ZeroDivisionError: division by zero
None
The program completes successfully.
```

Using the else Block

Notice the program logic in the previous program and consider the division operation again. You understand that if a runtime error occurs during the division operation, the program does not print the result. This logic is correct, but you can beautify your code. It is a better idea to put the

236

CHAPTER 8   EXCEPTION MANAGEMENT

result of the division in an else block. It can show whether the code in the try block can pass without an issue. As a next step, the program control enters the else block. So, in this example, I've moved the line print(f"The result of the division is: {result}") into the else block.

Demonstration 8.3

Here is the complete demonstration with the key change in bold:

```
print("The following program can handle two different errors.")
a = input("Enter the dividend: ")
b = input("Enter the divisor: ")
try:
    result = int(a) / int(b)
except ZeroDivisionError as e:
    print("Invalid input! Your divisor becomes zero!")
    print(f"Error details: {e}")
except ValueError as e:
    print("Invalid input! Provide a correct input next time!")
    print(f"Error details: {e}")
else:
    print(f"The result of the division is: {result}")
finally:
    print("The program completes successfully.")
```

Output

If you test this modified program with different inputs (that were used in Demonstrations 8.2), you'll notice the same behavior.

237

CHAPTER 8   EXCEPTION MANAGEMENT

POINTS TO REMEMBER

When you assume that a particular segment of code may raise a runtime error or exception, you place that segment of code into a **try** block. To handle a specific runtime error, you place an appropriate **except** block to handle the error, print user-friendly messages, and suppress important details to prevent malicious attacks. Finally, if there are codes that depend on the successful completion of the **try** block, you place them into the **else** block. In short, keeping this information in mind, you can design a **try-except-else** block.

Q&A Session

Q8.7 How does the else block differ from the finally block?

The else block executes if the try block does not raise any exception. You'd like to use this block to separate the "successful execution" logic from the "potential error" logic and the "cleanup" logic. On the contrary, the finally block always executes. So you put the cleanup codes in the finally block.

Using the pass Statement

If needed, you can hide the exception details and allow the program to fail silently. You may do this to give the user an impression that everything is fine.

To illustrate, the upcoming program calculates the aggregate of two valid numbers. If the user passes any invalid input, you catch the exception but silently skip the exception details by using the pass statement.

238

CHAPTER 8   EXCEPTION MANAGEMENT

Demonstration 8.4

The following demonstration describes such a scenario:

```
total = 0  #default value
try:
    a = float(first_input)
    b = float(second_input)
except ValueError as e:
    pass
else:
    total = a + b
    print(f"The sum of numbers: {total}")
finally:
    print("The program completes successfully.")
```

Output

If you supply valid inputs such as 25.5 and 12, everything seems to work fine. Here is the output:

```
This program prints the sum of two valid numbers.
Enter a valid number: 25.5
Enter another valid number: 12
The sum of numbers: 37.5
The program completes successfully.
```

Let's supply 27 and abc now. Here is the output:

```
This program prints the sum of two valid numbers.
Enter a valid number: 27
Enter another valid number: abc
The program completes successfully.
```

239

CHAPTER 8 EXCEPTION MANAGEMENT

Analysis

Notice that the previous output does not display the total. The program logic tells us that if everything goes well inside the try block, you calculate the aggregate of the valid numbers inside the else block. But it was NOT the case here because you supplied a string, abc, which cannot be converted into a valid floating-point number.

Arranging Multiple except Blocks

In a program, you can expect different errors, and you guard them with appropriate except blocks. But you may not anticipate everything in advance. So you may want to have a general except block that can handle remaining exceptional situations. For example, in Demonstration 8.2, you handled both ZeroDivisionError and ValueError, but what happens if a different exception occurs in your program? In such a case, you can use a general except block to catch the remaining errors. Here is such an example where I catch **all built-in non-system-exiting exceptions** after all the anticipated except blocks as follows:

```
try:
    # Some code
except ZeroDivisionError as e:
    print(f"Error details:{e}")
except ValueError as e:
    print(f"Error details:{e}")
except Exception as e:
    print(f"Error details:{e}")
```

This arrangement is important. If you place a more generic or broader except block before a specific except block, your code will NOT reach the specific except block. Just like if you already recognize a bus, you do not need to test whether it is a vehicle.

240

CHAPTER 8   EXCEPTION MANAGEMENT

Q&A Session

Q8.8 "If you place a more generic or broader except block before a specific except block, your code will NOT reach the specific except block." Can you give an example?

Let's execute the following program where the arrangement of the except blocks is not proper:

```
print("The following program can handle the non-system-exiting
exceptions.")
a = input("Enter the dividend: ")
b = input("Enter the divisor: ")
try:
    result = int(a) / int(b)
# The incorrect arrangement of the except blocks
except Exception as e:
    print(f"An unexpected error has occurred. Error
      details: {e}")
except ZeroDivisionError as e:
    print("Invalid input! Your divisor becomes zero!")
    print(f"Error details: {e}")
except ValueError as e:
    print("Invalid input! Provide a correct input next time!")
    print(f"Error details: {e}")
# except Exception as e:
#     print(f"An unexpected error has occurred. Error details: {e}")
else:
    print(f"The result of the division is: {result}")
finally:
    print("The program completes successfully.")
```

241

CHAPTER 8 EXCEPTION MANAGEMENT

Let's run the program against inputs 7 and 0. Here is the output:

```
The following program can handle the non-system-exiting
exceptions.
Enter the dividend: 7
Enter the divisor: 0
An unexpected error has occurred. Error details: division by zero
The program completes successfully.
```

Let's execute the program again, but this time, you supply 5 and abc. Here is the output:

```
The following program can handle the non-system-exiting exceptions.
Enter the dividend: 5
Enter the divisor: abc
An unexpected error has occurred. Error details: invalid
   literal for int() with base 10: 'abc'
The program completes successfully.
```

In both cases, the program terminates gracefully. However, instead of seeing specific error messages like "Invalid input! Your divisor becomes zero!" or "Invalid input! Provide a correct input next time!", you see a generic message "**An unexpected error has occurred ...**" in the output. It is because the top-level except block was able to handle both kinds of errors. So, if you want to see those specific messages, you need to place the except blocks properly. For example, here is a correct arrangement:

```
except ZeroDivisionError as e:
    print("Invalid input! Your divisor becomes zero!")
    print(f"Error details: {e}")
```

242

CHAPTER 8   EXCEPTION MANAGEMENT

```
except ValueError as e:
    print("Invalid input! Provide a correct input next time!")
    print(f"Error details: {e}")
except Exception as e:
    print(f"An unexpected error has occurred. Error details: {e}")
```

Author's note: You can download the file **ch08_arranging_multiple_ except_blocks.py** from the Apress website to see the complete program.

POINTS TO REMEMBER

When you deal with multiple except blocks, you need to place more specific except blocks first. In other words, you should place the except blocks from the most specific to the most general.

Q8.9 Can I create a custom exception?

Yes. Since I have not discussed classes and inheritance yet, I did not include this discussion yet. The online link `https://docs.python.org/3/ tutorial/errors.html#user-defined-exceptions` provides some useful guidelines for using the user-defined exceptions. Let me include the important ones:

- You should derive your exception class from the Exception class.

- You should keep it simple.

- While naming the exception, you should use the suffix "**Error**," similar to built-in exceptions.

To illustrate, let me demonstrate a simple program that is as follows (the program should be super easy for you once you understand inheritance that is discussed in Chapter 11).

243

CHAPTER 8 EXCEPTION MANAGEMENT

Demonstration 8.5

The following program asks for user input. To make the example short and simple, I assume that the user needs to supply an integer that is less than or equal to 100. Otherwise, the program raises a custom exception called GreaterThan100Error. In the previous chapter, you learned how to execute a program as the main program. While implementing the program, let's revise that concept one more time as well. Here is the complete demonstration.

```python
# The following example uses a custom exception
class GreaterThan100Error(Exception):
    """ This is a custom exception."""
    pass

def test_custom_exception():
    try:
        usr_input = float(input("Enter a number below 100: "))
        if usr_input >= 100:
            raise GreaterThan100Error(f"The input {usr_input}
            is NOT less than 100.")
    except GreaterThan100Error as e:
        print(f"The custom exception is raised:{e}")
    except ValueError as e:
        print(f"Error Details:{e}")
    else:
        print(f"Well done. You have entered: {usr_input}")

if __name__=="__main__":
    test_custom_exception()
```

244

CHAPTER 8   EXCEPTION MANAGEMENT

Output

Here is a sample output when the user supplies a number that is less than 100:

```
Enter a number below 100: 75.7
Well done. You have entered: 75.7
```

Here is another sample output. This time user supplies an integer that is greater than 100:

```
Enter a number below 100: 721
The custom exception is raised: The input 721.0 is NOT less
  than 100.
```

Here is another sample output. This time the user did not supply a number:

```
Enter a number below 100: abc
Error Details: could not convert string to float: 'abc'
```

I hope that you have enjoyed this chapter. Now it's time for exercises and projects.

Summary

This chapter discussed exception handling in detail. In brief, it answered the following questions:

- How can you handle exceptions in Python programming?

- How can you use the try, except, and finally blocks?

- How can an else block help you to write a concise try block?

- How can you use a custom exception in your code?

245

CHAPTER 8   EXCEPTION MANAGEMENT

- How do you use the pass statement?

- How should you arrange multiple except blocks?

Exercise 8

E8.1 Predict the output when you execute the following code:

```
try:
    result = 15/0
except ArithmeticError:
    print("Caught the ArithmeticError.Your divisor is zero.")
except ZeroDivisionError:
    print("Caught ZeroDivisionError.The divisor is zero.")
```

E8.2 Can you execute the following program?

```
print("The following program can handle two different errors.")
a = input("Enter the dividend: ")
b = input("Enter the divisor: ")
try:
    result = int(a) / int(b)
except (ZeroDivisionError,ValueError) as e:
    print(f"Error details: {e}")
else:
    print(f"The result of the division is: {result}")
finally:
    print("The program completes successfully.")
```

E8.3 Predict the output of the following program:

```
try:
    raise BaseException("BaseException raised.")
except Exception as e:
    print("Caught the BaseException")
```

CHAPTER 8   EXCEPTION MANAGEMENT

E8.4 Write a program that asks you to keep entering valid integers. However, the program should continue, even if the user provides an invalid input. The user can type "q" to quit the program. The program must evaluate every input and display the result as well.

Keys to Exercise 8

Here is a sample solution set.

E8.1

You'll see the following output:

```
Caught the ArithmeticError.Your divisor is zero.
```

Explanation: The ArithmeticError is a built-in exception. It can handle the exceptions when the code raises an arithmetic error. The built-in exceptions ZeroDivisionError, OverflowError, and FloatingPointError are the subcategories of **the** ArithmeticError.

Since I placed ArithmeticError before ZeroDivisionError, this program caught the error inside the ArithmeticError block. If you interchange these except blocks, you can see a different output:

```
Caught ZeroDivisionError.The divisor is zero.
```

I have shown you how to arrange multiple except blocks in your code. You can read that section again.

E8.2

Yes, it's a valid program that uses a single except block to handle both the ZeroDivisionError and ValueError.

247

CHAPTER 8   EXCEPTION MANAGEMENT

E8.3

The except block cannot catch the exception. It is because the BaseException is the parent class of Exception. Here is a sample output:

```
Traceback (most recent call last):
  File "E:\MyPrograms\PythonBootcamp\chapter8\ch08_e03.py",
line 2, in <module>
    raise BaseException("BaseException raised.")
BaseException: BaseException raised.
```

E8.4

Here is a sample program:

```
print("Exercise-8.4")

def test_input():
    flag = True
    while flag:
        user_input = input("Keep entering integers. (Type q to
        quit):")
        if user_input == 'q':
            break
        try:
            display_input = int(user_input)
        except Exception as e:
            print(f"Invalid input: {e}")
        else:
            print(f"Correct. You entered:{display_input}")
    # This statement is placed outside the while loop
    print("End of the exercise.")
if __name__ =="__main__":
    test_input()
```

248

CHAPTER 8   EXCEPTION MANAGEMENT

Here is a sample output:

```
Exercise-8.4
Keep entering integers. (Type q to quit):3
Correct. You entered:3
Keep entering integers. (Type q to quit):5.7
Invalid input: invalid literal for int() with base 10: '5.7'
Keep entering integers. (Type q to quit):abc
Invalid input: invalid literal for int() with base 10: 'abc'
Keep entering integers. (Type q to quit):105
Correct. You entered:105
Keep entering integers. (Type q to quit):q
End of the exercise.
```

Case Study

It's time for the case study. **Instead of trying to implement a new case study, I want you to update all the previous implementations, considering exception-handling mechanisms.** To begin with, you can try implementing the following.

CS8.1 Problem Statement

In CS7.1, you made a calculator that performs the basic operations: addition, subtraction, multiplication, and division. There, you protected your application against the invalid operator. Now you have learned about exception handling. So I want you to make a better implementation using this knowledge.

You understand that the output should not change for valid inputs. But for an invalid input, the application should raise an exception. Let me give you three sample outputs to understand it better.

249

CHAPTER 8   EXCEPTION MANAGEMENT

Here is **use case 1**. A user enters an invalid number. Since the number is invalid, you do not need to ask for an operator. In this case, you can report the issue immediately:

```
=========================
This is a simple calculator.
It supports the following operations:
i) Addition
ii) Subtraction
iii) Multiplication and
iv) Division.
=========================
Enter the first number:23
Enter the next number:asc
Invalid input.Details: could not convert string to float: 'asc'
```

Here is **use case 2**. A user enters an invalid operator:

```
# There is no change in the top-level output. It is not shown
# to avoid repetition.
=========================
Enter the first number:12.5
Enter the next number:3
Enter an operator(+,-,*,/): >?
Error details: Invalid operator.
```

Here is **use case 3**. A user tries to do an invalid operation:

```
# There is no change in the top-level output. It is not shown
# to avoid repetition.
=========================
Enter the first number:27.3
Enter the next number:0
Enter an operator(+,-,*,/): /
```

250

CHAPTER 8   EXCEPTION MANAGEMENT

Invalid Operation.Details: float division by zero

Sample Implementation

Let's see the sample implementation for the case study.

CS8.1 Implementation

Here is the solution to CS8.1. You can consider it as an improved solution for CS7.1 because it can report a wide range of invalid inputs.

Here is an improved and organized solution for CS7.1. The initial part is not shown to avoid repetitions. This time, you'll see the use of `try...` except statement. Let me show you the key changes in bold:

```python
# i.e. there is no change in the initial part that you saw
# in the implementation of CS7.1

def main():
    """
    This is the top-level function.
    It calls the compute() function.
    """
    try:
        usr_input1 = input("Enter the first number: ")
        first_number = float(usr_input1)
        usr_input2 = input("Enter the next number: ")
        second_number = float(usr_input2)
        usr_opr = input("Enter an operator(+,-,*,/): ")
        if usr_opr not in valid_operators:
            raise Exception("Invalid operator.")
        compute(first_number, usr_opr, second_number)
```

251

CHAPTER 8   EXCEPTION MANAGEMENT

```python
        except ZeroDivisionError as e:
            print(f"Invalid Operation.Details: {e}")
        except ValueError as e:
            print(f"Invalid input.Details: {e}")
        except Exception as e:
            print(f"Error details: {e}")
if __name__ == "__main__":
    main()
```

> **Note**   Download **ch08_cs01.py** from the Apress website to see the complete implementation.

CHAPTER 9

Programming with Files

Files are helpful in many scenarios. For example, if you need to process an enormous amount of data, manually supplying one input at a time makes the program execution slow. Alternatively, you can store the input data in a file and allow your program to read the data from it. This approach is undoubtedly faster than the previous approach. You can also save data by writing to a file. In this context, the use of logs is quite common in real-world scenarios.

Files can indeed be of different types. However, while dealing with them, you'll discover that in most cases, you need to be familiar with some fundamental operations such as reading from a file, writing to a file, handling exceptions during various operations, and so forth. This chapter focuses on those fundamental operations and tries to simplify the topic for you.

Processing Text Files

At a high level, you can consider two types of files: text files and non-text files, a.k.a. binary files (such as image files or videos). The first one is human-readable, while the other one is not. Let us start our discussion on programming with text files.

© Vaskaran Sarcar 2025
V. Sarcar, *Python Bootcamp*, https://doi.org/10.1007/979-8-8688-1516-4_9

CHAPTER 9   PROGRAMMING WITH FILES

To begin with, let us read from a text file that I saved as `OriginalFile.txt` in my preferred location: `E:\TestData`. Here is the content of the file:

```
This is a sample text file.
It is stored at E:\TestData in my system.
Let's enjoy learning.
```

POINT TO NOTE

Instead of seeing the file name with the absolute path, in many programs, you may see the file name only. Those programs can work if the programs and the corresponding files reside in the same location. To avoid confusion, I mentioned the complete file path in all demonstrations in this chapter. So, once you download these programs, you may need to adjust these locations.

Reading from a File

You can use a text editor to read the content of a text file. However, you are learning programming, so let's read the content using a Python program.

The upcoming program starts with the following lines:

```
location="e:\\TestData\\OriginalFile.txt"
file_object = open(location, "r")
```

POINTS TO NOTE

Many authors use single quotes (such as 'r' instead of "r") to describe modes. However, I'd like to use double quotes to be consistent with the mode literal. In fact, the PyCharm IDE also suggests the mode inside double quotes.

254

CHAPTER 9   PROGRAMMING WITH FILES

The official link Built-in Functions – Python 3.13.2 documentation describes the open function and its parameters as follows:

***open**(file, mode='r', buffering=-1, encoding=None, errors=None, newline=None, closefd=True, opener=None)*

Open the file and return a corresponding file object. If the file cannot be opened, an OSError is raised.

In the upcoming example, I passed only two arguments. However, you can see that while using the open function, passing the first argument was mandatory for me. In my example, it represents the location of the file.

I have also passed an optional string to represent the mode in which the file was opened. While reading a file, **you can omit this argument because the default mode is 'r', which means that the file is opened for reading in the text mode.** However, I kept it to make you accustomed to the mode parameter. It is because you'll see me using different modes in the examples of this chapter.

You can use the readline() function to read a complete line from a file. Since OriginalFile.txt has three lines, I used it three times in the following demonstration. Finally, I close the file using the close() method. It is important because you should always close your files.

Demonstration 9.1

Let's see the complete program now:

```python
location="e:\\TestData\\OriginalFile.txt"
file_object = open(location, "r")

# Approach-1: reading a file line by line
first_line = file_object.readline()
print(first_line)
second_line = file_object.readline()
print(second_line)
```

255

CHAPTER 9 PROGRAMMING WITH FILES

```
third_line = file_object.readline()
print(third_line)
file_object.close()
```

POINTS TO NOTE

In Chapter 7, you learned how to execute a program as a main program. If needed, you can restructure this demonstration and upcoming demonstrations in this book following that concept.

Output

Here is the output of the program:

```
This is a sample text file.

It is stored at E:\TestData in my system.

Let's enjoy learning.
```

Analysis

You can see two obvious issues in this demonstration:

- This program uses the readline function three times to read three lines. If the text file (OriginalFile.txt) contains many more lines, this approach is not convenient.

- **In the output, you can see the line breaks between the lines**. This is because readline() inserts a line break after each line.

Let's improve the program by tackling the mentioned issues.

256

CHAPTER 9   PROGRAMMING WITH FILES

Demonstration 9.2

This program overcomes the mentioned issues in the previous program as follows:

- It uses a for loop to avoid the repeated use of the readline() function.

- By default, the print function uses the new line character('\n'). This program uses the end parameter inside the print function to control the end of a line.

Let's see the updated program:

```
location="e:\\TestData\\OriginalFile.txt"
file_object = open(location, "r")

# Approach-2: reading a file using a for loop
for current_line in file_object:
    print(current_line, end=" ")
file_object.close()
```

Output

This time, you'd see the following output:

```
This is a sample text file.
It is stored at E:\TestData in my system.
Let's enjoy learning.
```

257

CHAPTER 9   PROGRAMMING WITH FILES

WARNING

The official link `https://docs.python.org/3/tutorial/`
`inputoutput.html#tut-files` warns us by stating the following:

*In text mode, the default when reading is to convert platform-specific line
endings (\n on Unix, \r\n on Windows) to just \n. When writing in text mode, the
default is to convert occurrences of \n back to platform-specific line endings.
This behind-the-scenes modification to file data is fine for text files, but will
corrupt binary data like that in JPEG or EXE files. Be very careful to use binary
mode when reading and writing such files.*

Demonstration 9.3

You can also use the read function to read the entire file. Let's see this in
the following program:

```
location="e:\\TestData\\OriginalFile.txt"
file_object = open(location, "r")
# Approach-3: reading a file using the read() function
content = file_object.read()
print(content)
file_object.close()
```

Output

Upon executing this program, you'll see the same output that you saw in
the previous demonstration. So I'll not repeat it here.

258

CHAPTER 9   PROGRAMMING WITH FILES

Using the with Keyword

Closing a file is an important activity. When you close a file, you free system resources. This activity also allows other code to use that file. If you forget to close a file, you may not see the immediate effect. However, if you have too many open files, you may see the impact of memory leaks, which may end your program abnormally. This is why **you should close the file properly to avoid unwanted situations.**

In the previous demonstrations, after opening a file, I used the `close()` function before quitting the programs. However, this approach suffers from a potential drawback. For example, if there is a bug that prevents the execution of the `close()` function, the file will not close. In that case, the data can be lost or corrupted. On the contrary, as a precautionary step, if you close the file early, your program may start working with a closed file. It also causes unexpected results. So, if you are unsure when to close a file, you can leave the decision to Python by using the `'with'` keyword. The official documentation 7. Input and Output – Python 3.13.2 documentation also states the following:

> *It is good practice to use the with keyword when dealing with file objects. The advantage is that the file is properly closed after its suite finishes, even if an exception is raised at some point. Using with is also much shorter than writing equivalent try-finally blocks.*

Demonstration 9.4

The first approach that I showed in Demonstration 9.1 was inefficient. So let's focus on the other approaches (that are shown in the previous two demonstrations) and improve the design following the recommended suggestion:

259

CHAPTER 9   PROGRAMMING WITH FILES

```python
# Using the 'with' keyword, updating the previous approaches.
# Now Python closes the file when it is no longer needed.

location="e:\\TestData\\OriginalFile.txt"
# Approach-2: reading a file using a for loop
with open(location, "r") as file_object:
    for current_line in file_object:
        print(current_line, end='')
print("-"*10)
# Approach-3: reading a file using the read() function
with open(location, 'r') as file_object:
    content= file_object.read()
print(content)
```

Output

Upon executing this program, you can verify that both approaches can print the content of the file successfully.

I hope you have got an idea about how to use the 'with' keyword in your program. **I recommend that you also use the 'with' keyword in your program and let Python decide when to close the file.**

Q&A Session

Q9.1 How many different modes can a file be opened in?
In the PyCharm IDE, if you right-click the open function and investigate the **Declaration or Usages (Ctrl+B)**, you'll navigate to the built-in **_io.py** file. This file describes the following characters to represent different modes as follows:

```
'r': open for reading (default)
'w': open for writing, truncating the file first
'x': create a new file and open it for writing
```

260

CHAPTER 9 PROGRAMMING WITH FILES

```
'a': open for writing, appending to the end of the file if
  it exists
'b': binary mode
't':  text mode (default)
'+':  open a disk file for updating (reading and writing)
```

You can find these descriptions from the online link 2. Built-in Functions – Python 3.3.7 documentation as well. This link also talks about an additional mode, 'U' (universal newlines mode), that was supposed to be used for that backward compatibility but should not be used in new code. At this stage, you do not need to memorize these modes. Upon practicing, you'll become familiar with them.

Writing to a File

Till now, you have seen how to open and read from a text file. In this section, let's write something to the file. **It is a common and useful activity because you can verify the result even after the program finishes executing.**

Since you'd like to write to a file, you need to open the file in a different mode. You learned that the **w** mode can be used for writing. Let's examine this in the following demonstration.

POINT TO REMEMBER

While using the "w" mode, if the file does not exist, the open function will create the file. However, if the file already exists, Python will erase the current content of the file. So you need to be careful.

CHAPTER 9 PROGRAMMING WITH FILES

Demonstration 9.5

At a high level, the following program can be divided into two parts: first, you write to a file, and next, you read its contents. The last part was not necessary to examine the write operation because you can go to the target location and verify the file contents. Still, I have kept this part so that you can see the modification immediately. Here is the complete program:

```
location="e:\\TestData\\NewFile.txt"
with open(location, "w") as file_object:
    file_object.write("Python is a programming language.  ")
    file_object.write("It supports object-oriented programming.")

print(f"Reading the content of {location} now.")
with open(location, "r") as file_object:
    content = file_object.read()
print(content)
```

Output

This program produces the following output.

```
Reading the content of e:\TestData\NewFile.txt now.
Python is a programming language. It supports object-oriented
programming.
```

Q&A Session

Q9.2 Can I avoid the repeated calling of the open function in this program?

Good catch! By changing the mode from **w** to **w+**, it could be done as follows:

262

CHAPTER 9 PROGRAMMING WITH FILES

```python
location="e:\\TestData\\NewFile.txt"
with open(location, "w+") as file_object:
    file_object.write("Python is a programming language.")
    file_object.write("It supports object-oriented
      programming.")
    file_object.seek(0) # moving the pointer at the beginning
    print(f"Reading the content of {location} now.")
    content= file_object.read()
print(content)
```

Q9.3 Can I use r+ instead of w+ in the previous code?
If the file already exists, you'll see the same output. However, if the file does not exist, using **r+** will raise an error. For example, while using the previous code (shown in the answer to **Q9.2**), if the file (NewFile.txt) does not exist, you'll see the error. Here is a sample for your reference:

```
Traceback (most recent call last):
  File "E:\MyPrograms\PythonBootcamp\chapter09\ch09_d05_
  writing_to_a_file.py", line 13, in <module>
    with open(location, 'r+') as file_object:
         ~~~~^^^^^^^^^^^^^^^^^^
FileNotFoundError: [Errno 2] No such file or directory:
'e:\\TestData\\NewFile.txt'
```

Now, if you change the mode from **r+** to **w+**, this program will execute without any error and produce the intended output:

```
Reading the content of e:\TestData\NewFile.txt now.
Python is a programming language. It supports object-oriented
programming.
```

Now, change the mode from **w+** to **r+** again. This time, you won't see any issues because the file was already created.

263

CHAPTER 9 PROGRAMMING WITH FILES

Q9.4 In the output, the last two lines are squished together. Is this correct behavior?

Yes. However, no one prevents you from adding a new line character at the end of a line. For example, if I use the following code in my Windows system

```
file_object.write("Python is a programming language. \n")
file_object.write("It supports object-oriented
  programming. \n")
```

I can see that the strings appear in different lines in the output.

Q9.5 How can I keep the existing content before writing new content to a file?

You can open the file in the append mode (a) and add the new content to the end of the file. Here is a sample program for your reference (you have already seen the contents of OriginalFile.txt that was saved at E:\TestData):

```
location="e:\\TestData\\OriginalFile.txt"
# Opening the file in 'a' mode and adding the content
with open(location, 'a') as file_object:
    file_object.write("Python supports object-oriented
        programming.")

# Verifying the file contents now
with open(location, 'r') as file_object:
    print(f"Reading the content of {location} now.")
    content= file_object.read()
    print(content)
```

264

CHAPTER 9 PROGRAMMING WITH FILES

Let's verify the sample output as well:

```
Reading the content of e:\TestData\OriginalFile.txt now.
This is a sample text file.
It is stored at E:\TestData in my system.
Let's enjoy learning.
Python supports object-oriented programming.
```

Author's note: You can download **ch09_appending_to_a_file.py** from the Apress website to execute the program.

Limiting the Size

Since Demonstration 9.3, you have seen me using the read function many times as follows: content = file_object.read(). Alternatively, I could use file_object.read(size), where size is an optional numeric argument. By default, it is -1, which means the entire file. So, to read the entire file contents, I did not pass any argument inside the read function.

In this context, the official documentation(7. Input and Output – Python 3.13.2 documentation) states the following:

When size is omitted or negative, the entire contents of the file will be read and returned; it's your problem if the file is twice as large as your machine's memory. Otherwise, at most size characters (in text mode) or size bytes (in binary mode) are read and returned. If the end of the file has been reached, f. read() will return an empty string ('').

This is useful information for you. This is because if you try loading a big file at once, you can face a memory shortage problem. To overcome the problem, while using the read() function, you can specify the size limit.

To illustrate, in the upcoming example, I'll use the file NewFile.txt, which was already created by Demonstration 9.5. Now, I specify that at most ten characters can be read at a time.

265

CHAPTER 9   PROGRAMMING WITH FILES

Demonstration 9.6

Here is the complete program:

```
location="e:\\TestData\\NewFile.txt"
with open(location, "r") as file_object:
    buffer=10
    content= file_object.read(buffer)
    while content:
        print(content)
        # print(content,end="")
        content = file_object.read(buffer)
```

Output

Here is a sample output:

```
Python is
a programm
ing langua
ge. It sup
ports obje
ct-oriente
d programm
ing.
```

Analysis

You can see that each line contains a maximum of ten characters. If you replace the line print(content) with `print(content,end="")`, you'll see that the contents are organized similarly to the input file as follows:

```
Python is a programming language. It supports object-oriented
programming.
```

CHAPTER 9   PROGRAMMING WITH FILES

Processing Binary Files

Till now, you have been working with simple text files. Let us now work with a binary file. A binary file is a non-text file, such as an image or a video. To do reading from a binary file, I stored a flower image, named flower.png, inside the location E:\TestData.

Copying an Image

Let's make a copy of the image flower.png. So, first, read the image file (flower.png) and then write the content to a new file (new_flower.png). Since we are processing a binary file, this time, you'll see me using the modes "**rb**" and "**wb**" instead of **"r"** and **"w"** modes. You understand the changes in modes are necessary because we are processing a binary file now.

Demonstration 9.7

Here is the complete program for you:

```
# Using two files-one for reading and one for writing
input_file="e:\\TestData\\flower.png"
output_file="e:\\TestData\\new_flower.png"

with open(input_file, "rb") as input_object:
    content=input_object.read()
    with open(output_file, "wb") as output_object:
        output_object.write(content)
```

Output

Execute the program and go to the output file location. You can see a new image called new_flower.png, which is a duplicate of the original image. I'm taking a partial snapshot from my machine to show this (see Figure 9-1).

267

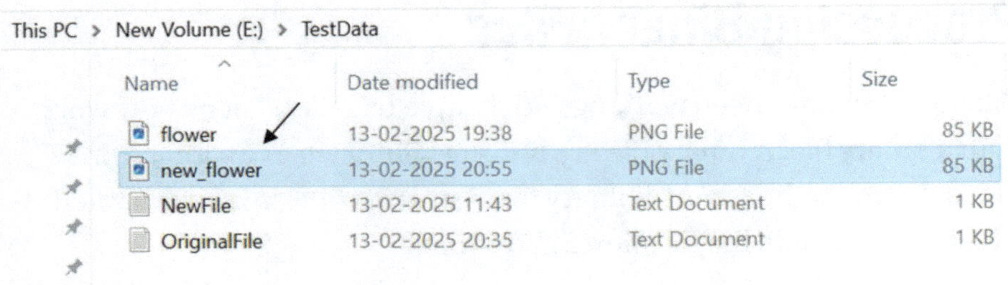

CHAPTER 9   PROGRAMMING WITH FILES

Figure 9-1. *The new image is created in the target location*

Pickling and Unpickling

Consider the following scenarios:

- There is a program that keeps generating a few random numbers, which are further processed. Assume a scenario while processing those numbers, your application reaches an inconsistent state.

- There is an application that keeps a record of the activities that individual users perform.

- You have an application that saves users' preferences and so forth.

From these examples, you understand that you may need to store data (even after closing the applications) for various reasons. Now, the question is: how do we store these data? There are different ways, such as using a text file, connecting to a database, and so on. However, this section discusses the binary files. So let's focus on them.

In the upcoming example, I'll show you the use of the **pickle** module. Let's know about it from the official documentation (pickle – Python object serialization – Python 3.13.2 documentation):

268

CHAPTER 9 PROGRAMMING WITH FILES

The pickle module implements binary protocols for serializing and de-serializing a Python object structure. "Pickling" is the process whereby a Python object hierarchy is converted into a byte stream, and "unpickling" is the inverse operation whereby a byte stream (from a binary file or bytes-like object) is converted back into an object hierarchy. Pickling (and unpickling) is alternatively known as "serialization", "marshalling," or "flattening"; however, to avoid confusion, the terms used here are "pickling" and "unpickling".

To illustrate pickling and unpickling, let me modify the previous demonstration that copied an image. This time, you'll see two steps:

- First, from the input image, you make a pickle file (commonly created with a .pickle extension for easier understanding).

- Second, from this pickle file, you can reconstruct the image whenever required.

POINT TO NOTE

I have seen that developers use different extensions for the pickle files such as **.pickle, .pkl , .pck,** and so on. I'd like you to note that Python 3 documentation (https://docs.python.org/3.13/library/pickle.html#examples) uses the **.pickle extension**. However, Python 2 used the .pkl extension (see https://docs.python.org/2/library/pickle.html#example).

CHAPTER 9 PROGRAMMING WITH FILES

Demonstration 9.8

This program creates a pickle file:

```
import pickle

input_file="e:\\TestData\\flower.png"
pickle_file="e:\\TestData\\flower_pickle.pickle"

with open(input_file, "rb") as ifile:
    content=ifile.read()
    with open(pickle_file, "wb") as pfile:
        pickle.dump(content,pfile)
```

Output

Execute the program and go to the output file location. You'll see a new file named **flower_pickle.pickle** is created. Here is a partial snapshot from my machine to show this (see Figure 9-2).

Name	Date modified	Type	Size
AdditionalImages	14-02-2025 11:09	File folder	
flower.PNG	13-02-2025 19:38	PNG File	85 KB
flower_pickle.pickle	15-02-2025 11:51	PICKLE File	85 KB
new_flower.png	15-02-2025 11:31	PNG File	85 KB
NewFile.txt	13-02-2025 11:43	Text Docume...	1 KB
OriginalFile.txt	13-02-2025 20:35	Text Docume...	1 KB

Figure 9-2. *A pickle file is created in the target location*

Demonstration 9.9

Since you have the pickle file (flower_pickle.pickle), you can reconstruct the image anytime. Let's see the following program:

270

CHAPTER 9   PROGRAMMING WITH FILES

```python
import pickle

pickle_file="e:\\TestData\\flower_pickle.pickle"
output_file="e:\\TestData\\flower_new.png"

with open(pickle_file, "rb") as pfile:
    content=pickle.load(pfile)
    with open(output_file, "wb") as ofile:
        ofile.write(content)
```

Output

Execute the program and go to the output file location. You'll see a new file named **flower_reconstructed.png** is created. Here is a partial snapshot from my machine (see Figure 9-3).

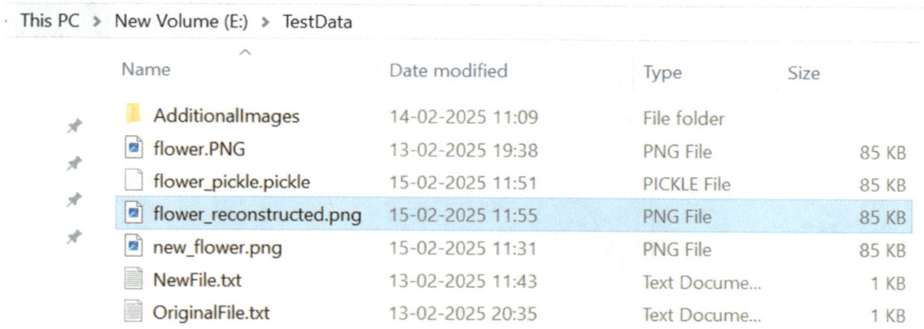

	Name	Date modified	Type	Size
	AdditionalImages	14-02-2025 11:09	File folder	
	flower.PNG	13-02-2025 19:38	PNG File	85 KB
	flower_pickle.pickle	15-02-2025 11:51	PICKLE File	85 KB
	flower_reconstructed.png	15-02-2025 11:55	PNG File	85 KB
	new_flower.png	15-02-2025 11:31	PNG File	85 KB
	NewFile.txt	13-02-2025 11:43	Text Docume...	1 KB
	OriginalFile.txt	13-02-2025 20:35	Text Docume...	1 KB

This PC > New Volume (E:) > TestData

Figure 9-3. *The image is reconstructed in the target location*

Analysis

To demonstrate the overall process, I used two demonstrations instead of one. In Demonstration 9.8, you stored the source data in a pickle file (flower_pickle.pickle), and in Demonstration 9.9, you reconstructed the image (flower_reconstructed.png) from the previously created pickle file.

271

CHAPTER 9   PROGRAMMING WITH FILES

By comparing Figures 9-2 and 9-3, you can also notice that the construction times of the pickle file and the newly created image file were different.

Q&A Session

Q9.6 Why did you use the pickle module instead of the json module in this chapter?
It's a choice! From the online link pickle – Python object serialization – Python 3.13.2 documentation, you'll know the pros/cons of these modules. However, I'd like you to note that since pickle's data format is Python-specific, you do not need to worry about the restrictions imposed by external standards (such as JSON). However, it is also true that non-Python programs may not be able to reconstruct pickled Python objects.

Finally, note that you were working with an image file (i.e., binary data). You can't directly insert an image into a `.json` file. Yes, there are some workarounds; however, you have seen that the `pickle` module made the process very easy for you.

Handling Exceptions

To make the programs short and simple, I didn't consider exception handling in the previous demonstrations. However, in real-world programming, you cannot ignore this activity. So, while coding, you should implement a proper exception-handling mechanism (you learned it in Chapter 8). **This comment applies to all programs in this book as well.**

FileNotFoundError

When you work with files, your program may not find a file for various reasons. Here are some of them:

272

CHAPTER 9   PROGRAMMING WITH FILES

- The file resides in a different location.

- You misspelled the file name.

- The intended file does not exist at all and so on.

So it's a better practice to put the code in the **try-except** block to avoid unexpected outcomes.

To illustrate, instead of using OriginalFile.txt in Demonstration 9.4, if you use a file (e.g., IncorrectFile.txt) that does not exist, you'll see the FileNotFoundError. Here is a sample:

```
Traceback (most recent call last):
  File "E:\MyPrograms\PythonBootcamp\chapter09\ch09_d10_
  exception_handling.py",
  line 4, in <module>
    with open(location, 'r') as file_object:
         ~~~~^^^^^^^^^^^^^^^^
```

FileNotFoundError: [Errno 2] No such file or directory: 'e:\\TestData\\IncorrectFile.txt'

Demonstration 9.10

To handle this error, let's update the implementation as follows:

```
location="e:\\TestData\\OriginalFile.txt"
# location="e:\\TestData\\IncorrectFile.txt" # incorrect
file name
try:
    with open(location, 'r') as file_object:
        content = file_object.read()
except FileNotFoundError as e:
    print(f"The file is not found at {location}")
else:
    print(content+"\n")
```

273

CHAPTER 9   PROGRAMMING WITH FILES

Output

There is no surprise that if the file is found, the program will print the content of the file. However, if you use an incorrect file name (as shown in the commented code), you'll see a user-friendly message:

```
The file is not found at e:\TestData\IncorrectFile.txt
```

Summary

This chapter discussed file handling in detail. In brief, it answered the following questions:

- How can you process text and binary files?

- How can you avoid memory leaks while processing files?

- How can you handle exceptions (such as FileNotFoundError) while processing files?

- How can you use the pickle module to perform pickling and unpickling?

Exercise 9

E9.1 Write a program to print the first "n" lines from a text file. A user can supply the value of "n."

E9.2 Write a program that generates ten random integers. Create a list to hold these integers and dump the data into a new file that holds the data in a binary format. Then, retrieve the list from this file again and display the content.

(Hint: Use the concept of pickling/unpickling.)

274

CHAPTER 9   PROGRAMMING WITH FILES

E9.3 In Chapter 7, you learned how to execute a program as the main program. Can you refactor Demonstration 9.10 using that concept?

E9.4 Can you write a program to count an approximate number of words in a text file.?

E9.5 The json module also has the dump() and load() functions. Similar to the pickle module, the dump() function can be used to store the data in JSON format, and the load() function can be used to retrieve the data from the JSON format. The file extension .json is used to indicate a file that maintains JSON format. In Exercise 9.2, you tried pickling and unpickling. Can you do a similar exercise using the json module with its dump() and load() functions?

Keys to Exercise 9

Here is a sample solution set for the exercises in this chapter.

E9.1

Here is a sample implementation (I used the file OriginalFile.txt for this example. You saw this file at the beginning of the chapter.):

```
location = "e:\\TestData\\OriginalFile.txt"

def print_lines(input_file, lines):
    """ This function prints the first 'n' lines from a
    file."""
    try:
        with open(input_file, "r") as file_object:
            count = 0
            while count < lines:
                line_content = file_object.readline()
                print(line_content,end='')
```

275

CHAPTER 9   PROGRAMMING WITH FILES

```
            count += 1
    except FileNotFoundError as ex:
        print(f"The file {input_file} is not found.")
        print(f"Error details:{ex}")
try:
    user_input = input('Enter how many lines you want to print
      from the file? ')
    number_of_lines = int(user_input)
    print_lines(location,number_of_lines)
except ValueError as e:
    print("Invalid input! Provide the correct input next time!")
    print(f"Error details:{e}")
except Exception as e:
    print("An unknown error occurred.")
    print(f"Error details:{e}")
```

Here is a sample output for a positive input:

```
Enter how many lines you want to print from the file? 2
This is a sample text file.
It is stored at E:\TestData in my system.
```

Here is a sample output for a negative input:

```
Enter how many lines you want to print from the file? 2.3
Invalid input! Provide the correct input next time!
Error details:invalid literal for int() with base 10: '2.3'
```

Author's comment:
You can make a better solution by considering the file name as a user
input. I left this exercise for you.

276

CHAPTER 9 PROGRAMMING WITH FILES

E9.2

Here is a sample implementation:

```python
import pickle
import random

pickle_file="numbers.pickle"
numbers=[]
for i in range(1,11):
    number=random.randint(1,500)
    numbers.append(number)
print("The random numbers are:")
print(numbers)
# Dumping/storing the numbers in binary format
with open(pickle_file,"wb") as file:
        pickle.dump(numbers,file)

# Retrieving the data from the pickle file
with open(pickle_file, "rb") as file:
    content=pickle.load(file)
    print("The retrieved numbers:")
    print(content)
```

Here is a sample output:

```
The random numbers are:
[311, 98, 189, 198, 128, 333, 447, 305, 490, 238]
The retrieved numbers are:
[311, 98, 189, 198, 128, 333, 447, 305, 490, 238]
```

Author's comment:
I kept this program and the pickle file (**numbers.pickle**) in the same directory. I believe that I do not need to mention that you can store the pickle file in your preferred location as well. By considering exception handling, you can further improve the solution.

CHAPTER 9   PROGRAMMING WITH FILES

E9.3

Here is the refactored code:

```python
def main():
    location="e:\\TestData\\OriginalFile.txt"
    # location="e:\\TestData\\IncorrectFile.txt" # incorrect
    file name
    try:
        with open(location, "r") as file_object:
            content = file_object.read()
    except FileNotFoundError as e:
        print(f"The file is not found at {location}")
    else:
        print(content+"\n")

if __name__ == "__main__":
    main()
```

E9.4

I created a small text file, called **sample_text_file.txt**, in the same directory where this program resides. This file has the following contents:

```
The sky is blue.
Apple is red.
Sam is a good boy.
```

I used this file for the following implementation:

```python
def count_words(input_file):
    """

    This function counts the approximate number
    of words in a text file.
    """
```

278

CHAPTER 9   PROGRAMMING WITH FILES

```python
try:
    with open(input_file,"r") as file_object:
        file_content = file_object.read()

except FileNotFoundError as e:
    print(f"The file {input_file} is not found.")
    print(f"Error details:{e}")
else:
    separate_words = file_content.split()
    word_count = len(separate_words)
    print("The content of the file:")
    print("-" * 20)
    print(file_content)
    print("-"*20)
    print(f" The file has {word_count} words (approx).")
def main():
    count_words("sample_text_file.txt")

if __name__ == "__main__":
    main()
```

Here is a sample output:

The content of the file:

The sky is blue.
Apple is red.
Sam is a good boy.

The file has 12 words (approx).

Author's comment:

279

CHAPTER 9   PROGRAMMING WITH FILES

You can avoid using the built-in len function in this implementation.
How? You can use a for loop to calculate the word count as follows:

```
# word_count = len(separate_words)
# Alternative solution
word_count = 0
for word in separate_words:
    word_count += 1
# There is no change in the remaining code.
```

You can also enhance this solution by asking the user to input the file
name. I left this exercise for you.

E9.5

Here is a sample implementation with the key lines in bold:

```
import json
import random

# The json module uses demo
json_file="numbers.json"
numbers=[]
for i in range(1,11):
    number=random.randint(1,500)
    numbers.append(number)
print("The random numbers are:")
print(numbers)
# Dumping/storing the numbers in the JSON format
with open(json_file,"w") as file:
        json.dump(numbers,file)

# Retrieving the data from the json file
with open(json_file, "r") as file:
```

280

CHAPTER 9   PROGRAMMING WITH FILES

```
content=json.load(file)
print("The retrieved numbers are:")
print(content)
```

Author's comment:
Similar to the solution of E9.2, I kept this program and the JSON file (**numbers.json**) in the same directory. If needed, you can choose a different location for the JSON file as well. By considering exception handling, you can further improve the solution.

Case Study

Let's try to make solutions for the following case studies.

CS9.1 Problem Statement

Create a program that asks for three user inputs to create three registered user IDs. You use a list to hold these inputs. Then, create a binary file (say registered_users.pickle) to save the data. Here is a sample output:

```
Enter user1: Jack123
Enter user2: Kate25#
Enter user3: Bob07$
3 registered user IDs are saved.
```

After this activity, create another program that asks the user to enter his ID. Once the user enters the ID, you load the binary file again to verify whether it is a registered ID. Here is a sample when the user ID is not saved in the file:

```
Enter the user ID: Sam01#
Verifying the user...
Sorry. You are not a registered user.
```

281

CHAPTER 9   PROGRAMMING WITH FILES

Here is another sample where the user ID is found in the file:

```
Enter the user ID: Bob07$
Verifying the user...
Welcome Bob07$! You are a verified user.
```

CS9.2 Problem Statement

This time, you make a report card of students. Assume that a student joins a beginner's course in Python. To get a grade card, a student needs to meet the following criteria:

- The student needs to submit two assignments (50 marks each) before appearing in the final examination (which is 100 marks).

- You calculate the final score based on these assignment scores and the final examination score. Consider 25% of the total marks in the assignment and 75% of the final examination score to prepare the grade card. When a student scores more than 90, he gets an A+, which means Outstanding. If he scores more than 80, he gets an A, which means Very Good. If the score is 70 or above, he gets a B, which means Good. Consider a score that is less than 70 as a Fail.

- If any of the assignment scores are found to be greater than 50, your application should report an error. The same rule applies if anyone inputs a final examination score greater than 100.

- You save these student records in text files that have names like student_name.txt. You store these files in a separate folder. You can name it *GradeScores*.

282

CHAPTER 9   PROGRAMMING WITH FILES

Let me show you three sample outputs:

Here is **sample 1**. A user enters valid inputs:

```
Enter the student's name: Ravi S
Assignment-1 score: 25.5
Assignment-2 score: 34.5
Exam score: 87
Final score: 80.25
Grade: A(Very Good)
Get the report card at:
E:\MyPrograms\PythonBootcamp\chapter09\GradeScores\Ravi S.txt
```

Here is a sample report card that you store. The content of the text file **Ravi S.txt** may look like the following:

```
***Report Card***
***Course name: Python for Beginners***
==================================================
Student Name: Ravi S
Assignment-1 score: 25.5
Assignment-2 score: 34.5
Exam Score: 87.0
Final score: 80.25
Grade/Remark: A(Very Good)
```

Here is **sample 2**. A user enters an assignment score that is above 50:

```
Enter the student's name: John
Assignment-1 score: 23
Assignment-2 score: 51.5
Error: Assignment 2 score cannot be greater than 50.
Provide the correct input next time!
```

CHAPTER 9   PROGRAMMING WITH FILES

Here is **sample 3**. A user enters the final examination score that is above 100:

```
Enter the student's name: Kate
Assignment-1 score:23
Assignment-2 score:45.3
Exam score:105
Error: Final exam score cannot be greater than 100.
Provide the correct input next time!
```

Sample Implementations

Let's see the sample implementations.

CS9.1 Implementation

Here is a sample implementation for the **first part** of the case study:

```python
import pickle
def main():
    users=[]
    for i in range(1,4):
        name=input(f"Enter user{i}: ")
        users.append(name)

    with open("registered_users.pickle","wb") as f:
        pickle.dump(users,f)
        print(f"{len(users)} registered user IDs are saved.")

if __name__ == "__main__":
    main()
```

284

CHAPTER 9   PROGRAMMING WITH FILES

Here is a sample implementation for the **second part** of the case study:

```python
import pickle

def verify_user(user):
    print("Verifying the user...")
    with open("registered_users.pickle","rb") as f:
        users=pickle.load(f)

    if user in users:
        print(f"Welcome {user}! You are a verified user.")
    else:
        print(f"Sorry. You are not a registered user.")

def main():
    current_user=input("Enter the user ID: ")
    verify_user(current_user)

if __name__ == "__main__":
    main()
```

CS9.2 Implementation

In this implementation, I imported the os module at the beginning of this implementation and used the makedirs() function. Let's see the function documentation from the PyCharm IDE for your immediate reference:

```python
def makedirs(name, mode=0o777, exist_ok=False):
    """makedirs(name [, mode=0o777][, exist_ok=False])

    Super-mkdir; create a leaf directory and all intermediate
    ones.  Works like mkdir, except that any intermediate path
    segment (not just the rightmost)will be created if it does
```

285

CHAPTER 9   PROGRAMMING WITH FILES

```
not exist. If the target directory already exists, raise an
OSError if exist_ok is False. Otherwise, no exception is
raised.  This is recursive.
"""
```

I added a relative path to the current working directory. **Though it was not necessary, I stored these grade cards in a separate directory to keep the current working directory clean.** This is why you'll see the following code segment:

```python
# Retrieve the current working directory
current_path = os.getcwd()

# Adding a relative path to the current path
relative_path = "GradeScores"
new_path = os.path.join(current_path, relative_path)
# Making the directory if it does not exist
if not os.path.exists(new_path):
    os.makedirs(new_path)
new_path = new_path + '\\' + name + '.txt'
print("Get the report card at:")
print(new_path)
```

You should not find any difficulties in understanding the remaining segments because those are already discussed in this chapter and the previous chapters. Here is the complete implementation for you:

```python
import os

class ScoreExceedsError(Exception):
    """ This is a custom exception."""
    pass

def calculate_grade(a1_score, a2_score, e_score):
    """
```

286

CHAPTER 9   PROGRAMMING WITH FILES

```python
    This function calculates the final score.
    Here is the consideration:
    25% of the total marks in assignments and
    75% of the total marks make the grade card.
    """

    final_score = (a1_score + a2_score) * .25 + e_score * .75
    return final_score

def make_grade(score):
    """ This function makes the grade."""
    grade = ""
    if score > 90:
        grade = "A+(Outstanding)"
    elif score > 80:
        grade = "A(Very Good)"
    elif score >= 70:
        grade = "B(Good)"
    else:
        grade = "F(Fail)"
    return grade

def save_scores(name,assign1,assign2,exam,score,grade):
    """

    This function stores the result in a text file.
    It picks the current working directory. Then create a
    directory(if it does not exist),called GradeScores.
    All records are stored as test files inside
    this directory.
    """

    try:
        # Retrieve the current working directory
        current_path = os.getcwd()
        # print("The current working directory:")
```

287

CHAPTER 9   PROGRAMMING WITH FILES

```python
        # print(current_path)
        # Adding a relative path to the current path
        relative_path = "GradeScores"
        new_path = os.path.join(current_path, relative_path)
        # Making the directory if it does not exist
        if not os.path.exists(new_path):
            os.makedirs(new_path)
        new_path = new_path + '\\' + name + '.txt'
        print("Get the report card at:")
        print(new_path)
        with open(new_path,'w') as file_object:
            file_object.write("***Report Card***")
            file_object.write("\n***Course name: Python for
                Beginners***\n")
            file_object.write("=" * 50)
            file_object.write(f"\nStudent Name: {name}")
            file_object.write(f"\nAssignment-1 score: {assign1}")
            file_object.write(f"\nAssignment-2 score: {assign2}")
            file_object.write(f"\nExam Score: {exam}")
            file_object.write(f"\nFinal score: {score}")
            file_object.write(f"\nGrade/Remark: {grade}")
    except FileNotFoundError as e:
        print(f"The file is missing.Details:{e}")
    except Exception as e:
        print(f"Error details: {e}")

def main():
    """
    It is the top-level function for this application.
    """
    try:
        student_name = input("Enter the student's name: ")
```

288

CHAPTER 9   PROGRAMMING WITH FILES

```python
        assign1 = float(input("Assignment-1 score: "))
        if assign1 > 50:
            raise ScoreExceedsError("Assignment1 score cannot
                be greater than 50.")
        assign2 = float(input("Assignment-2 score: "))
        if assign2 > 50:
            raise ScoreExceedsError("Assignment2 score cannot
                be greater than 50.")
        exam = float(input("Exam score: "))
        if exam > 100:
            raise ScoreExceedsError("Final exam score cannot be
                greater than 100.")
    except ValueError as e:
        print(f"Invalid input.Details:{e}")
    except ScoreExceedsError as e:
        print(f"Error: {e}")
        print("Provide the correct input next time!")
    except Exception as e:
        print(f"Error details: {e}")
    else:
        final_score = calculate_grade(assign1,assign2,exam)
        print(f"Final score: {final_score}")
        grade_score = make_grade(final_score)
        print(f"Grade: {grade_score}")
        save_scores(student_name,assign1,assign2,exam,final_
            score,grade_score)

if __name__ == "__main__":
    main()
```

289

PART III

Introduction to OOP

Object-oriented programming (OOP) is a programming paradigm centered around objects and classes. It promotes code reusability, modularity, and abstraction through key concepts like inheritance, encapsulation, and polymorphism. Python's OOP approach allows developers to model real-world entities effectively, making complex programs more organized, scalable, and easier to maintain.

This part will give you a quick overview of OOP using classes, objects, and inheritance.

CHAPTER 10

Classes and Objects

Classes and objects are the foundation of object-oriented programming (OOP). This chapter discusses their usage in Python programming.

Basic Concepts and Common Terms

To represent a real-world entity, we first create a class and then create objects from it. Since we create objects of a particular class, we define the common behavior of these objects within the class. Let me emphasize the following points that can help you avoid any confusion in the future:

- A class is the architectural blueprint that defines the structure and behavior of the objects. From a single blueprint, you can create multiple buildings. Similarly, you can construct multiple objects (or instances) from a single class. (I ignore some typical corner cases when I make this statement. For example, a true singleton class cannot have multiple instances.)

- Developers often refer to the terms *function* and *method* interchangeably. Conventionally, a function defined in a class is termed a **method**. So your previous knowledge about functions will be useful while you exercise OOP as well. We expose object behaviors through these methods. You may note that a method can access the data that is contained in a class.

© Vaskaran Sarcar 2025
V. Sarcar, *Python Bootcamp*, https://doi.org/10.1007/979-8-8688-1516-4_10

CHAPTER 10   CLASSES AND OBJECTS

- We refer to the process of creating an object from a class as **instantiation**. This is why the words *objects* and *instances* are often used interchangeably.

POINT TO NOTE

Classes provide the structure (or template), and objects are the actual entities created based on that structure. However, objects are self-contained; they hold the data. Interestingly, in the discussion of OOP, developers often use fields, variables, and attributes to mean the same thing. The same is true for methods and functions as well.

Modeling a Class

Normally, a class contains both variables and methods. To begin with, let me show you a simple class that contains only a method.

To illustrate, let us model a simple class for any student in this world. You can safely assume that a student must study before appearing for an examination. Based on this assumption, you can make the following class called Student:

```python
class Student:
    """ This is a simple class to model a student"""
    def describe(self):
        """ A simple method to describe the behavior of a
            student."""
        print(f"A student must study before an examination.")
```

294

CHAPTER 10   CLASSES AND OBJECTS

From this segment of the code, I want to draw your attention to the following points:

- You need to use the **class** keyword to create a class. The class has a name, and the line ends with a colon (:).

- The indented code shows the class body.

- At the beginning, I used a docstring, which tells about the class. In real-world programming, docstrings are used to specify what a class can do in your code.

POINT TO NOTE

Once you dive deep into OOP, you'll see the usages of different kinds of methods, such as instance methods, static methods, and class methods. In OOP, the instance methods are most common. This chapter and the next chapter (Chapter 11) will use the instance methods only. The PEP 8 – Style Guide for Python Code I peps.python.org suggests that you always use **self** for the first argument to instance methods. In Appendix A, you'll learn about static methods and class methods.

Creating Objects

Till now, you have the class definition only; it does not allocate any computer memory. However, since I have created a class called Student, I can create an instance, named sam, from it as follows:

```
# Creating an object from the Student class
sam= Student()
```

CHAPTER 10   CLASSES AND OBJECTS

Now, I can invoke the `describe` method as follows:

```
# Invoking the method
sam.describe()
```

This code will output the following:

```
A student must study before an examination.
```

Alternative Code

You could invoke the `describe` method in an alternative way. Let me show you that as well:

```
# Invoking the method in a different way
Student.describe(sam)
```

This code will also produce the same output. However, in most cases, developers use the other approach that I discussed before.

Q&A Session

Q10.1 The describe method had a parameter called self. In the first approach, without passing this parameter, how could you invoke the "describe" method?

It is true that at this stage, the alternative code does not create any confusion, but the first approach may look surprising. When you called the instance method using the code **sam.describe()**, behind the scenes, the current instance (**sam**) was passed automatically as an argument. It was possible because the `self` parameter is a reference to the instance itself.

You'll always notice that the "self" parameter appears before any other parameter(s) in the method definition. It is useful because a ***Python method requires the object to be passed as the first argument to a class to distinguish the object from other objects of the class.*** (For a static method, "`self`" is not required. You can skip that part for now.)

296

CHAPTER 10   CLASSES AND OBJECTS

POINT TO NOTE

The PEP 8 – Style Guide for Python Code | peps.python.org suggests the following:

Always use $self$ for the first argument to instance methods.

Author's note: If you are familiar with Java or C#, you'll find that **self** in Python is similar to **this** in Java or C#.

Q10.2 Between the code sam.describe() and Student.describe(sam), which one would you like to use?

I prefer the first one. For example, notice how I used the built-in methods in Chapter 3. Here is a sample where I called the built-in **isdigit** method that was defined in the **str** class: `print(f"Is 25 a valid number? {"25".isdigit()}")`. If you spend a little time on this, you'll see that other developers follow the same approach as well.

Q10.3 Do I need to follow any specific conventions while modeling a class?

In a class name, the first letter of each word is capitalized, and you should not separate words using underscores. For example, `MyClass, Student,` and `ColorContainer` are examples of some standard class names. Instance names are lowercase letters, and you can have underscores between the words. In addition, it's a better practice to maintain a meaningful docstring in your class and methods(s). I recommend you to follow this practice. However, to type less, in the remaining chapter, I use some code fragments without docstrings. There I focus on some other aspects of a class.

Hope you have got the idea! Now you are ready to execute your first object-oriented program. Download the complete program **ch10_class_and_objects_intro.py** from the Apress website and run it. Since each part of the program is discussed, I am not showing it again to avoid repetitions.

297

CHAPTER 10   CLASSES AND OBJECTS

POINTS TO REMEMBER

A class is a logical entity. Once you instantiate a class, you create objects. These objects occupy memories in your system. So the objects are physical entities.

Initializer

So far, I have created only one object from the Student class. As said before, you can create any number of objects from this class. For example, if you now exercise the following code

```
# Creating another object from the Student class
kate= Student()
# Invoking the method
kate.describe()
```

once again, you'll see the following output:

```
A student must study before an examination.
```

Notice that for each of these objects, the describe method always displays the same output. In other words, each object describes the same behavior. It is okay to a certain extent. For example, each man walks, each player plays, each student has a roll number, and so forth. However, it is also true that each man walks at varying speeds, each player plays a game in different ways, and each student has a unique roll number. Let's examine how you can model these situations.

298

CHAPTER 10   CLASSES AND OBJECTS

Using Initializers

You can use constructors (aka initializers) to run initialization codes and create the objects. Constructors can be both parameterized and non-parameterized. When you use a parameterized constructor, you can pass the necessary arguments to it.

In Python, there is a special method, called **__init__()**. It runs automatically whenever you create an instance from the class. Following the convention, this method has two leading and two trailing underscores.

Here is an example of a non-parameterized constructor in a class. Ideally, "non-parameterized" means that there is no parameter. But in Python, __init__(self) takes the argument self automatically, and you do not need to pass anything inside it. So we often refer to the following constructor as a non-parameterized constructor:

```
def __init__(self):
    print("You do not need to supply any parameter.")
```

Now let me show you a constructor that I can use to initialize two variables name and roll_number as follows:

```
def __init__(self,name,roll_number):
    self.name=name
    self.roll_number=roll_number
```

POINT TO NOTE

I have seen authors who dislike using the word "constructor" in Python programming. They would simply avoid this word by saying _init_ adds new attributes to an object. They also explain why they believe that Python developers should not refer to the _init_ as a constructor. However, "constructor"

299

CHAPTER 10   CLASSES AND OBJECTS

is a common term in well-known object-oriented programming languages.
I have also seen that in many places of the official documentation, the word
"constructor" is used. So I'll use the term "constructor" as well. I believe that at
this moment, you do not need to worry much whether the term "constructor" is
absolutely perfect. Still, if you want to avoid the term "constructor", you can call
it "initializer".

Let me use this constructor in the following program.

Demonstration 10.1

Let me show you a program using the constructor that I just discussed.
Here is the complete program:

```python
class Student:
    """ This is a simple class to model a student"""
    def __init__(self,name,roll_number):
        self.name=name
        self.roll_number=roll_number

    def describe(self):
        """ A simple method to describe a student."""
        print(f"{self.name} has been assigned roll number
        {self.roll_number}")

# Creating two objects from the Student class
sam= Student("Sam", 1)
kate= Student("Kate", 2)

# Describing the students
sam.describe()
kate.describe()
```

300

CHAPTER 10   CLASSES AND OBJECTS

Output

When you run this program, you see the following output:

```
Sam has been assigned roll number 1
Kate has been assigned roll number 2
```

Analysis

Notice that the Student class used a constructor to initialize the name and roll number of a student. This program also demonstrated that you can make different objects by initializing different values of the attributes. Now let us have a close look at certain portions of this program.

A variable prefixed with self is available to every method in the class. So when I used these lines

```
self.name=name
self.roll_number=roll_number
```

the values associated with the parameters name and roll_number were assigned to the corresponding variable names and attached to the instance being created. **This is why whenever I created an object, these variables were initialized.**

Note   The named elements' name and roll_number are normally termed as **attributes** of this Student class.

In addition, have you noticed that I didn't declare the variables name and roll_number in advance in the Student class? In Python programming, you can create data fields on the fly. This is why if you use the following lines inside the constructor

```
self.name=name
self.roll_number=roll_number
```

301

CHAPTER 10   CLASSES AND OBJECTS

there is no problem though you did not declare these variables
earlier.

Changing an Attribute Value

You can update the attribute value inside an object (or instance). For
example, earlier, you created an instance called sam as follows:

```
sam= Student("Sam", 1)
```

Notice that inside sam, the attribute name had the value Sam, and the
attribute roll_number had the value 1. You can assign different values in
this instance. The easiest way is to directly access the attribute, say roll_
number, and change the value. Here is an example:

```
# Updating the roll_number
sam.roll_number=11
```

Note   I intentionally updated the roll number but not the name. You
understand that sam is a better name than object1 or object2, but
it doesn't look good if you replace the name Sam with Bob (for the
object called sam). So I suggest that you prefer a meaningful name
for your object.

Alternatively, you can define a method inside your class to update an
instance value. Once you initialize the object, you can use this instance
method to update the attribute value.

302

CHAPTER 10   CLASSES AND OBJECTS

Demonstration 10.2

In this demonstration, I updated a student's roll number multiple times using the approaches that I already discussed. Let's see the complete demonstration:

```
class Student:
    """ This is a simple class to model a student"""
    def __init__(self,name,roll_number):
        self.name=name
        self.roll_number=roll_number

    def describe(self):
        """ A simple method to describe a student."""
        print(f"{self.name}'s current roll number is {self.
          roll_number}")

    def update_roll_number(self, roll_number):
        """ Updating the roll number of a student."""
        self.roll_number=roll_number
        print(f"{self.name}'s roll number has been updated to
          {self.roll_number}")

# Creating an object and showing the details
sam= Student("Sam", 1)
sam.describe()
print("-"*10)

print("Updating the roll number and showing the details:")
sam.roll_number=11
sam.describe()
print("-"*10)
```

303

CHAPTER 10   CLASSES AND OBJECTS

```
print("Updating the roll number again and showing the
details:")
sam.update_roll_number(21)
sam.describe()
print("-"*10)
```

Output

Upon executing this program, you'll see the following output:

```
Sam's current roll number is 1
----------
Updating the roll number and showing the details:
Sam's current roll number is 11
----------
Updating the roll number again and showing the details:
Sam's roll number has been updated to 21
Sam's current roll number is 21
----------
```

Default Attributes

Until now, you saw me passing the values for the attributes. But it is not mandatory. Instead, you can set a default value for an attribute. Let's see an example.

Applying the Concept

Consider a case where all these students belong to the same institution. Here, you do not need to pass the institution's name repeatedly. For example, let's assume our students belong to a college called St. Stephen. In this case, I can set this default value inside a constructor.

304

CHAPTER 10   CLASSES AND OBJECTS

Demonstration 10.3

The following example shows such a case:

```python
class Student:
    """ This is a simple class to model a student"""
    def __init__(self,name,roll_number):
        self.name=name
        self.roll_number=roll_number
        self.institution="St. Stephen's"

    def describe(self):
        """ A simple method to describe a student."""
        print(f"Name: {self.name}")
        print(f"Roll number: {self.roll_number}")
        print(f"Institution: {self.institution}")

# Creating two objects from the Student class
sam= Student("Sam", 1)
kate= Student("Kate", 2)

# Displaying the student details
sam.describe()
print("*"*10)
kate.describe()
```

Output

Here is the output of the program:

```
Name: Sam
Roll number: 1
Institution: St. Stephen's
**********
```

305

CHAPTER 10   CLASSES AND OBJECTS

```
Name: Kate
Roll number: 2
Institution: St. Stephen's
```

Analysis

Notice that while creating a Student object, you did not pass the institution name. This is because the default value for the institution was set inside the constructor.

Class Variables versus Instance Variables

The official documentation (https://docs.python.org/3/tutorial/classes.html) states that

> *Generally speaking, instance variables are for data unique to each instance and class variables are for attributes and methods shared by all instances of the class.*

In the previous demonstration, name, roll_number, and institution are instance variables; these are unique to each instance. Since the institution name does not vary, you could use the institution as a class variable and rewrite the Student class as follows (I have commented out the old code and highlighted the new code; I also marked the variable types with inline comments for your easy reference):

```
class Student:
    """ This is a simple class to model a student"""
    institution="St.Stephen's"  # class variable
    def __init__(self,name,roll_number):
        self.name=name # instance variable
        self.roll_number=roll_number # instance variable
        # self.institution="St. Stephen's" # instance variable
    # There is no change in the remaining code
```

306

CHAPTER 10   CLASSES AND OBJECTS

Q&A Session

Q10.4 Instead of using "institution" as a class variable, why did you use it as an instance variable in the previous program (Demonstration 10.3)?

I used `institution` as an instance variable because it is unlikely that all students in this world belong to the same institution.

Importing Classes

In a complex real-world application, the code size is gigantic. If you write the entire code into a single file, you create a huge file. This kind of practice is commonly discouraged. Instead, Python allows you to store and segregate your code in modules.

Importing a Single Class

In Chapter 7, I told you that a module can contain many things such as variables, functions, and classes. In this chapter, our focus is on classes. So here I show you how to import classes from a module.

You have seen the `Student` class in the previous demonstration. Let's move this class to a separate file named **ch10_student_module**. (I used the prefix **ch10_** to indicate that this program belongs to Chapter 10.) It's a good practice to use a module-level docstring that can describe the module. So I have also added a docstring at the top of the file. The **ch10_student_module.py** looks like

```
"""
This module is useful to create a student
and display the necessary information.
"""
```

307

CHAPTER 10   CLASSES AND OBJECTS

```python
class Student:
    """ This is a simple class to model a student"""
    def __init__(self,name,roll_number):
        self.name=name
      # The remaining code is not shown
```

Demonstration 10.4

Create a new Python file. Save it with a new name, say
ch10_d04__importing_single_class.py, and type the following lines
into it:

```python
from ch10_student_module import Student
# Creating two objects from the Student class
sam= Student("Sam", 1)
kate= Student("Kate", 2)

# Displaying the student details
sam.describe()
print("*"*10)
kate.describe()
```

Output

The program will produce the same output that you saw in the previous
demonstration. To avoid repetition, I did not show it again.

Analysis

Since I moved the Student class to a separate module and imported the
module, this program produced the same output. However, this time,
the main program file is much cleaner, concise, and easy to read. This
gives you a clue that you can separate the program logic and focus on the
higher-level logic in the main program.

308

CHAPTER 10 CLASSES AND OBJECTS

Importing Multiple Classes

To import multiple classes from a module, your module should have multiple classes. Since our imported module had only one class (Student), let's add one more class, called Stream, inside the file **ch10_student_module.py** that I used earlier:

```python
class Stream:
    """ Initializes the student's stream """
    def __init__(self, student, stream):
        self.roll_number=student.roll_number
        self.stream=stream

    def display(self):
        """ Return the student details. """
        return f"Roll number {self.roll_number} belongs to the {self.stream} stream."
```

Demonstration 10.5

Create a new Python file. Save it with a new name (I used the name **ch10_d05_importing_multiple_classes.py**) and type the following lines into it:

```python
from ch10_student_module import Student, Stream

# Creating a Student instance and displaying the info
sam= Student("Sam", 1)
sam.describe()

stream_sam=Stream(sam,"Science")
print(stream_sam.display())
```

309

CHAPTER 10   CLASSES AND OBJECTS

Output

Once you execute the program, you'll see the following output:

```
Name: Sam
Roll number: 1
Institution: St. Stephen's
Roll number 1 belongs to the Science stream.
```

Note   In our examples, the imported module contains the Student class and the Stream class. These two classes are related to each other. It is recommended that you create modules with related classes.

Importing the Whole Module

You can import the whole module. How to access the classes in the modules? Chapter 7 gave you the clue! In this case, you can access the classes using the dot notation.

Demonstration 10.6

To illustrate, consider the following example, which is an alternative version of the previous demonstration (notice the key changes in bold):

```
import ch10_student_module

# Creating a Student instance and displaying the info
sam= ch10_student_module.Student("Sam", 1)
sam.describe()

stream_sam= ch10_student_module.Stream(sam, "Science")
print(stream_sam.display())
```

310

CHAPTER 10   CLASSES AND OBJECTS

Output

If you run this program, you'll see the same output that you saw in the previous demonstration.

Alternative Code

Let me show you another way of importing classes from a module. Though **it is not a recommended practice**, I present this to you for the sake of completeness. Here is an alternative version of the previous program:

```
from ch10_student_module import *
```

```
# Creating a Student instance and displaying the info
sam= Student("Sam", 1)
sam.describe()
```

```
stream_sam= Stream(sam, "Science")
print(stream_sam.display())
```

This program can produce the same output that you saw in the previous demonstrations. Now, see the first line of this program: in Chapter 7, I also told you not to use this kind of import statement. Let me remind you of some of the typical problems that are as follows:

- It is difficult for readers to identify the source.

- There is a possibility of name collisions.

Q&A Session

Q10.5 It'll be helpful if you explain the previous bullet points with a program.

You know that the Student class is already included in ch10_student_ module. Let's add another class that has the same name in the **current file** as follows:

311

CHAPTER 10   CLASSES AND OBJECTS

```
from ch10_student_module import * # Not a recommended practice

class Student:
    pass

# There will be a name collision after the addition
# of the Student class in the current file

# Creating a Student instance and displaying the info
sam= Student("Sam", 1)
#   The remaining code...
```

If you run this program now, you'll see the following:

```
 TypeError: Student() takes no arguments
```

Author's note: You can download the file ch10_not_recommended.py from the Apress website to examine this error.

Q10.6 Is there any way to use this new Student class in the current file? You can import the entire module and use the dot notation to point to the correct class. Let me show you how to use the following program.

Demonstration 10.7

Now I added a few lines of code in Demonstration 10.6 and demonstrated the usage of the new class as follows (notice the changes in bold):

```
import ch10_student_module

class Student:
    def __init__(self):
        print("Using the new Student class of the current
            file now.")

# Creating a Student instance and displaying the info
sam= ch10_student_module.Student("Sam", 1)
```

312

CHAPTER 10   CLASSES AND OBJECTS

```
sam.describe()

stream_sam= ch10_student_module.Stream(sam, "Science")
print(stream_sam.display())

# Using the Student class of the current file
jack=Student()
```

Output

Upon executing the program, you'll see the following output:

```
Name: Sam
Roll number: 1
Institution: St. Stephen's
Roll number 1 belongs to the Science stream.
Using the new Student class of the current file now.
```

The last line of output shows the usage of the new Student class that was placed in the current file.

Summary

Classes and objects are the foundation of object-oriented programming (OOP). This chapter explained them with different code examples. Upon completion of this chapter, you shouldn't find any problem answering the following questions:

- What is a class?

- What is an object?

- How can you use constructors?

- How can you change the attribute values?

313

CHAPTER 10   CLASSES AND OBJECTS

- How can you use the default attributes?

- How can you reuse the code by importing classes?

Exercise 10

Let's solve the following exercises.

E10.1 Can you predict the output of the following code segment?

```
class Employee:
    def __init__(self,id,name="Anonymous"):
        self.name=name
        self.id = id
    def describe(self):
        return f"{self.name} is an employee with ID: {self.id}"

mike= Employee(1,"Mike")
print(mike.describe())
```

E10.2 Now replace the following line in E10.1

```
mike= Employee(1,"Mike")
```

with the following line:

```
mike=Employee(1)
```

Can you predict the output?

E10.3 If you replace the following line in E10.1

```
def __init__(self,id,name="Anonymous"):
```

with the following line

```
def __init__(self, name="Anonymous",id):
```

can you predict the output?

314

CHAPTER 10   CLASSES AND OBJECTS

E10.4 Can you predict the output of the following program?

```python
class Employee:
    id=0
    def __init__(self, name="Anonymous"):
        self.name=name
    def describe(self):
        return f"{self.name} is an employee with ID: {self.id}"

kate= Employee("Kate")
print(kate.describe())
```

E10.5 Can you predict the output of the following program?

```python
class Employee:
    id=0
    def __init__(self, name="Anonymous"):
        self.name=name
    def update_id(self):
        self.id = 100
    def describe(self):
        self.update_id()
        return f"{self.name} is an employee with ID: {self.id}"

jack= Employee("Jack")
print(jack.describe())
```

Keys to Exercise 10

Here is a sample solution set for the exercises in this chapter.

E10.1

The program will produce the following output:

```
Mike is an employee with ID: 1
```

315

CHAPTER 10   CLASSES AND OBJECTS

E10.2

This code segment uses the default values. If you do not pass the employee's name, it accepts the default name "Anonymous." However, you need to supply the ID; you cannot bypass this activity. Here is the output:

```
Anonymous is an employee with ID: 1
```

E10.3

In the function definition, a non-default argument cannot be placed after a default argument. In this case, you'll encounter the following error:

```
SyntaxError: parameter without a default follows parameter with
a default
```

E10.4

The program shows the usage of a class variable id and it will produce the following output:

```
Kate is an employee with ID: 0
```

E10.5

The update_id method updates the ID to 100. Since the describe method calls the update_id method before returning the information of the employee, you'll see the following output:

```
Jack is an employee with ID: 100
```

Case Study

You have just started object-oriented programming. Let's work on some simple case studies, which are as follows.

CHAPTER 10 CLASSES AND OBJECTS

CS10.1 Problem Statement

Let's model a class to represent a car. To simplify things, let's assume this class has two attributes: one to display the model of the car and another to display the manufacturer's name. Once the class is made, create a few instances and display the details.

CS10.2 Problem Statement

A car manufacturing company can design different car models. Upon completing the previous case study, I would like you to write a function that creates at least two different car models from two distinct companies. Let's store the company-specific models in a list and then use a dictionary to store those models along with the manufacturer's name. Finally, display the car details.

Sample Implementations

Here are the sample implementations for the case studies.

CS10.1 Implementation

Here is a sample implementation:

```
class Car:
    def __init__(self,company,model):
        self.company=company
        self.model=model
    def display_car(self):
        print(f"Company: {self.company}, Model: {self.model}")
```

317

CHAPTER 10   CLASSES AND OBJECTS

```python
def main():
  glanza= Car("Toyota","Glanza")
  glanza.display_car()
  mustang= Car("Ford", "Shelby Mustang")
  mustang.display_car()

if __name__ == "__main__":
  main()
```

This program will produce the following output:

```
Company: Toyota, Model: Glanza
Company: Ford, Model: Shelby Mustang
```

CS10.2 Implementation

Here is a sample implementation:

```python
class Car:
    def __init__(self,company,model):
        self.company=company
        self.model=model
    def display_car(self):
        print(f"Company:{self.company}, Model: {self.model}")

def cars_info():
    # Making Toyota cars
    glanza= Car("Toyota","Glanza")
    rumion = Car("Toyota", "Rumion")
    # Listing Toyota models
    toyota_models = [glanza.model, rumion.model]

    # Making Ford cars
    mustang= Car("Ford", "Shelby Mustang")
```

318

CHAPTER 10 CLASSES AND OBJECTS

```python
    gt40=Car("Ford","Ford GT40")
    fiesta=Car("Ford","Ford Fiesta")
    # Listing Ford models
    ford_models=[mustang.model,gt40.model,fiesta.model]

    # Storing the models along with the company names
    cars = {"Toyota": toyota_models,
 "Ford": ford_models}
    # Traversing the dictionary and displaying the details
    for key,value in cars.items():
        print(f"{key} models: {value}")

if __name__ == "__main__":
  cars_info()
```

This program will produce the following output:

```
Toyota models: ['Glanza', 'Rumion']
Ford models: ['Shelby Mustang', 'Ford GT40', 'Ford Fiesta']
```

319

CHAPTER 11

Inheritance

Every time you do not need to start from scratch to model a class. Instead, you can consider an existing class and make a specialized version of it using inheritance. The primary aim of inheritance is to promote reusability and eliminate redundancy in code. It also shows how a child class can get the features (or characteristics) of its parent class. This chapter focuses on this topic.

Basic Concepts and Terminologies

Let's understand the concept using some examples. Suppose you already have a `Vehicle` class to represent any vehicle in this world. Later, you need to design a `Bus` class to represent any bus in this world. However, you know a bus is nothing but a special type of vehicle. So, instead of designing from scratch, you can make a class that is a specialized version of `Vehicle` and call it `Bus`. By doing this, you can type less and avoid lots of duplicate code in a program.

Developers may refer to the existing class and the new specialized class using different names. In our example, since the `Bus` class (the new class) derives from the `Vehicle` class (the existing class), the `Vehicle` class is termed as the **parent class, base class,** or **superclass** (a C# programmer often calls a parent class a base class, but a Java programmer refers to it as a superclass), and the Bus class is termed as the **child class**, or **derived class**.

© Vaskaran Sarcar 2025
V. Sarcar, *Python Bootcamp*, https://doi.org/10.1007/979-8-8688-1516-4_11

CHAPTER 11 INHERITANCE

Note Inheritance represents the **IS-A** relationship. Notice that in our example, a bus **is a** vehicle, but the reverse is not necessarily true.

While coding, you place a parent class one level up from a derived class in a hierarchical chain. Then you can add or change the functionalities (methods) inside a derived class. When you change a parent class functionality inside a child class, you say "I'm **overriding** the functionality into the child class." Ideally, these modifications should be meaningful, and they should not change the original architecture.

In some scenarios, instead of replacing a specific functionality of the parent class, a derived class can **extend** that functionality. How? It can invoke the base class functionality just before adding something new to that functionality. Do not worry! Shortly, you'll see the code examples.

POINTS TO REMEMBER

Using inheritance, you avoid writing the code from scratch. Instead, you make a specialized version of a parent class and can use the attributes and methods of the parent class. A child class can use any number of attributes or methods of the parent class. It can also define new attributes and methods of its own.

Types of Inheritance

There are different kinds of inheritance. Let's examine them.

322

CHAPTER 11   INHERITANCE

Single Inheritance

In the simplest form of inheritance, a child class derives from a parent class. In Demonstration 10.3 of the previous chapter (Chapter 10), you saw the following class:

```
class Student:
    """ This is a simple class to model a student """
    def __init__(self,name,roll_number):
        self.name=name
        self.roll_number=roll_number
        self.institution="St. Stephen's"

    def describe(self):
        """ A simple method to describe a student."""
        print(f"Name: {self.name}")
        print(f"Roll number: {self.roll_number}")
        print(f"Institution: {self.institution}")
```

We know that in a college or institution, students can enroll in different departments. **So let's model a scenario where, along with the previous information, you also print which department a student belongs to.** The following diagram (Figure 11-1) will help you visualize the model.

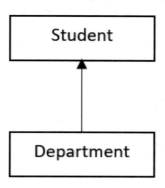

Figure 11-1. Single inheritance

323

CHAPTER 11   INHERITANCE

Understanding the Super Call

In the upcoming program, you'll see the use of the super method. It allows you to call a parent class method. For example, see the following code:

```
class Department(Student):
    def __init__(self, name, roll_number, dept):
        """ Initializing the parent class attributes. """
        super().__init__(name, roll_number)
        self.dept=dept
```

This code segment tells us the following points:

- The Department class inherits from the Student class.

- Before it initializes the specialized attribute dept, it initializes other attributes (name and roll_number) of the Student class.

Now you should not find any difficulties in understanding the following program.

Demonstration 11.1

Since there is no change in the Student class, it is not shown to avoid repetition. Let's focus on the new code segment now:

```
# There is no change in the Student class

class Department(Student):
    def __init__(self, name, roll_number, dept):
        super().__init__(name, roll_number)
        self.dept=dept
```

324

CHAPTER 11   INHERITANCE

```python
    def describe(self):
        """ A specialized method to describe a student."""
        super().describe()
        print(f"Department: {self.dept}")

# Creating two objects from the Student class
sam= Department("Sam", 1,"Physics")
kate= Department("Kate", 2,"Computer Science")

# Displaying the student details
sam.describe()
print("*"*10)
kate.describe()
```

Output

This time, upon executing the program, you'll be able to see the department info as well:

```
Name: Sam
Roll number: 1
Institution: St. Stephen's
Department: Physics
**********
Name: Kate
Roll number: 2
Institution: St. Stephen's
Department: Computer Science
```

Analysis

Apart from initializing the parent class attributes, the Department class also overrides the parent class method describe(). This is why you can see the student's details along with the department info.

325

CHAPTER 11   INHERITANCE

Q&A Session

Q11.1 What do you mean by method overriding?

Notice that the parent class (Student) and the child class (Department) both include the same-named method: describe(). Programmatically, when the child class redefines the parent class method, we call it method overriding.

Q11.2 Instead of defining a new method, why did you override the describe method?

It makes more sense when you describe a similar behavior. So there is no problem if you execute the following code:

```
sam= Student("Sam", 1)
sam.describe()
sam= Department("Sam", 1,"Physics")
sam.describe()
```

However, if you use a different method name that is specific to the Department class, a Student class instance cannot invoke that method.

Q11.3 It will be helpful if you clarify the last line of the previous answer.

Let's add the following method in the Department class:

```
def show_elective_paper(self,subject):
    """ A specialized method to mention the elective papers."""
    print(f"{self.name} has taken {subject} as an elective
      subject. ")
```

Now the following code can work:

```
sam= Department("Sam", 1,"Physics")
sam.show_elective_paper("Nuclear Physics")
```

However, the following code will not work:

```
sam= Student("Sam", 1)
sam.show_elective_paper("Nuclear Physics") # Error
```

326

This is because the show_elective_paper method was not available in the Student class.

Q11.4 It appears to me that I can avoid the super call. For example, in Demonstration 11.1, if you replace the line super().__init__(name, roll_number) with the line Student.__init__(self,name, roll_number), you can get the same output. Is this correct?

This is not a standard practice, and it is not suitable in the long run. Since you hard-coded the inherited class name, refactoring the code can be challenging for you in the future (you may need to refactor the code to accommodate a change in the design or inheritance hierarchy for various reasons).

This is why expert programmers prefer to invoke the super function in their code. This approach promotes indirection because we do not need to mention the delegate class by name.

Multiple Inheritance

In the case of multiple inheritance, a child class can derive from multiple parent classes. Here is a sample diagram (see Figure 11-2) for your reference.

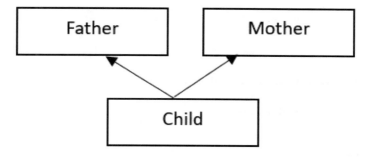

Figure 11-2. Multiple inheritance

CHAPTER 11   INHERITANCE

Programming languages like C# and Java do not support multiple inheritance directly (through class) to avoid ambiguity and complexity. Those languages tackle the situation using a different mechanism (you need to understand interfaces). However, Python allows this. Let's discuss how Python tackles the challenges that may arise due to multiple inheritance.

Demonstration 11.2

First, execute the following program, and analyze the output:

```python
class Father:
    def describe(self):
        print("The father is an employee.")
class Mother:
    def describe(self):
        print("The mother is a housewife.")
class Child(Father,Mother):
    def describe(self):
        print("The child is a student.")

child=Child()
child.describe()
```

Output

This program will produce the following output:

```
The child is a student.
```

Analysis

Let's replace the describe method inside the Child class with a pass statement as follows

328

CHAPTER 11   INHERITANCE

```
class Child(Father,Mother):
    # def describe(self):
    #     print("The child is a student.")
    pass
```

and execute the program again. You can use a pass statement when a statement is required syntactically, but your program does not need to take any action. You can consider it as a placeholder that can be replaced with a code block in the future. This time, you'll see the following output:

```
The father is an employee.
```

Method Resolution Order

Now let me ask you: why do you see this output? Is this output arbitrary? Or why do you not see the line "The mother is a housewife." in the output? To answer these questions, you need to understand method resolution order (MRO). In simple terms, it is the order in which Python searches a method in an inheritance hierarchy. The basic scheme is **depth-first, left-to-right**.

POINT TO NOTE

If you have the following code

class DerivedClassName(Base1, Base2, Base3):

<statements>

the official doc (`https://docs.python.org/3/tutorial/classes.html#inheritance`) states the following:

For most purposes, in the simplest cases, you can think of the search for attributes inherited from a parent class as depth-first, left-to-right, not searching twice in the same class where there is an overlap in the

329

CHAPTER 11   INHERITANCE

hierarchy. Thus, if an attribute is not found in DerivedClassName, it is searched for in Base1, then (recursively) in the base classes of Base1, and if it was not found there, it was searched for in Base2, and so on.

There are many articles/blog posts on the topic, but I recommend you first read Guido's post: `https://python-history.blogspot.com/2010/06/method-resolution-order.html`.

To illustrate, in our program, when you use the line child.describe()

- First, it searches for the `describe` method in the `Child` class (since `child` is a `Child` class object).

- If it is not found, it will search in the parent class. However, in our example, the `Child` class has two parent classes, named `Father` and `Mother`. Following the "**depth-first, left-to-right**" rule, it will start searching the `describe` method inside `Father`. If the method is not found in the `Father` class, it will then search for this method in the `Mother` class.

You can also verify this claim by executing the line print(Child.mro()), which will print the output

```
[<class '__main__.Child'>, <class '__main__.Father'>, <class '__main__.Mother'>, <class 'object'>]
```

Q&A Session

Q11.5 Is there any way to change the search order? For example, if the describe method is not found in the Child class, I'd like to check the Mother class before the Father class.

You can replace the line class Child(**Father**,Mother) with the following one

```
class Child(Mother,Father):
```

330

CHAPTER 11   INHERITANCE

to fulfill your demand. You may also note that after this change, print(Child.mro()) will print the following:

```
[<class '__main__.Child'>, <class '__main__.Mother'>, <class
'__main__.Father'>, <class 'object'>]
```

Q11.6 Why do I see <class 'object'> in the previous output?
It is the ultimate parent class in the class hierarchy. You can examine this by investigating **builtins.py**. There, you'll see the following documentation as well:

```
class object:
    """

    The base class of the class hierarchy.
    When called, it accepts no arguments and returns a new
    featureless instance that has no instance attributes and
    cannot be given any.
    """

# The remaining portions are not shown
```

Investigating the Super Call

It is interesting to note that a super call does not go to the object's parent class; it passes the control to the next thing that is placed in the object's MRO. How can you verify this? Let's run the following program.

Demonstration 11.3

To discuss the topic, I have introduced a new class named Grandfathers. Both the Father and Mother classes inherit from this class. The remaining code is almost similar to the previous demonstration, except this time, the Father class's describe method made a super call, but the Mother class's describe method did not make such a call. Here is the complete program:

331

CHAPTER 11   INHERITANCE

```python
class Grandfathers:
    def describe(self):
        print("Both grandfathers are artists.")

class Father(Grandfathers):
    def describe(self):
        print("The father is an employee.")
        super().describe()

class Mother(Grandfathers):
    def describe(self):
        print("The mother is a housewife.")

class Child(Father,Mother):
    pass

child=Child()
child.describe()
print(Child.mro())
```

Output

This program will produce the following output:

```
The father is an employee.
The mother is a housewife.
[<class '__main__.Child'>, <class '__main__.Father'>, <class
'__main__.Mother'>, <class '__main__.Grandfathers'>, <class
'object'>]
```

Analysis

This time, the output is interesting. Since the Child class did not have
the describe method, the control needed to search for this method in its
parent classes (Father and Mother). However, as per the MRO, it searched

332

CHAPTER 11   INHERITANCE

the Father class before the Mother class and, eventually, got the method and displayed the content. So, there is no problem understanding the first line of the output.

However, the second line in this output is interesting: notice that from the Father class, the super call did not go to its parent class, Grandfathers; instead, it went to the Mother class. Why? Look into the MRO again, and you'll understand that it's the expected behavior.

You may also note that the describe method of the Mother class made no more super calls; so there is no more output from the invocation of child.describe().

However, if you add a super call in the describe method of the Mother class as follows (the bold line is added)

```
class Mother(Grandfathers):
    def describe(self):
        print("The mother is a housewife.")
        super().describe()
```

you'll see the following output (notice the change in bold):

```
The father is an employee.
The mother is a housewife.
Both grandfathers are artists.
[<class '__main__.Child'>, <class '__main__.Father'>, <class
'__main__.Mother'>, <class '__main__.Grandfathers'>, <class
'object'>]
```

By looking at the MRO, you know that this time this new super call was supposed to be moved to the Grandfathers class from the Mother class. Hence, there is no confusion!

333

CHAPTER 11 INHERITANCE

> **POINT TO REMEMBER**
>
> Now you understand that a super call does not necessarily go to the object's parent class; it passes the control to the next thing that is placed in the object's MRO.

Hierarchical Inheritance

In hierarchical inheritance, multiple child classes can derive from one parent class. For example, you know that a bus is one type of vehicle. Similarly, a train is another type of vehicle. So you can design a Bus class and a Train class by deriving from the Vehicle class. Here is a sample diagram for your reference (see Figure 11-3).

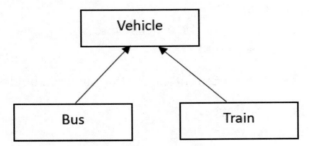

Figure 11-3. *Hierarchical inheritance*

Multilevel Inheritance

In multilevel inheritance, a child class derives from a parent class that, in turn, derives from another parent class. In other words, a child class has a grandfather. For example, a "goods train" is different from a "passenger train," but they both fulfill the basic criteria of a train, which in turn is a vehicle. To design this scenario, you can start with a Vehicle class. Then you create a child class, called Train, that derives from the Vehicle class.

334

CHAPTER 11   INHERITANCE

Finally, you can derive a child class, say `GoodsTrain` or `PassengerTrain`, which derives from the `Train` class. Here is a sample diagram (see Figure 11-4) for your reference.

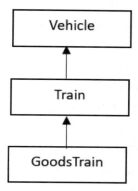

Figure 11-4. *Multilevel inheritance*

Hybrid Inheritance

There is another type of inheritance known as hybrid inheritance. It is a combination of two or more types of inheritance.

POINT TO NOTE

If you can model single and multiple inheritance, you should not have any difficulties modeling the other types, such as hierarchical or multilevel inheritance. The same comment applies when you model a hybrid inheritance as well. I leave these exercises to you. If you still find any difficulties in implementing these ideas, you can refer to the exercises E11.3 and E11.4 of this chapter.

CHAPTER 11   INHERITANCE

Private Variables and Methods

If you are familiar with object-oriented programming languages like Java, C#, C++, etc., you will notice the use of public, private, and protected variables (and methods). If not, let me give you the idea with simple examples.

Consider your ATM card or credit card credentials. You do not share this information with anybody else. These are your private data.

You must keep these cards in a place that is unknown to an outsider. However, your spouse may know about these cards and the place where you keep them. You can consider that place as a protected area for your cards. In programming languages like Java, apart from the containing class, the child classes can access the protected variables (and methods). In simple words, you extend the visibility to some extent, but not to everyone.

On the other hand, anyone can access public information. For example, an advertisement in a newspaper or visiting hours mentioned in a hospital's notice board represent public data. In programming, public data has maximum visibility.

Does Python Have Private Variables?

In Java, C#, or C++, declaring a variable public, private, or protected is straightforward. For example, you use the keyword "private" to declare a private variable. However, **Python does not have real private variables**. The official source 9. Classes – Python 3.13.3 documentation states:

> *"Private" instance variables that cannot be accessed except from inside an object don't exist in Python.*

Interestingly, this link also acknowledges that we may need class-private members in certain scenarios. How to handle those situations? The official documentation 6. Expressions – Python 3.13.3 documentation states:

336

CHAPTER 11   INHERITANCE

When an identifier that textually occurs in a class definition begins with two or more underscore characters and does not end in two or more underscores, it is considered a private name of that class.

Once you mark a variable (or method) private following this suggestion, you cannot access the variable (or the method) in the usual way.

Now you have got the clue! **You can use the underscore(s) in a similar context to get a behavior close to the private variable concept.** Let us examine this with an example.

If you execute the following code

```
class Person:
    def __init__(self,name):
        self.name=name
        self.designation= "Teacher"
        self.__salary = 10000.5  # acts like a private variable

amit=Person("Amit")
print(amit.name) # OK
print(amit.designation) # OK
```

there is no surprise that you'd see the following output:

```
Amit
Teacher
```

However, if you write the following

```
print(amit.__salary) # Error
```

you'll see the following:

```
AttributeError: 'Person' object has no attribute '__salary'
```

337

CHAPTER 11   INHERITANCE

Accessing Private Data

Then how can you access the __salary attribute? Let me show you some approaches:

You can introduce a method inside the Person class that can access the __salary attribute. Here is a sample:

```
def display_salary(self):
    print(f"{self.name} earns ${self.__salary} per month.")
```

Now the code amit.display_salary() can display the required information in the output: Amit earns $10000.5 per month.

There is an alternative way! The official documentation 9. Classes – Python 3.13.3 documentation states:

> *Since there is a valid use-case for class-private members (namely to avoid name clashes of names with names defined by subclasses), there is limited support for such a mechanism, called* **name mangling**. *Any identifier of the form __spam (at least two leading underscores, at most one trailing underscore) is textually replaced with _classname__spam, where classname is the current class name with leading underscore(s) stripped.*

Now you understand that you can use the following code

```
print(amit._Person__salary)
```

to display Amit's salary as well. Let's review all these concepts using the following demonstration.

Demonstration 11.4

Now I present a complete demonstration with supportive comments. If you uncomment the corresponding codes, you will get errors. I have kept them for your reference:

338

CHAPTER 11   INHERITANCE

```python
class Person:
    def __init__(self,name):
        self.name =name
        self.designation = "Teacher"
        self.__salary = 10000.5  # acts like a private variable

    def display_salary(self):
        print(f"{self.name} earns ${self.__salary} per month.")
amit=Person("Amit")
print(amit.name) # OK
print(amit.designation) # OK

# print(amit.__salary) # Error
amit.display_salary() # OK
print(amit._Person__salary) # OK too
```

Output

Here is the output:

```
Amit
Teacher
Amit earns $10000.5 per month.
10000.5
```

Q&A Session

Q11.7 How does name mangling help?
It helps you avoid name clashes between a parent class and its derived
class. Particularly, it helps your subclasses override methods without
breaking intraclass method calls.

339

CHAPTER 11   INHERITANCE

Q11.8 Can you show me a program that explains the last line of the previous answer?

Consider the following program (you can download **ch10_ understanding_name_mangling.py** from the Apress website) where both the parent class and the derived class contain a method named `display`:

```
class Parent:
    def __init__(self):
        print("Invoking the display method...")
        self.display()
    def display(self):
        print("The parent.display is called.")

class Child(Parent):
    def display(self):
        print("The child.display is called.")

child=Child()
```

If you execute this program, you'll see the following output:

```
Invoking the display method...
```
The child.display is called.

Notice that since the Child class does not have a constructor, the control reaches the parent class constructor. However, the parent class constructor invoked the `display` method of the derived class, though it was supposed to call its own `display` method (notice that the code in the parent class was self.display()).

Now introduce some changes in the Parent class as follows:

```
class Parent:
    def __init__(self):
        print("Invoking the display method...")
        # self.display()
```

340

CHAPTER 11   INHERITANCE

```python
    self.__display()
def display(self):
    print("The parent.display is called.")
__display=display
# There is no change in the remaining code
```

Upon executing the modified program, you'll see the following output:

```
Invoking the display method...
The parent.display is called.
```

You can see that this time the display method of the Parent class is called from the Parent class constructor, which means that **the "intraclass method call" is not broken now.**

You may also note that at present, the child class instance cannot call the parent class's display using the following line:

```
child.__display()  # error
```

Author's note: Though name mangling is a big and complex topic, I wanted to give you an overview of it. In general, the mangling rules are designed to avoid accidents. You can find many online lectures on this topic. If interested, you can go through those lectures. However, I recommend you visit the online link https://www.youtube.com/watch?v=0hrEaA3N3lk to explore some interesting cases related to this topic. Normally, to make things simple, I try to avoid the double underscore prefix in my code.

Final Thoughts

Inheritance is undoubtedly helpful. However, it's possible to abuse inheritance and create unrelated hierarchies. Also, by breaking a system into many small pieces, you can complicate the integration and testing

CHAPTER 11   INHERITANCE

processes. As you learn more, you'll also identify that "**has-a**" relationships (compositions) can serve you better than the "**is-a**" relationships (inheritance) in many different scenarios, particularly when you investigate the design patterns. Despite these challenges, inheritance has its own significance and usefulness. No one can ignore this fact!

Summary

This chapter gave you an overview of inheritance and answered the following questions:

- How does inheritance help you in OOP?

- What are the different types of inheritances? How can you implement them?

- What is method overriding?

- What is method resolution order (MRO) in Python?

- How does name mangling work in Python?

Exercise 11

E11.1 Can you predict the output of the following code segment?

```
class Vehicle:
    def __init__(self):
        print("A vehicle is created.")
class Bus(Vehicle):
    def __init__(self):
        super().__init__()
        print("A bus is created.")

vehicle=Bus()
```

342

CHAPTER 11   INHERITANCE

E11.2 If you comment out the line super().__init__() in the previous exercise (E11.1), what will be the output?

E11.3 Can you predict the output of the following code segment?

```python
class Grandfather:
    def __init__(self,grandfather):
        print(f"Grandfather: {grandfather}")

class Father(Grandfather):
    def __init__(self, father, grandfather):
        super().__init__(grandfather)
        print(f"Father: {father}")

class Child(Father):
    def __init__(self,name,father,grandfather):
        super().__init__(father,grandfather)
        print(f"Child: {name}")

jack=Child("Jack","Robert","Smith")
```

E11.4 Can you predict the output of the following code segment?

```python
class Car:
    def __init__(self):
        print("It is a car.")

class ElectricCar(Car):
    def __init__(self):
        super().__init__()
        print("It uses an electric motor. ")

class DieselCar(Car):
    def __init__(self):
        super().__init__()
        print("It uses a diesel engine. ")
```

343

CHAPTER 11 INHERITANCE

```python
first_car= ElectricCar()
print("-"*10)
second_car= DieselCar()
```

E11.5 Can you predict the output of the following code segment?

```python
class Quadrilateral:
    def show(self):
        print("I am a quadrilateral.")

class Parallelogram(Quadrilateral):
    def show(self):
        print("I am a parallelogram.")

shape=Parallelogram()
shape.show()
```

E11.6 Can you predict the output of the following code segment?

```python
class Parent:
    pass
class Child(Parent):
    def display(self):
        print("Child.display")
parent=Parent()
parent.display()
```

E11.7 Can you predict the output of the following code segment?

```python
class A:
    def display(self):
        print("A.display")

class B(A):
    def display(self):
```

CHAPTER 11   INHERITANCE

```python
        print("B.display")
        super().display()

class C(A):
    def display(self):
        print("C.display")

class D(C, B):
    pass

d=D()
d.display()
print(D.mro())
```

E11.8 Predict the output when you use the following definition of D in the previous exercise (E11.7):

```python
class D(B,C):
    pass
```

E11.9 Can you predict the output of the following code segment?

```python
class Calculator:
    def sum(self,a,b):
        return a+b

class AdvancedCalculator(Calculator):

    def sum(self, a, b,c):
        return a+b+c

calc = AdvancedCalculator()
print(f"2 + 3.5 + 7 = {calc.sum(2,3.5,7)}")
print(f"2 + 3.5 = {calc.sum(2,3.5)}")
```

345

CHAPTER 11   INHERITANCE

E11.10 Given the following code

```
class A:
    a=1
    _b=2
    __c=3
    __d_=4
    __e__=5
```

can you point out the erroneous lines of code in the following segment?

```
object1=A()
print(object1.a)
print(object1._b)
print(object1.__c)
print(object1._A__c)
print(object1.__d_)
print(object1._A__d_)
print(object1.__e__)
```

E11.11 Can you predict the output of the following code segment?

```
class Parent:
    def show(self):
        return "Parent.show"
    __show=show

class Child(Parent):
    def show(self):
        return "Child.show"

child=Child()
print(child.show())
print(child._Parent__show())
```

346

CHAPTER 11   INHERITANCE

Keys to Exercises 11

Here is a sample solution set for the exercises in this chapter.

E11.1

This program will produce the following output:

```
A vehicle is created.
A bus is created.
```

E11.2

Since you do not use the super call inside the derived class constructor, this time you'll see the following output:

```
A bus is created.
```

E11.3

This program shows an example of multilevel inheritance. Here is the output:

```
Grandfather: Smith
Father: Robert
Child: Jack
```

E11.4

This program shows an example of hierarchical inheritance. Here is the output:

```
It is a car.
It uses an electric motor.
----------
It is a car.
It uses a diesel engine.
```

347

CHAPTER 11 INHERITANCE

Notice that when you create an `ElectricCar` instance, it does not provide any information about a diesel car. Similarly, when you create a `DieselCar` instance, it does not provide any information about an electric car.

E11.5

If you understood method overriding, you'd not face any difficulties in understanding the following output:

```
I am a parallelogram.
```

E11.6

You'll see the following error:

```
AttributeError: 'Parent' object has no attribute 'display'
```

Explanation: In Q11.3, you've seen that a parent class object cannot access the method that is specific to the child class. The same concept applies here. In other words, a derived class can access the features of the parent class, but the reverse is not true.

E11.7

If you understood method resolution order (MRO), you would not face any difficulties in understanding the following output:

```
C.display
[<class '__main__.D'>, <class '__main__.C'>, <class
'__main__.B'>, <class '__main__.A'>, <class 'object'>]
```

Explanation: Notice that the D class did have the display method. So the control needed to search for this method in its parent classes (C and B). However, as per the MRO, it searched the C class before the B class and, eventually, got the method and displayed the content.

348

CHAPTER 11   INHERITANCE

E11.8

If you understood method resolution order (MRO), you would not face any difficulties in understanding that this time, the program will produce the following output:

```
B.display
C.display
[<class '__main__.D'>, <class '__main__.B'>, <class
'__main__.C'>, <class '__main__.A'>, <class 'object'>]
```

Additional note: However, if you redefine the C class in this program as follows (the bold line is added)

```
class C(A):
    def display(self):
        print("C.display")
        super().display()
```

you'll see the following output (notice the change in bold):

```
B.display
C.display
A.display
[<class '__main__.D'>, <class '__main__.B'>, <class
'__main__.C'>, <class '__main__.A'>, <class 'object'>]
```

By looking at the MRO, you know that this time the super call was supposed to be moved to the A class.

E11.9

You know that Python does not support method overloading. So the last line of the program will raise an error. Here is a sample output for your reference:

349

CHAPTER 11   INHERITANCE

```
2 + 3.5 + 7= 12.5
Traceback (most recent call last):
  File "E:\MyPrograms\PythonBootcamp\chapter11\ch11_e09.py",
  line 11, in <module>
    print(f"2+3.5= {calc.sum(2,3.5)}") # Error
                    ~~~~~~~~~~^^^^^^^
TypeError: AdvancedCalculator.sum() missing 1 required
positional argument: 'c'
```

However, you can provide a workaround by redefining the sum method in the child class (AdvancedCalculator) as follows:

```
def sum(self, a, b, c=0):
        return a+b+c
```

After making this change, the program can execute without the issue and produce the following output:

```
2 + 3.5 + 7= 12.5
2 + 3.5 = 5.5
```

You can make this sum method even better by making it capable of processing a variable number of arguments as follows:

```
def sum(self, *numbers):
    total=0
    for number in args:
        total += number
    return total
```

E11.10

The erroneous lines are highlighted in bold. For the remaining lines, the corresponding output is shown in inline comments:

CHAPTER 11   INHERITANCE

```
print(object1.a) # Outputs 1
print(object1._b) # Outputs 2
print(object1.__c) # Error
print(object1._A__c) # Outputs 3
print(object1.__d_) # Error
print(object1._A__d_) # Outputs 4
print(object1.__e__) # Outputs 5
```

E11.11

This program will show the following output:

```
Child.show
Parent.show
```

Case Study

Let's try to make solutions for the following case studies.

CS11.1 Problem Statement

Let's create an animal hierarchy and describe them. First, create an `Animal` class at the top of the hierarchy. Let's assume that this class has two attributes, named `type` and `sound`. To describe the animal behavior, let's create a method, called `describe`, in this class as well.

Once the Animal class is ready, derive two classes, named `Dog` and `Tiger`, from it and update the attributes along with the behavior. Now create one instance from each of the specialized classes and display the details. Here is a sample output for your reference:

351

CHAPTER 11   INHERITANCE

```
Dogs are domestic animals.
They prefer barking.

Tigers are wild animals.
They prefer roaring.
```

CS11.2 Problem Statement

Create an application that can design computer science courses that can vary across institutions. Here are the assumptions:

- The course includes three subjects. Two subjects are common in all institutions. Let us assume these two subjects are Mathematics and Artificial Intelligence. However, the third one is an elective paper that can vary across institutions.

- While initiating the course, the user needs to supply the institution name along with the elective paper. To reduce the code size, you can assume there is no invalid user input to consider.

Here is a sample input:

```
Enter the institution name: St. Stephens College
Enter the elective paper: Python Programming
```

Here is a sample output:

```
**********
Institution name: St. Stephens College
Computer science course includes:
1:Mathematics.
2:Artificial Intelligence.
3:Python Programming
**********
```

352

CHAPTER 11 INHERITANCE

Sample Implementations

Let's see the sample implementations.

CS11.1 Implementation

Here is a sample implementation:

```
class Animal:
    def __init__(self):
        self.type = "unknown"
        self.sound = "unknown"

    def describe(self):
        print(f"Different animals make different sounds.\n")

class Dog(Animal):
    def __init__(self):
        self.type = "domestic"
        self.sound = "barking"
    def describe(self):
        print(f"Dogs are {self.type} animals. ")
        print(f"They prefer {self.sound}.\n")

class Tiger(Animal):
    def __init__(self):
        self.type = "wild"
        self.sound = "roaring"
    def describe(self):
        print(f"Tigers are {self.type} animals. ")
        print(f"They prefer {self.sound}.\n")
```

353

CHAPTER 11   INHERITANCE

```
animal=Dog()
animal.describe()

animal=Tiger()
animal.describe()
```

CS11.2 Implementation

Here is a sample implementation:

```
class Engineering:
    """ Engineering is the parent class. """
    def __init__(self,institution):
        # Initializes the common subjects
        self.institution = institution
        self.subject_1 = "Mathematics."
        self.subject_2 = "Artificial Intelligence."

class ComputerScience(Engineering):
    """
    The ComputerScience class inherits from
    the Engineering class.
    """

    def __init__(self,institution, elective):
        """ Initialize starts from parent class."""
        super().__init__(institution)
        self.subject_3 = elective

    def course_details(self):
        """ Prints the course details of an institution. """
        print("*"*10)
        print(f"Institution name: {self.institution}")
        print("Computer science course includes:")
```

354

CHAPTER 11   INHERITANCE

```python
        print(f"1:{self.subject_1}")
        print(f"2:{self.subject_2}")
        print(f"3:{self.subject_3}")
        print("*" * 10)

# Supply the institution name
institution_name = input("Enter the institution name: ")
# Enter the elective paper
elective_paper = input("Enter the elective paper: ")
cs_course= ComputerScience(institution_name,elective_paper)
cs_course.course_details()
```

Gentle Reminder: By considering the exception-handling mechanism, you can improve these implementations. In addition, while implementing the case studies in this chapter, I have not used the construct if __name__ == "__main__":. However, if needed, you can always control the program executions using this construct. I leave these exercises to you.

355

APPENDIX A

Supplementary Material

Chapter 2 discussed operators. This appendix provides a detailed discussion on them. In Chapter 10, you were introduced to the OOP principles. Thereafter, you used instance methods in many demonstrations. Once you deep dive into Python programming, you'll also see the use of static methods and class methods. This appendix discusses how to use them as well.

More on Operators

Let us test some common operators. These are easy to understand. I'm about to execute them in the PyCharm Terminal.

Arithmetic Operators

These are used to perform common mathematical operations. Probably, most of us are familiar with these operators. Before I use the arithmetic operators, I use two variables, x and y. I assign them the initial values 25 and 10 as follows:

```
>>> x=25
>>> y=10
```

© Vaskaran Sarcar 2025
V. Sarcar, *Python Bootcamp*, https://doi.org/10.1007/979-8-8688-1516-4

APPENDIX A   SUPPLEMENTARY MATERIAL

Addition operator (+):

```
>>> x+y
35
```

Subtraction operator (-):

```
>>> x-y
15
```

Multiplication operator (*):

```
>>> x*y
250
```

Division operator (/):

```
>>> x/y
2.5
```

Modulus (or remainder) operator (%):

```
>>> x%y
5
```

Explanation: If you divide 25 by 10, 5 is the remainder.

Exponentiation operator (**):

```
>>> y**4
10000
```

Explanation: 10*10*10*10=10000

Floor division (//) operator:

```
>>> print(x//y)
2
```

Explanation: You get the answer to the nearest whole number. Consider another example: 14/3=4.666 (approx). So 14//3 gives you the answer as 4.

APPENDIX A   SUPPLEMENTARY MATERIAL

Assignment Operators

You can use these operators to assign some values to the variables. Typically, you use them to assign the value of the right side of the expression to the left side of the operand. For example, to assign 5 to x, you write x=5.

Often, you use them to type less as well. For example, x+=3 is shorthand for x = x+3. Similarly, x -=5 is a shorthand for x = x-5.

Let us test the common assignment operators:

Assign 3 to x and verify the result:

```
>>> x=3
>>> x
3
```

Now, assign 10 to a new variable (a). Assign this new variable to the latest value of x and verify the result:

```
>>> a=10
>>> x=a
>>> x
10
```

Increment the latest value of x by 2:

```
>>> x+=2
>>> x
12
```

Decrement the latest value of x by 3:

```
>>> x-=3
>>> x
9
```

APPENDIX A   SUPPLEMENTARY MATERIAL

Multiply the latest value of x by 7:

```
>>> x*=7
>>> x
63
```

Divide the latest value of x by 10:

```
>>> x/=10
>>> x
6.3
```

Set a new value (13) to x and apply the modulus assignment operator (%=):

```
>>> x=13
>>> x%=5
>>> x
3
```

Set a new value (25) to x and apply the floor division operator (//=):

```
>>> x=25
>>> x//=7
>>> x
3
```

Set two values to x and y and test exponentiation assignment:

```
>>> x=5
>>> y=4
>>> x**=y
>>> x
625
```

Explanation: If you multiply 5 four times, you'll get 5*5*5*5=625.

360

APPENDIX A   SUPPLEMENTARY MATERIAL

Comparison (or Relational) Operators

These operators are used to compare the equality (or inequality) of two values (or operands). The result of the comparison is a Boolean value, i.e., either True or False. You can use **Table A-1** for your reference.

Table A-1. *The relational operators*

Operator Name	Operator Symbol	Example	Expected Result
Strictly greater than	>	10>7	True
Strictly less than	<	10<7	False
Greater than or equal	>=	19>=12	True
Less than or equal	<=	19<=12	False
Equal	==	25 == (18+7)	True
Not equal	! =	25 != (18+7)	False

Assign 7 to x and 5 to y, and then, let's do some exercises on the comparison operators:

```
>>> x=7
>>> y=5
>>> x==y
False
>>> x!=y
True
>>> x==y+2
True
>>> x!=y+2
False
```

APPENDIX A   SUPPLEMENTARY MATERIAL

Logical Operators

You can use these operators when you work on conditional statements. You can make a complex Boolean expression by combining simple Boolean expressions using "**logical AND**," "**logical OR**," and "**logical NOT**" operators. To understand these, let us suppose you are testing two statements:

- In the case of a logical OR, if at least one statement is true, the combined result is True; otherwise, it is False. You use or to denote logical OR.

- In the case of a logical AND, if both statements are true, the combined result is True; otherwise, it is False. You use and to denote logical AND.

- The logical NOT does the opposite – it reverses the result. For example, if the result is True, it reverses it to False and vice versa. You use **not** to denote logical NOT.

Let me show you some examples in a Python shell:

```
>>> 25>21 and 34>29.5
True
>>> 25>21 and 34<29.5
False
>>> 25>21 or 34<29.5
True
>>> not(45>23)
False
>>> not(25.2>34 and 12<5)
True
>>> x,y=10,20
>>> x>3 and y>19
True
```

362

APPENDIX A   SUPPLEMENTARY MATERIAL

```
>>> not (x>3 or y<15)
False
```

Identity Operators

You can test an object's identity using the operators is and is not. Let's understand their usage.

The following program defines a class Student. Then it creates two Student objects jack and bob. Finally, it verifies whether these are the same object. Here is the complete program with the supporting comments:

```
# Defining the Student class
class Student:
    def __init__(self,name):
        self.name= name

# Creating two objects
jack = Student("Jack")
bob = Student("Bob")

# Verifying the object's identity
print(f"Are jack and bob the same object? {jack is bob}")
print(f"Is jack different from bob ? {jack is not bob}")
```

Upon executing this program, you should see the following output:

```
Are jack and bob the same object? False
Is jack different from bob ? True
```

Now create another object jack2 as follows:

```
jack2=Student("Jack")
```

363

APPENDIX A   SUPPLEMENTARY MATERIAL

You can see that both jack and jack2 have the same name: **Jack**. **However, are they the same?** Let's verify by executing the following line of code:

```
print(f"Are jack and jack2 the same object? {jack is jack2}")
```

The previous line will produce the output

```
Are jack and jack2 the same object? False
```

Are you surprised? Let us visit the official documentation page (6. Expressions – Python 3.13.3 documentation) that states:

> *The operators **is** and **is not** test for an object's identity: x is y is true if and only if x and y are the same object. **An Object's identity is determined using the id() function.** x is not y yields the inverse truth value.*

How does the id() function work? Let me pick the function documentation from the builtins.py:

```
def id(*args, **kwargs): # real signature unknown
    """

    Return the identity of an object.

    This is guaranteed to be unique among simultaneously
        existing objects.
    (CPython uses the object's memory address.)
    """

    pass
```

The function documentation is self-explanatory. To confirm, let's try to print the IDs of the objects, jack and jack2, by executing the following code:

```
print(f"The ID of jack is {id(jack)}")
print(f"The ID of jack2 is {id(jack2)}")
```

364

APPENDIX A   SUPPLEMENTARY MATERIAL

Here is a sample output (the ID can vary on your computer):

```
The ID of jack is 2198121512112
The ID of jack2 is 2198124721360
```

Now you understand that jack and jack2 point to different memory locations. Hence, they are not the same!

Interestingly, you can also use the is and is not operators to check if the variable is of a certain type. For example, if you now examine the following lines of code

```
print(f"Is jack a Student object? {type(jack) is Student}")
print(f"Is jack an int type? {type(jack) is int}")
print(f"Is bob not an int type? {type(bob) is not int}")
```

you'll see the output

```
Is jack a Student object? True
Is jack an int type? False
Is bob not an int type? True
```

Author's note: You can download the program **app1_d01_identity_operator.py** to execute the complete program.

POINT TO NOTE

In certain cases, you may notice an unusual behavior of the is operator. The official documentation 6. Expressions – Python 3.13.3 documentation mentions this by stating the following:

Due to automatic garbage-collection, free lists, and the dynamic nature of descriptors, you may notice seemingly unusual behaviour in certain uses of the is operator, like those involving comparisons between instance methods or constants. Check their documentation for more info.

APPENDIX A   SUPPLEMENTARY MATERIAL

Membership Operators

You can use "in" and "not in" to test whether an element is present
(or absent) in a sequence such as a string, list, tuple, or dictionary. The
in operator returns **True** if the element is found in the sequence and
False otherwise. The not in operator does the opposite. In Chapter 6,
you already saw a usage when I presented you the following code and
associated output.

Code:

```
# Checking whether an element is present inside a list
names = ["John", "Sam","Bob", "Ester"]
print(f"Is 'Sam' present on the list? {'Sam' in names} ")
print(f"Is 'sam' present on the list? {'sam' in names} ")
# Checking whether an element is absent in this list
print(f"Is 'Jeniffer' missing from the list? {'Jennifer' not in
  names}")
```

Output:

```
Is 'Sam' present on the list? True
Is 'sam' present on the list? False
Is 'Jeniffer' missing from the list? True
```

Let us perform similar tests with a string, a tuple, and a dictionary as
well. Let's execute the following code (the associated output is shown in
inline comments):

```
# String
message = "Welcome"
print(f"The string is: {message}")
print(f"Is 'com' present in the string? {'com' in message}")
print(f"Is 'com' absent in the string? {'com' not in message}")
print("-"*10)
```

366

APPENDIX A   SUPPLEMENTARY MATERIAL

```python
# Tuple
numbers = (1, 2, 3)
print(f"The contents of the tuple are: {numbers}")
print(f"Is 1 present in the tuple? {1 in numbers}")
print(f"Is 2 absent in the tuple? {2 not in numbers}")
print("-"*10)

# Dictionary
sample_dict = {"key1": 10, "key2": 25}
print(f"The contents of the dictionary are: {sample_dict}")
print(f"Is key1 a key in the dictionary? {'key1' in
    sample_dict}")
print(f"Is 20 a value in the dictionary? {20 in sample_dict.
    values()}")
```

Here is the output:

```
The string is: Welcome
Is 'com' present in the string? True
Is 'com' absent in the string? False
----------
The contents of the tuple are: (1, 2, 3)
Is 1 present in the tuple? True
Is 2 absent in the tuple? False
----------
Is key1 a key in the dictionary? True
Is 20 a value in the dictionary? False
```

Author's note: You can download **app1_d02_membership_operators.py** from the Apress website to execute this program.

367

APPENDIX A   SUPPLEMENTARY MATERIAL

Bitwise Operators

We use these operators for binary numbers. Here, operands are integers, but Python treats them as binary digits. Since we compare bit by bit of the binary codes, we call them bitwise operators. The common bitwise operators are

- **Bitwise or**: You use "|" to denote bitwise **or**. When you compare two bits, the resultant bit is 1 if at least one of the two bits is 1.

- **Bitwise and**: You use "**&**" to denote bitwise **and**. When you compare two bits, the resultant bit is 1 if both bits are 1.

- **Bitwise exclusive or**: You use "^" to denote bitwise **exclusive or**. When you compare two bits, the resultant bit is 1 if ONLY one of the two bits is 1.

- **Bitwise inversion:** You use "~" to denote bitwise **not**. This operator inverts all the bits in a binary number (i.e., you change 1 to 0 and 0 to 1 for each bit).

- **Left shift:** You use "<<" to denote the zero-fill left shift operator. Here, x<<y simply means that the resultant x will appear with the bits shifted to the left by y places. The 0s are inserted as new bits on the right-hand side.

- **Right shift**: You use ">>" to denote the signed right shift operator. Here x>>y simply means that the resultant x will appear with the bits shifted to the right by y places and fills 0 on voids.

Let us understand this better. Consider two numbers 3 and 5. In an 8-bit number system, 3 can be represented in binary as 0000 0011. Similarly, 5 can be represented in binary as 0000 0101. You may use the

368

APPENDIX A   SUPPLEMENTARY MATERIAL

bin() function to convert from a decimal number to a binary number. For example, see the following code that was executed in a Python shell:

```
>>> bin(3)
'0b11'
>>> bin(5)
'0b101'
```

Special Notes

The online link https://wiki.python.org/moin/BitwiseOperators states:

Python considers two's complement binary form, which is the same as the classical binary representation for positive integers, but is slightly different for negative numbers.

The previous link also confirms that

Python doesn't use 8-bit numbers. It USED to use however many bits were native to your machine, but since that was non-portable, since Python 3 ints are arbitrary precision. Thus the number -5 is treated by bitwise operators as if it were written "...1111111111111111111011".

As you can easily understand that to make the discussion easy, I started the discussion with the classical binary form and 8-bit number system. Let's start examining the operators.

First, let's apply the "bitwise or" operator on these numbers:

```
0000 0011
0000 0101
```
———————————
```
0000 0111
```

So the result will be $1*2^0+ 1* 2^1 +1* 2^2 =1+2+4=7$.

369

APPENDIX A   SUPPLEMENTARY MATERIAL

Let us test this in the Python shell now:

```
>>> 3|5
7
```

Let's apply the "bitwise and" operator on the numbers (3 and 5) now:

```
0000  0011
0000  0101
```
_____
```
0000  0001
```

So the result will be $1*2^0 =1$.

Let us test this in the Python shell now:

```
>>> 3&5
1
```

Let's apply the "bitwise exclusive or" on the numbers (3 and 5) now:

```
0000  0011
0000  0101
```
_____
```
0000  0110
```

So the result will be $0*2^0+ 1*2^1 +1*2^2 =0+2+4=6$.

Therefore, in the Python shell, you'll see the following results:

```
>>> 3^5
6
```

Let's apply the << operator on the numbers 3 and 5:

3 in binary is 0000 0011

Now 3<<2 becomes: 0000 1100, i.e.,12

5 in binary is 0000 0101

So, 5<<1 becomes 0000 1010, i.e., 10

370

APPENDIX A   SUPPLEMENTARY MATERIAL

Therefore, in the Python shell, you'll see the following results:

```
>>> 3<<2
12
>>> 5<<1
10
```

Let's apply the >> operator on the numbers 3 and 5:
3 in binary is 0000 0011
Now 3>>2 becomes: 0000 0000 ,i.e.,0

In the same way, 5>>2 becomes 0000 0001, i.e., 1
In the same way, 5>>1 becomes 0000 0010, i.e., 2

Let us test this in the Python shell now:

```
>>> 3>>2
0
>>> 5>>2
1
>>> 5>>1
2
```

Understanding the "**bitwise not**" operator is not always easy. The link BitwiseOperators - Python Wiki explains the following point:

Negative numbers are written with a leading one instead of a leading zero. So, if you are using only 8 bits for your twos-complement numbers, then you treat patterns from "00000000" to "01111111" as the whole numbers from 0 to 127, and reserve "1xxxxxxx" for writing negative numbers. A negative number, -x, is written using the bit pattern for (x-1) with all the bits complemented (switched from 1 to 0 or 0 to 1). So, -1 is complement (1 - 1) = complement (0) = "11111111", and -10 is complement (10 - 1) = complement (9) = complement ("00001001") = "11110110". This means that negative numbers go all the way down to -128 ("10000000").

371

APPENDIX A   SUPPLEMENTARY MATERIAL

As per the previous information, you can say that

-4 = Complement for (4-1)= 3, which says ~**3** is **-4**

-6 = Complement for (6-1)= 5, which says ~**5** is **-6**

Therefore, in the Python shell, you see the following results:

```
>>> ~5
-6
>>> ~3
-4
```

Static Methods

In OOP, the usage of instance methods is common, and you are already familiar with that. Now I show you static methods and Python-specific class methods. These are useful when you learn advanced programming in Python. It may seem complicated at the beginning, but a careful analysis can make things easier for you.

Let us begin with a class with an initializer and an instance method:

```python
class Color:
    fav_color = "Green"

    def __init__(self, color):
        self.fav_color = color

    def instance_method(self):
        print("The instance method is called.")
        print(f"My favorite color is: {self.fav_color}")
```

You know that you can create an object of the Color class and call the instance_method. Here is a sample code segment:

372

APPENDIX A   SUPPLEMENTARY MATERIAL

```
# Creating an object from the Color class
favorite_color = Color("Blue")
# Calling the instance method
favorite_color.instance_method()
```

If you run this code, you can get the following output:

```
The instance method is called.
My favorite color is: Blue
```

How to Use?

Till this point, everything is straightforward. Now I introduce a static method inside the Color class. Python's static methods have the following characteristics:

- There is a decorator @staticmethod before the method definition.

- There is no self parameter in the class definition.

- A static method can be called without creating an object of the class. You use the class name to invoke the static method.

POINT TO NOTE

Static methods are useful for **utility functions** (or operations) that make sense in the context of the class. These methods don't need access to any instance/class attributes.

373

APPENDIX A   SUPPLEMENTARY MATERIAL

Here is a sample:

```python
@staticmethod
def static_method():
    print("The static method is called.")
    print("You can call me without creating an instance.")
    print(f"My favorite color is: {Color.fav_color}")
```

If the Color class contains this static method, the following code segment can invoke this method as follows:

```python
Color.static_method()
```

and produce the following output:

```
The static method is called.
You can call me without creating an instance.
My favorite color is: Green
```

Note   The concept of static method is also present in many other programming languages, such as Java and C#.

Q&A Session

QA1.1 When should I consider using static methods?

You have seen that the static methods can be called without creating any instances. It means these are not instance-specific. This gives you a clue that if you need a function that logically belongs to a class but does not need to access or modify the state of an instance, you can make it static. For example, if you make a Person class and want to check whether a person is an adult, you can make the function static. It is because the criterion of becoming an adult is not specific to a person; it applies to every person.

374

APPENDIX A   SUPPLEMENTARY MATERIAL

Author's note: Overuse of static methods goes against the principles of OOP. So make a function static only when it makes sense.

Class Methods

Now I introduce a class method inside the Color class. It's a special inclusion in Python programming. Notice the following points in this segment:

- You use a decorator @classmethod before the method definition.

- Again, the self parameter is absent in the method definition.

- A class method can also be called without creating an object of the class. You use the class name to invoke the class method.

- Now the question is: how does a class method differ from a static method? The class method must have a reference to the class object as the first parameter, usually denoted with cls, whereas a static method can have no parameters at all.

   Let's see a class method:

```
@classmethod
def class_method(cls):
    print("The class method is called.")
    print("You can call me without creating an instance.")
    print(f"My favorite color is: {cls.fav_color}")
```

375

APPENDIX A   SUPPLEMENTARY MATERIAL

POINT TO NOTE

The PEP 8 – Style Guide for Python Code I peps.python.org suggests the following:

- Always use `self` for the first argument to instance methods.

- Always use `cls` for the first argument to class methods.

How to Use?

If the `Color` class contains this class method, the following code segment can invoke this method as follows

```
Color.class_method()
```

and produce the following output:

```
The class method is called.
You can call me without creating an instance.
My favorite color is: Green
```

Author's note: I chose the parameter name "cls" following the convention. If you use any other name, that will work too, but experts do not recommend that.

Q&A Session

QA1.2 From the previous outputs, apart from some syntactical differences, I could not figure out how a class method, a static method, and an instance method differ from each other. Can you throw some light on this?

Let us assume the `Color` class has an instance method, a static method, and a class method as follows:

376

APPENDIX A   SUPPLEMENTARY MATERIAL

```python
class Color:
    fav_color = "Green"

    def __init__(self, color):
        self.fav_color = color

    def instance_method(self):
        print("The instance method is called.")
        print(f"My favorite color is: {self.fav_color}")
        print("-"*15)

    @staticmethod
    def static_method():
        print("The static method is called.")
        print("You can call me without creating an instance.")
        print(f"My favorite color is: {Color.fav_color}")
        print("-"*15)

    @classmethod
    def class_method(cls):
        print("The class method is called.")
        print("You can call me without creating an instance.")
        print(f"My favorite color is: {cls.fav_color}")
        print("-" * 15)
```

Let me set a new color through an instance of the Color class and invoke these methods as follows:

```python
# Creating an object from the Color class
favorite_color = Color("Blue")
# Calling the instance method
favorite_color.instance_method()
# Calling the static method
Color.static_method()
```

377

APPENDIX A   SUPPLEMENTARY MATERIAL

```
# Calling the class method
Color.class_method()
```

There is no surprise that you'll see the following output:

```
The instance method is called.
My favorite color is: Blue
---------------
The static method is called.
You can call me without creating an instance.
My favorite color is: Green
---------------
The class method is called.
You can call me without creating an instance.
My favorite color is: Green
---------------
```

Notice that the color "**Blue**" is reflected when you use the instance method. But the static method or the class method did not change the "**Green**" color (the value of the class-level variable fav_color). It is because both the class method and the static method are bound to the class, but not to an object. I hope that this is clear and **you can see how a class method (or static method) differs from an instance method**.

Author's note: You can download **app1_d03_investigating methods.py** from the Apress website to execute this program.

Let's do some more analysis. This time, I made the Color class simpler. It has a class variable color, an instance method display, and a class method update_color. The class looks as follows:

```
class Color:
  color = "Green"
  def display(self):
    print(f"My favorite color is: {self.color}")
```

378

APPENDIX A   SUPPLEMENTARY MATERIAL

```python
@classmethod
def update_color(cls, newcolor):
    cls.color = newcolor
    print(f"The default color is updated to {newcolor}.")
```

Let us now exercise the following code:

```python
print(f"The current default is: {Color.color}")
# making an instance of the Color class
color1= Color()
color1.display()
color1.update_color("Blue")
color1.display()
print(f"The current default is: {Color.color}")
```

Upon executing the previous segment, you should see the following output:

```
The current default is: Green
My favorite color is: Green
The default color is updated to Blue.
My favorite color is: Blue
The current default is: Blue
```

Notice the first and the last line of the output. **You can see that the default value of the class variable (color) is updated from Green to Blue**.

Now, remove the @classmethod decorator of the update_color method in the Color class and execute the previous code again. This time, you'll see the following output (notice the change in bold):

```
The current default is: Green
My favorite color is: Green
The default color is updated to Blue.
```

379

APPENDIX A   SUPPLEMENTARY MATERIAL

```
My favorite color is: Blue
The current default is: Green
```

Notice that though an instance of the `Color` class changed its default color, **the value of the class variable is unchanged.**

You can see that a class method can access class attributes and modify them. On the contrary, since a static method does not have an implicit first argument like `cls`, it cannot modify the class-level variables. A static method does not take a `self` argument as well. So you can use a static method as a utility method that does not require instance data or class-level data.

Finally, though an instance method can access the attributes and modify them, the changes are specific to an instance. So, if you need to modify class-level data, you must opt for the class methods.

Author's note: You can download **app1_d04_investigation_continued.py** from the Apress website to execute the program that we just discussed.

Before I finish this discussion, I want to draw your attention to the following statements from Built-in Functions – Python 3.13.3 documentation:

> *A class method can be called either on the class (such as C.f())*
> *or on an instance (such as C().f()). The instance is ignored*
> *except for its class. If a class method is called for a derived*
> *class, the derived class object is passed as the implied first*
> *argument.*

This is a useful piece of information when you work on inheritance. To illustrate, let us consider the following program where I invoke different methods using objects. (I know invoking class methods and static methods using objects may seem to be unusual. However, for the sake of discussion, let us do this.)

380

APPENDIX A SUPPLEMENTARY MATERIAL

```python
class Parent:
    def instance_method(self):
        print(f"The instance method is called.{self}")
    @staticmethod
    def static_method():
        print("The static method is called.")
    @classmethod
    def class_method(cls):
        print(f"The class method is called.{cls}")

class Child(Parent):
    """ This is a Child class."""
    pass

# Creating an object from the Parent class
sample_object = Parent()
sample_object.instance_method()
# Parent.static_method()
sample_object.static_method() # Also ok
# Parent.class_method()
sample_object.class_method() # Also ok

print("*"*20)


# Using the Child class object now,
sample_object = Child()
sample_object.instance_method()

# Child.static_method()
sample_object.static_method() # Also ok

# Child.class_method()
sample_object.class_method() # Also ok
```

381

APPENDIX A   SUPPLEMENTARY MATERIAL

Author's note: You can download **app1_d05_class_method_contd.py** from the Apress website to execute this program.

Here is a sample output from my computer:

```
The instance method is called.<__main__.Parent object at
0x0000016610677CB0>
The static method is called.
The class method is called.<class '__main__.Parent'>
********************
The instance method is called.<__main__.Child object at
0x0000016610677E00>
The static method is called.
The class method is called.<class '__main__.Child'>
```

By looking at this output, you can tell whether the Parent class object called the class method or the derived class object called it. You'll find this mechanism useful when you make an advanced application. But static methods do not tell any such information. It is another important difference between a class method and a static method.

Finally, from this output, you can see that behind the scenes

- The invocation of sample_object.instance_method() transformed the code to instance_method(sample_object).

- The invocation of sample_object.static_method() transformed to static_method().It means no additional argument is added in the function call.

- The invocation of sample_object.class_method() transformed to class_method(type(cls)).

382

APPENDIX A   SUPPLEMENTARY MATERIAL

Conclusion

Both the class method and the static method are bound to a class, but not to an object. You do not use a class name to invoke an instance method. However, in general, you use class names to invoke a class method or a static method.

APPENDIX B

What's Next?

Python is a useful programming language that is gaining popularity every day. After finishing this book, I hope you have a solid understanding of it. Now I encourage you to read related topics from other books, articles, or blogs. Most importantly, keep experimenting with new code and continue learning. As we all know, practice makes perfect.

I too consistently experiment with programs and learn from others. Below is a list of recommended books, courses, and articles from which I have gained valuable insights. I believe that these materials (or their updated editions) will be equally beneficial to you.

Books

Here is my recommended list of books:

- *Think Python* by Allen Downey (O'Reilly Media; third edition, 2024)

- *Python Crash Course* by Eric Matthes (No Starch Press; third edition, 2023)

- *Python Workout* by Reuven M. Lerner (Manning; first edition, 2020)

- *Python Projects for Beginners* by Connor P. Milliken (Apress, 2019)

© Vaskaran Sarcar 2025
V. Sarcar, *Python Bootcamp*, https://doi.org/10.1007/979-8-8688-1516-4

APPENDIX B   WHAT'S NEXT?

- *The Quick Python Book* by Naomi Ceder (Manning; third edition, 2018)

- *Learning Python* by Mark Lutz (O'Reilly Media; fifth edition, 2013)

Courses

The following list includes two helpful online courses covering a wide range of topics. At the time of writing, the second course in this list is not free, but you may find promotional discounts occasionally:

```
https://www.youtube.com/watch?v=QXeEoDOpB3E&list=PLsyeobzWxl7p
oL9JTVyndKe62ieoN-MZ3
```

```
https://www.linkedin.com/learning/learning-python-14393370
```

Other Resources

Throughout the book, you have seen various online resources in the discussions and the "Q&A Sessions." Be sure to explore those resources to enhance your learning further.

APPENDIX C

Other Books by the Author

The following list includes other Apress books by the author:

- *Creational Design Patterns in C#* (Apress, 2025)

- *Task Programming in C# and .NET* (Apress, 2025)

- *Parallel Programming with C# and .NET* (Apress, 2024)

- *Introducing Functional Programming Using C#* (Apress, 2023)

- *Simple and Efficient Programming with C#* Second Edition (Apress, 2022)

- *Test Your Skills in C# Programming* (Apress, 2022)

- *Java Design Patterns* Third Edition (Apress, 2022)

- *Simple and Efficient Programming with C#* (Apress, 2021)

- *Design Patterns in C#* Second Edition (Apress, 2020)

- *Getting Started with Advanced C#* (Apress, 2020)

- *Interactive Object-Oriented Programming in Java* Second Edition (Apress, 2019)

© Vaskaran Sarcar 2025
V. Sarcar, *Python Bootcamp*, https://doi.org/10.1007/979-8-8688-1516-4

APPENDIX C   OTHER BOOKS BY THE AUTHOR

- *Java Design Patterns* Second Edition (Apress, 2019)

- *Design Patterns in C#* (Apress, 2018)

- *Interactive C#* (Apress, 2017)

- *Interactive Object-Oriented Programming in Java* (Apress, 2016)

- *Java Design Patterns* (Apress, 2016)

To learn more about these books and the author's non-Apress books, you can refer to the following links:

- https://amazon.com/author/vaskaran_sarcar

- https://link.springer.com/search?newsearch=true &query=vaskaran+sarcar&content-type=book&dateFr om=&dateTo=&sortBy=newestFirst

Index

A

Actual parameters, 188
Alias, 205, 206
append(), 162
Arguments, 187, 189
Arithmetic operators, 357–358
Assignment operators, 359, 360
Associativity, 55–56

B

Base class/superclass, 321
Binary files
  copying image, 267
    analysis, 271
    demonstration, 267
    output, 267
    pickle files, 269, 270
    pickle module, 272
    pickling/unpickling,
      268, 269
    reconstructing, 270, 271
  dump() and load() functions,
    274, 280
  random integers, 274, 276, 277
Bitwise operators, 54, 56, 368–371
Boolean data type, 84
Boolean variables, 85

Break statement, 136–138
Built-in functions, 29,
  67–74, 79, 139

C

Case study, 91, 116, 146, 178, 216,
  249, 280, 316, 351
Catching, 225
Child class/derived class, 321
Class, 227, 298, 375
  definition, 293
  importing
    alternative code, 311–313
    multiple classes, 309, 310
    single class, 307, 308
    whole module, 310
  instance value, 302
  modeling, 294, 295, 297
Class methods, 372, 375
  class attributes, 380
  @classmethod, 380
  cls, 376
  Color class, 376, 377
  inheritance, 381
  and instance method, 378, 380
  and objects, 381
  parent class, 382

© Vaskaran Sarcar 2025
V. Sarcar, *Python Bootcamp*, https://doi.org/10.1007/979-8-8688-1516-4

INDEX

Class methods (*cont.*)
   vs. static method, 375, 382
   update_color method, 379
Code reuse concept, 194
Coding, 33, 223, 322
Command-line interface (CLI), 5, 9
Comments, 23–25, 29
Comparison operators, 99, 102, 361
Computer programming, 3, 143
Constructors, 299
   analysis, 301
   definition, 299
   demonstration, 300
   non-parameterized, 299
   variables, 299
Contradictions, 111
current_number, 126

D

Default attributes
   analysis, 306
   concept, 304
   demonstration, 305
   outupt, 305, 306
Default values, 190, 192
Demonstration, 20, 26, 33, 41, 87,
       100–102, 104, 105, 107–109,
       133, 134, 138, 139, 185, 190,
       194, 195, 197, 201, 203, 205,
       228, 233, 237, 239, 244, 259,
       262, 266, 267, 270, 273, 300,
       303, 305, 308–310, 312,
       324, 338

Dictionaries, 172
   characteristics, 172
   code, 172, 173
   output, 173, 174
   sample implementations, 180

E

elif statements, 99, 102, 103, 105,
      106, 118
else, 99, 100, 102, 105–107, 118, 121,
      218, 220, 237, 238, 240, 336
employee_names, 134, 135
eval(), 120
Exception handler, 225
Exception handling, 223
   arithmetic problem, 225
   documentation, 233
   else block, 237
      demonstration, 237
      output, 237
      Q&A session, 238
   errors, 224
   except blocks, 240
      arrangement, 240
      custom exception, 243
      demonstration, 244
      generic/broader, 241–243
      output, 245
   exercises, 246, 247
   FileNotFoundError, 273, 274
   hierarchical structure, 226
      demonstration, 228
      output, 228–230

390

INDEX

parent–child relationship, 227
Q&A session, 230, 231, 233
subset, 226
vehicle, 228
ZeroDivisionError, 227
key points, 231, 232
operations, 224
pass statement, 238
analysis, 240
demonstration, 239
output, 239
pass statement demonstration, 239
problem statement, 249–251
purpose, 224
Python, 226
sample implementation, 251, 252
secure application, 224
solution to exercises, 247–249
try block, 238
try-catch-finally, 233
demonstration, 233, 234
output, 234, 235
Q&A session, 235, 236
unwanted situations, 224

F, G

FileNotFoundError, 272–274
Files, 253
binary files (*see* Binary files)
text files (*see* Text files)
types, 253

Float, 38, 46, 250, 251
foreach loop, 133
for loop, 129
Formal parameters, 188
Function arguments, 188
keyword arguments, 189–192
positional arguments, 189
variable, 193–196
Functions, 293
case studies, 216–218
characteristics
analysis, 186
def keyword, 184
demonstration, 185
documentation, 185
output, 186
print_details, 184
print_hello(), 184
print(print_details.__doc__), 185
logical set of statements, 183
sample implementations, case studies, 218–222

H

hello_world.py file, 20

I, J

IDE, 12–15, 81, 223
Identity operators, 363–365
IDLE, 10–12, 15, 66

391

INDEX

if-else, 99, 100, 102, 105, 218
index() function, 73
Inheritance, 321, 334, 341
    case studies, 351–355
    hierarchical inheritance, 334
    hybrid inheritance, 335
    is-a relationships, 342
    multilevel inheritance, 334
    multiple inheritance, 327
        analysis, 328
        attributes, 329
        child.describe(), 330
        demonstration, 328
        <class 'object'>, 331
        MRO, 329
        search order, 330
    single inheritance, 323
        analysis, 325
        department class, 326
        describe method, 326
        overriding, 326
        student class, 324, 325, 327
    super call, 324, 331, 333
initial_list, 195
Instance, 297
Instantiation, 294
int() function, 40, 46, 79, 88, 115
IS-A relationship, 322
isdigit() function, 79, 80
islower() function, 71
iterable_element, 134
iterable object, 139
Iteration, 123, 138

K

Keyword arguments
    default values, 190
    demonstration, 190
    output, 191
    warning, 192

L

Lambda functions
    def keyword, 197
    demonstration,
        197, 198
    lambda keyword, 197
    output, 197, 199
len() function, 174, 181
Lists, 151
    append(), 162
    code, 162
    code, 151–161
    list.sort() method, 164
    max() and min()
        functions, 159
    output, 162, 163
    output, 152–161
    remove, 158
    sort() function, 163
list.sort() method, 164
Logical operators, 362
for loop, 129
Loop statements, 124
    while loop, 125
lower(), 70

INDEX

M

__main__, 208, 209
makedirs() function, 285
make_double(), 195
map function, 198
Mathematical functions, 82
Membership operators, 51, 366, 367
__init__() method, 299
Method resolution order
        (MRO), 329
module_name.function_
        name, 204
Modules, 199
    alias
        demonstration, 205
        output, 206
    bootcamp_library.py, 200
    create, 200
    definition, 199
    demonstration, 201
    general form, import, 206
    import entire contents
        bootcamp_library.py, 202
        demonstration, 203
    output, 202
MRO, *see* Method resolution
        order (MRO)
Multiple Python versions, 8

N

__name__, 208
Naming conventions, 43–48
Nested loop, 141–142

O

Object-oriented programming
        (OOP), 227, 293, 295,
        313, 316–318
Objects, 294
    attribute value, 302
        output, 304
        student's roll number, 303
    creation, 295, 296
        alternative code, 296
        describe method, 296
        sam.describe()/Student.
            describe(sam), 297
        describe method, 298
Operators, 50, 51, 55, 357, 359,
        361–363, 366, 368
    arithmetic operators, 357, 358
    assignment operators, 359, 360
    bitwise operators, 368–371
    comparison operators, 361
    identity operators, 363–365
    logical operators, 362
    membership operators, 366, 367

P, Q

Parentheses, 51, 53, 137, 171
Parameters, 67, 120, 187, 188
Parent class, 321, 322, 324–326, 330,
        340, 341
Pass statement, 238, 328, 329
Path environment variable, 7
Positional arguments, 188, 189
Print function, 142, 257

393

INDEX

print_details(), 184, 186, 188
Private variables and methods
   ATM card/credit card, 336
   private data, accessing, 338
      amit.display_salary(), 338
      child class, 340
      demonstration, 338
      display method, 340, 341
      name clashes, 339
      output, 339
      parent class, 340
   public information, 336
   underscore(s), 337
Program execution
   as the main program,
      207–209
   as main program, refactored
      code, 274, 277
   problems, 223
Programming languages, 69, 102,
      133, 328, 336
Programs
   report card, 281
      outputs, 282, 283
      sample implementation,
        285, 286, 288, 289
      student_name.txt, 282
   user IDs, 281
      sample implementation,
        284, 285
PyCharm, 15–17, 20, 21, 36, 37, 68,
      79, 128, 184, 223
PyCharm Terminal Window
      shell, 46

Python, 3, 5, 7, 8, 12, 86, 109, 131,
      141, 385
   code, 8
   command prompt, 9
   download, 5
   download and install, 6
   IDLE, 10
   installer, 4
   interpreter and install, 4
   "shells" and "terminals", 9, 12
   version, 4, 6, 9
   Windows, 6
PythonBootcamp, 15, 17, 18
Python command shell, 66
Python expression, 56, 120
Python file, 19, 20, 87, 208, 209,
      308, 309
Python module/package, 208
Python programming, 12, 15, 35,
      43, 301, 375
Python programs, 8, 12, 14, 20, 21,
      146, 272
Python scripts, 12, 14–16, 27
Python shell, 9, 33, 36, 45, 81,
      90, 369–371
Python standard library, 108, 199

R

Raises, 225
randint() function, 119, 149
Remove, 46, 158, 166, 175, 212, 266
repeat_sum function, 194, 195
Return value, 193, 195

INDEX

S

sample_text_file.txt file, 278

Solution, 58, 90, 114, 347

Solution to exercises, 90, 94, 114, 117, 315, 347, 354

sort() function, 163

Static methods, 372
- characteristics, 373
- color class, 372, 373
- instance method, 372
- instances, 375
- output, 373
- utility functions, 374

Strings, 64, 68
- numbers, 76

Student class, 298, 301, 306–308, 311, 312, 324, 326, 327

T

Tautology, 111–112

text1.upper(), 70, 71

Text files
- approximate number of words, 274, 278
- content, 254
- first "n" lines, 274–276
- programs, 254
- reading
  - analysis, 256
  - approaches, 259, 260
  - arguments, 255
  - issues, 257
  - keyword, 259
  - modes, 260
  - open function, 255
  - program, 254–256
  - read function, 258
  - readline() function, 255
  - warning, 258
- writing
  - analysis, 266
  - contents, 264
  - demonstration, 262, 266
  - modes, 261
  - open function, 262
  - output, 262, 264, 266
  - r+/w+ modes, 263
  - size limitation, 265

Total variable, 195

tuple() function, 168

Tuples, 165, 167, 168
- code, 166–170
- error, 166
- output, 166–170
- round brackets, 165
- slice operator, 166

U

upper(), 70

V

Variable, 31, 35
- assigning, 31
- assignment operator, 31
- class *vs.* instances, 306, 307

395

INDEX

Variable (*cont.*)
    float, 40
    programming, 33
    reassign, 40, 41
Variable arguments
    analysis, 194, 196
    calculate_sum
        function, 193
    demonstration, 194, 195

    error, 193
    output, 194, 196
Vehicle class, 321, 334

W, X, Y, Z

while loop, 124, 128, 129, 149
    characteristics, 125
    flowchart, 126

Printed in the United States
by Baker & Taylor Publisher Services